LOOK AT THE DIRT

LOOK AT THE DIRT

THE STORY OF BORDER PATROL AGENTS THROUGH THEIR OWN EYES

PAUL EBERLE

Library of Congress Control Number: 2022922106
ISBN: 979-8-9871423-0-1

Contents

Acknowledgments

Someone better than me said that nobody writes a book alone. First and foremost, thanks to my lovely wife who has fully supported me through two careers and maybe now a third. I don't deserve you.

Thanks to my parents for (among other things) raising readers in a house full of books and my whole family for the support and constructive criticism. It is greatly appreciated.

To my editor Jody Bennett, you were and are fantastic, I cannot thank you enough.

I also deeply appreciate the incredible generosity, encouragement, and inspiration received from John Caprarelli, author of *Uniform Decisions*, and his wife Lynn. Also, to Todd Bensmann author of *America's Covert Border War* and *Overrun*, thanks for trying! To John Stryker Meyer, author of *Across the Fence: America's Secret War in Vietnam*, *On the Ground*, and *The SOG Chronicles*, you and your guys were my superheroes growing up.

Books comprising eyewitness accounts such as *Nam* by Mark Baker, *Everything We Had* by Al Santoli, the World War II oral history books by Gerald Astor, and the historical fiction of Steven Pressfield, among others, affected me greatly.

Some of the podcasts I listened to over the years, especially the author interviews, also helped a lot. John Caprarelli was unknown to me until he was interviewed by Arik Levy on *Firearms Nation*; likewise, Mike Wood, the author of *Newhall Shooting: A Tactical Analysis*. As a firearms instructor, I was already familiar with the famous Miami FBI shootout in 1986 but first heard from Ed Mireles on Royce Bartlett's *Shooting Straight Radio Podcast*. The *Jocko Podcast* with Jocko Willink and *Danger Close* with Jack Carr regularly feature authors and books well worth reading.

Most of all, thanks to the agents. Those who served and

those who are still out there. It will get worse before it gets better. Whether you agreed to have your stories in here or not, I will always be grateful to and for you. So are many other people from all over the world who are only alive today because of you.

Apologies for anyone I missed, anything I got wrong, or stories I didn't get to. This project grew quickly, and almost got away from me. There is more than enough for another book!

I. Introduction

About The Title

"Look at the dirt" is a Border Patrol colloquialism meaning to look at the ground for signs of passage, otherwise known as "cutting sign." I first heard it from an old Vietnam veteran, Supervisory Border Patrol Agent Tom Johnson, retired now for over twenty years and held in high esteem by everyone I know who also knew him. I met him only a couple of times when I was a trainee, and he impressed me greatly. (Certainly, the reverse was not true!) His weather-beaten, sunburnt face and gravelly voice would make the Marlboro Man proud. He looked like what I always thought a cowboy would; a wiry little tough guy, indestructible, with a hard bark on him. He called everyone "Peckerhead," sometimes even on the radio. Occasionally, younger newer guys, eager to make an impression, would "get on sign" and try to run it down. This almost never worked, and SBPA Johnson would remind them, "Look at the dirt Peckerhead, and you won't need to run!"

Mr. Johnson, you were the first Border Patrol role model I ever had though you didn't know it. You could walk all day with very little water, smoking the entire time. You were a guy who went south, did the work, and to hell with everyone else. You were always in the field, as opposed to speaking to a captive audience of agents giving them your philosophy of life or in the office making pie charts and bar graphs. Agents like you embody the Border Patrol ethos as I understand it. Thanks.

Foreword

This is the story of Border Patrol Agents through their own eyes. Their job can be filthy, smelly, sometimes funny, sometimes boring, and other times dangerous. Their memories might differ, and they may or may not come from contemporaneous notes and reports, but the stories here are all true. Some have multiple viewpoints presented; as any cop will tell you, multiple eyewitnesses can have different recollections of the same incident that happened right in front of them.

Their story is also my story. I joined the Border Patrol (BP) in 1997 when it was still part of the Immigration and Naturalization Service, a component of the US Department of Justice. I came from working in nightclubs and bars, in both the Los Angeles and Phoenix areas. Before that, the Marines. I wanted excitement but with a little more job security than the bar scene. The Border Patrol promised and delivered both of these things. There was the excitement of the chase, an element of danger, and the security of an ongoing immigration problem that our elected officials did not seem too keen on solving.

For those readers who are not agents, I appreciate you spending your time riding along with us. Hopefully, you will come away with a sense of the job Border Patrol Agents do, all day, every day, on behalf of the United States. You may wish to refer to the rank structure below, as well as the glossary in the back, for the meanings of various acronyms and abbreviations, though I will try to explain them as we go along. If you are an agent, I hope that this book is an appropriate tribute.

Border Patrol Agents are frequently portrayed in the mass media as racist bullies rounding up poor migrants to harass or beat them up. Nothing could be further from the truth. Nowhere has this false media narrative been more evident than the recent media coverage of the Del Rio Sector in the summer of 2021. Agents of the Horse Patrol, a specialized unit of Border Patrol Agents on horseback, were filmed while interdicting groups of illegal aliens wading the Rio Grande. In a weekend, 1500 became 15,000. HPU personnel appeared to be twirling the split reins of their mounts in a way that was reported by multiple news outlets to be "strapping" or "whipping" the aliens, who in this case were dark-complected Haitians. These pictures were used as race-bait for the racists to cry racism. In fact, the twirling of the reins is a method of controlling the horse, and not a single alien was struck with the heavy reins. If they had been, it would have left a mark. Ask anyone who handles horses; they will tell you. In one media clip, I could hear an agent saying unkind things to an alien who appeared to be placing a woman between himself and the agents. That is the only thing I might have addressed as a supervisor, and then only to advise him to chill out. It is not an issue for an investigation. The subject of upper Border Patrol management not standing up for their agents, another sore spot from this episode, is another feature of life as a working agent.

The subject of illegal immigration is not about race. Those who try to make it so are racists, and view or want others to view the issue through the lens of race. This is a red herring; the product of race-baiting shakedown artists, both right and left-wing. Many of them make big money fomenting hate; you probably know their names. Forget race; we do not care.

For instance, you encounter BP Agents one night after crawling under, climbing over, or otherwise breaching the International Boundary Fence. You were not born or naturalized in the United States, nor were your parents. Maybe you are in the trunk of a car with another alien. Maybe you are packed like a sardine, with 80-100 others in the back of a semi-trailer in Texas. Did you ask permission to enter? Did you present yourself for inspection? Were you lawfully admitted? If not, you're an illegal alien from the Border Patrol Agent's perspective. Again, as to race, we do not care.

Except for about a year in 2002-03, when I went to another

agency, I stayed with the BP until November of 2021, serving as a Supervisory Border Patrol Agent for my last fourteen years. Never an operational genius or a strategist, just another agent/supervisor; I was doing the job that never really changed.

Looking back, not much has been achieved. There are a whole lot more illegal aliens in the United States, and a lot more (and cheaper!) drugs of all kinds, than there were twenty-four years ago. This is despite a massive National Security Apparatus that tracks and stores nearly every legal activity we engage in for possible reference later on, and almost completely ignores the border. Yet somehow, they manage to regularly miss terrorist plots and school shooters who are specifically reported to them. Illegal immigration also provides a nice source of demagoguery for politicians right and left. It is too good a problem to solve when you can raise money on it. As the jaded agents would say over the years, "job security."

While I am critical of the Border Patrol, it is because I love the Border Patrol, especially my fellow agents. The thrust of this book is not what a great job the United States Government is doing to protect your border. As I write this in the winter of 2021-22, it is not. What this book is about is the great job your Border Patrol Agents are doing in the field, in spite of the inability and/or unwillingness of Executive Branch political appointees (of both main parties) and their lickspittles, to see that the laws passed by Congress are faithfully executed.

I have changed, left out, or made up some of the names and places in these stories (stories in first-person narrative are not necessarily mine) to protect the agents involved. Many of them are still working and many opinions expressed herein could possibly hurt someone's feelings. Names and specific places are not terribly important to this book as it is meant to convey the job. The job is pretty much the same wherever aliens are crossing the border illegally - between the lawful Ports of Entry. Specific names and places are mentioned whenever possible, for authenticity, and with permission from the agents themselves.

As far as tactics, techniques, and procedures (TTP if you're a government employee), there is no breaking news here. Line agents featured here are not using any top-secret space-age technology that has not already been shown off in the media. The art of man-tracking is almost as old as humanity itself, as is the art of escape and evasion. Profiling drivers' behavior at a checkpoint, or the subject's reactions to interview questions, is as old as police work. Yes, I said profiling: this means profiling *behavior*, not racial profiling. There is nothing in here that isn't already in the public domain.

Here are your Border Patrol Agents, the agents who actually do the work, the ones who "go south." They are not the professional management and union types who fight their battles in the office and generally "stay north." Of course, we need everyone; but I think the ones who go south, *the ones who look at dirt*, are the agents we need most and should celebrate and retain. Right, wrong, or indifferent, that is my opinion.

A note to some who are easily offended, looking to be offended, or can't handle dark humor or foul language, this book is not for you. If you are looking for sensitive commentary, political correctness, glorious victories, and prettily gift-wrapped felony cases, you will be disappointed. There are plenty of sanitized and tidied-up accounts of Border Patrol operations out there, and that is great, I will refer to some of them. Trying to minimize the politics surrounding Immigration Law, except as it affects the agents portrayed herein, was a mostly losing battle. Everything is political today and often driven by the narrative that the reporter wishes you to embrace. Learn both sides of any newsworthy issue (from both actual sides, not just YouTube videos or Facebook), then watch the news corporations' coverage of that issue, and you will understand.

This book is by and for Border Patrol Agents, those who might consider becoming agents, and interested folks who wish to learn what real agents do in the field.

Border Patrol Mission

Pre-9/11:

"The Border Patrol's mission specifically was to prevent, detect, and apprehend those illegally entering the United States between the Ports of Entry." From MEMORANDUM FOR THE RECORD, GUS DE LA VINA, BORDER PATROL CHIEF, November 19, 2003.

Post-9/11:

"The priority mission of the Border Patrol is preventing terrorists and terrorist weapons, including weapons of mass destruction, from entering the United States..." From www.cbp.gov

From that to this, more recently, after the unprecedented collapse of border security in 2021:

"The primary mission of the Border Patrol is to protect our nation by *reducing the likelihood* that dangerous people and capabilities enter the United States between the ports of entry." (Emphasis mine.)

It goes on and on; the main mission never changes, only the way management defines it. As you can see, they are changing the wording all the time. In my opinion, the latest definition is an attempt to redefine failure as success. How do you disprove a reduction in likelihood?

Recently, the current Chief of the Border Patrol, along with the current Secretary of Homeland Security, addressed a group of frustrated Border Patrol Agents in Yuma. The agents were apparently exasperated at the jaw-dropping denial of reality coming from D.C. and expressed themselves respectfully. In reply, the Chief yelled at them, reminding them how much time he has in (31 years). This is a common tactic used by failing agents to brush out their shortcomings; an attempt by the speaker to make himself feel superior, to make the audience feel inferior, or to change the subject.

It always fails. I learned as a young 18-year-old Marine:

"You can't bullshit the troops."

See the cbp.gov website for a thorough, official introduction to the US Border Patrol.

Keep reading for what they, the real agents, actually do every day.

Ranks and Titles

Border Patrol ranks and titles follow; there is some overlap and a little confusion as they have changed over the years. Their Police Department equivalents are very rough, as each Department differs, and the US Border Patrol has a different focus than regular "real police" agencies.

Border Patrol Agent(t), BPA(t) - a trainee, pay grade GS-5, 7, 9, to 11. Equivalent to a probationary Police Officer or Patrolman. No rank on the collar.

Border Patrol Agent, BPA - after a couple of years, BPAs that achieve expectations receive bumps in pay grade until they reach full performance level, or "journeyman" status. Nowadays, agent full performance level is GS-12. In the 1990s, this level was at GS-9 and was followed by several raises in the 2000s in order to encourage retention. Equivalent to a Patrolman or basic Police Officer in a police department. No rank on the collar.

Senior Patrol Agent, SPA, pay grade GS-11. While journeyman agents were limited to GS-9 status, they could compete for a limited number of slots as Senior Patrol Agents, who were expected to lead casework, generate intelligence, and act in the place of Supervisors when none were available. This title went away with all of the pay raises and with it, a source of on-call leadership in the field that has been missed ever since. SPAs had gravitas and were looked up to because they earned it; it wasn't just handed to them. Roughly equivalent to a Senior Police Officer or Police

Corporal. They wore no rank on the collar.

Supervisory Border Patrol Agent, SBPA, pay grade GS-12 until around 2008, then GS-13. Also known as first-liners or sups, these are the supervisors who run operations in the field. Each generally has a few BPAs assigned to him administratively for whom he is responsible for performance reviews, serving disciplinary notices, and so forth, but in practice, there are only a few and every sup supervises every agent in his or her area. Roughly equivalent to a Police Sergeant. Two bars are worn on each side of the collar (military folks will recognize them as "Captain's bars") and a shield/eagle ornament on the shoulder straps of their uniforms. They are black in rough duty uniform, silver for dress.

Field Operations Supervisor, FOS, pay grade GS-13 until phased out and replaced by Watch Commanders. FOSs acted as Watch Commanders, or second-line supervisors, one or two of them per shift or Patrol Group. They ran operations for the Patrol Agent in Charge of the station. Roughly equivalent to a Police Lieutenant. FOSs and Watch Commanders wear a black or gold oak leaf on their collars and the shield/eagle ornament on their shoulder straps. These are subdued gold for rough duty, shiny for dress.

Watch Commander, WC, pay grade GS-14. After 2012, WCs replaced the FOS as the leader of a shift or Patrol Group. FOSs were either promoted (they had to compete for the WC jobs) or busted back down to Supervisors. This resulted in some hurt feelings. Watch Commander is the highest rank that has daily contact with agents in the field. Sometimes, they even make it south. Roughly equivalent to a Police Lieutenant. Rank insignia, same as above.

Special Operations Supervisor, SOS, a GS-13 position with the same pay as a supervisor, but more responsibility. SOSs take care of non-Patrol Group administration and operations around the station. There are usually one or two of these. Could be a Police Lieutenant or Captain. These agents wear the same rank as FOS/Watch Commanders.

Deputy Patrol Agent in Charge, DPAIC, a GS-14 position. The deputy for the Patrol Agent in Charge. At big stations, there are two of these; one for operations and one for administration. Roughly equivalent to a Police Lieutenant or Captain. Same rank insignia as FOS/Watch Commanders.

Patrol Agent in Charge, PAIC, a GS-14 or 15 position. There can be only one. Each PAIC is supposedly the captain of his or her "ship," the "ship" being the station. In practice this is debatable. With advances in communications and technology, it is a lot easier to micromanage than it used to be. My intel suggests that Associate Chiefs, Assistant Chiefs, Branch Chiefs, Deputy Chiefs, and Chief Patrol Agents who live at Sector Headquarters and above are not generally shy about this. PAICs are the rough equivalent of a Police Captain or Major in charge of a precinct or station. They wear black or silver eagles on their collars along with the eagle/shield device on shoulder straps.

For the main purpose of this book, we are not too concerned with any of the higher-ranking management personnel. They were all Border Patrol Agents once, but when you promote beyond Watch Commander, your relationship with the agents and the dirt they work diminishes greatly, and you become a "big picture" type. Even if you're a born leader, this is natural, and some are better at it than others.

No one is more surprised than I that my favorite Chief Patrol Agent the Border Patrol ever had in the last twenty-five years was the former FBI Deputy Director Mark Morgan. Chief Morgan was never a PA until he became Chief. I wanted to hate him, but after he demonstrated the ability and willingness to fight for the Border Patrol mission in Congress and in the media, he completely won me over. He is still out there trying to fight for the Patrol, and the agents appreciate it. The politicians and their appointees probably do not. Other outstanding Chiefs? In the Sectors where I have worked, those who the agents really trusted, were the Chiefs Colburn, Gilbert, and Barlow. I'm sure there were more, but Chiefs like that are few in my opinion.

Organization

The US Border Patrol is a large and complex organization with many stovepipes, niches, and fiefdoms. Your typical agent probably cannot draw you an org chart, nor would they care to. The only units of the patrol that really matter for the purposes of this work are the Stations, Patrol Groups, and agents. That is where the work gets done for the most part, although there are exceptions. The Border Patrol Headquarters is in Washington, D.C.; this is where the Chief and his crew must fight for resources to enforce the laws passed by Congress and signed by the President. The Border Patrol Academy is now in Artesia, New Mexico. A desolate wasteland except for the oil, it is the perfect spot for agents' basic training. There are Sectors all along the land and sea border of the United States, with the main strength of the USBP being stationed in the Southwest between Imperial Beach to the west to Brownsville at the very tip of Texas. Each Sector has stations that it manages.

There are interior stations, though not many, and checkpoint stations. There are national-level teams, such as the Border Patrol Search, Trauma, and Rescue (BORSTAR - they are EMTs that work to rescue agents and aliens that are in distress), the Border Patrol Tactical Team (BORTAC - they are like a national-level Border Patrol SWAT team for standoffs and high-risk warrants), that do other work besides the "line" stations. There are also Resident Agents that work out of Sheriffs' Offices or their homes in rural areas to assist local law enforcement with illegal aliens and to conduct jail checks.

Every station I ever worked was a line station, divided among three or four shifts, or Patrol Groups, each with a Watch Commander. Each station has a few special units, such as Horse

Patrol, ATVU, ASID, or Disrupt, who report to an SOS, a Command Staff with a crew of admin agents, who make the bar graphs and pie charts, and otherwise serve the PAIC. These days the processing is so complicated and ever-changing that many stations have moved to a semi-permanent processing unit that also answers to an SOS.

The Patrol Groups are where most Border Patrol work gets done, and the entire rest of the agency should be devoted to assisting and servicing them. Surely there are many great people at Headquarters; we could use their greatness on the border. For the scammers and hangers-on, they could at least be used for transport.

Uniform and Equipment

Border Patrol Uniforms consist of the "Rough Duty Uniform," or RDU, which is analogous to the US Military's Battle Dress Utilities (BDU), and the dress uniform, which is apparently modeled after World War I doughboy greens. When I came in, the RDU consisted of heavy polyester pants with zero give in the crotch which frequently ripped open revealing the black reinforcement material covering the gap under the green fabric, and a slightly less constricting button-down shirt. The RDU trousers were constantly having to be repaired, so often that many gave up repairing them and just wore them with the open hole exposing the black material underneath.

The RDU is currently a proprietary olive-green cotton-poly two-pocket shirt over six-pocket BDU-style trousers; very comfortable and breathable, and when you get wet or sweat through it, the uniform dries quickly. Very important. On the shirt, there is a CBP Patch on one sleeve and the Border Patrol Patch on the other. The patches are bordered in gold with gold lettering on a dark blue field. In front, the cloth badge in gold rests over the heart, and the Velcro name tape is on the right.

Agents can also wear a "Performance Patrol Shirt," which is basically a dark green polo shirt that can only be worn underneath the approved external body-armor carriers, with appropriate badging and name tape. There are many different kinds of outerwear, such as light to heavy jackets, parkas, and a thermal vest. All sport the same branding to facilitate agent ID. Agents wear ball caps, beanies, or "Boonie hats" as well, which must bear the Border Patrol logo in front.

Black nylon duty belts carry the agent's pistol, ammunition, "less-than-lethal" device (pepper spray, Taser, or collapsible steel baton), handcuffs, and a small flashlight, as well as sometimes a tourniquet. Many agents carry as much as possible off of their hips and utilize pouches mounted to their external body armor carriers. This can save the hips and (to a lesser extent) lower back later on in life. Every agent must carry on his or her person the pistol, two spare magazines, a radio, one pair of handcuffs, and a less-than-lethal use of force device. Most also have a pocketknife, multi-tool, a little pouch for nitrile gloves, and an extra set of cuffs.

Boots could be black when I was working. Nylon sneaker-type boots were sometimes used but not all of them were authorized. The heavy and very rugged Danner Acadias were state-of-the-art for a while but are now giving way to the lightweight and more comfortable Lowe and Salomon products, however, given the desert environs most agents are operating in, a cactus spine through the toe can instantly and decisively adjust one's way of thinking regarding these lightweight boots.

The uniform is said to be changing soon to a lighter, green-colored BDU style. Boots are already being authorized in a more sensible tan color. Feet required to stand at a checkpoint in 120-degree heat will appreciate this.

In the mid-1990s, the Border Patrol adopted the Beretta Brigadier .40 caliber pistol, with the SIG-Sauer P229 .40 as a personal-purchase option. The Berettas did not hold up; in approximately five years I went through several Berettas, mostly due to cracked frames. They simply were not designed for the .40 caliber pistol round, and in spite of a few "fixes," they had to be discarded. In the early 2000s, we began transitioning to the Heckler and Koch USP and P2000 compact pistols, also in .40. Agents were allowed to purchase the USP Compact for duty carry as well. The Remington 870 12-gauge shotguns and M4 5.56mm Carbines were, and still are, the authorized long arms. With Remington now defunct, the future of the 870 shotguns in Border Patrol service is in doubt. Since 2020, the Glock 47 full-sized and Glock 19 compact pistols in 9mm are issued to agents. Interestingly, the Customs and Border Protection only adopted these pistols after a long and excruciating testing process to include a survey of field agents as to what they wished for in a handgun. This was a huge turnaround for upper management, asking the field agents for input, and a very welcome one. No personal-purchase weapons are authorized.

In the 1990s, for patrol vehicles, the Ford Bronco and Chevrolet Tahoe 4x4 SUVs were standard. There are 14-passenger vans and Ford Crown Victoria sedans for support. Some agents rode lightweight ATVs. Later, we went to Ford and Chevy 1500 series 1/2-ton and 3/4-ton pickup trucks (some with boxes in the bed for the aliens, called "ice cream trucks" or "dog-catchers"), and for a short time, Jeeps. Terrain, infrastructure, and distances within each station's area dictate what works best. These days, the Border Patrol uses a combination of 1500 and 2500 series pickup trucks, Tahoe SUVs, and vans to get the job done. Special units still have horses, motorcycles, and the Honda Rincon and Yamaha Grizzly ATVs to get to hard-to-reach areas.

On the subject of vehicles, the Ford Raptor (V8) pickup trucks were hands-down the finest off-road patrol vehicle the Border Patrol ever purchased. I was assigned a 2014 model and put over 100,000 very hard miles on it before they took it away for auction. The only thing that was ever replaced on it was the front A-arms. In contrast, the newer Ford F150 1/2-ton pickup trucks, while they get good gas mileage, are fragile and are having durability problems. The Quigley-modified Ford 4x4 vans were the best transport vans we ever got. These two vehicles were so well-adapted for our operations, and so durable, that their purchase (during the Obama administration) must have been an accident.

New for the Border Patrol is the Small Unmanned Aerial Systems, or SUAS drones. Launched by teams of two to three agents, these little remote-controlled aircraft can operate in limited areas for a limited time and are quite useful. Helicopters, fixed-wing aircraft, and full-sized drones are of limited availability. Allegedly, under the tactical control of the Sector Chief Patrol Agents, they all officially work for the Office of Air and Marine, or OAM, a separate component.

II. Getting There

Why the Border Patrol?

My whole life I wanted to be in the military. I read a ton of books, saw a lot of movies, and had a keen interest in all things military. Even as a teenager, when nature assigned me a new interest, it was in the back of my mind that I would be a military man. School was only interesting because that was where the girls were, and sports were required to look good for the girls (Although smart, I wasn't a good student; though big and strong, I was a terrible athlete). As it happened, the Army recruiter was an electrician, and the Marine recruiter was a sniper. It would be the Marines.

The Marine Corps was an eye-opening experience that I would not trade for anything. There were some fantastic people and amazing places, but it was not for me. My undistinguished service ended with a knee injury that has plagued me ever since. By the time Saddam invaded Kuwait, I was just a couple of days from being out. I went to an officer to try to stay but was told to 'get the fuck out of here.' So that was that.

Once the Marines sent me my final pay, I was off to California where my cousin Mike got me a job as a doorman at a nightclub. On my first night, my trainer Alfie asked me if I had seen the movie *Road House*. Of course, I had. "It's just like that," Alfie said as he showed me around the club. "Just be nice. Even if you have to brawl." A few trips to the hospital aside, it was great fun. Every Wednesday was dollar drink night and there was a line of people around the parking lot waiting to get in, and the managers packed as many people into the place as possible. It was a good education on how to talk to people, what kind of body language to use or to watch for depending on the situation, and how much was too much to handle. We kept a bucket of water with bleach in it in the back to wash the blood off after the fights. It was interesting learning that most guys will be reasonable, especially if it makes them look cool doing so. I also learned (sometimes painfully) that some guys just want to fight you and they do not care who gets hurt. Furthermore, anyone, no matter what sex, how big or small they are, or what you think, can hurt you badly if you let them.

Promotions to bar back then bartender followed, but I still helped out the door staff when appropriate. I had met and married my dream girl during this time and it got me thinking grown-up thoughts: how long can this last, working in bars that can be shut down any day with no notice? There was no health insurance. Didn't seem like much of a future.

There was an ongoing ad in the Pennysaver (for those of you under 45, this was a free direct-mail paper of classified ads) for the Border Patrol test being given in nearby Los Angeles. I took the test and started the process. I had changed from one with political leftist views when I exited the Marines to one with independent political views. The Los Angeles riots clearly demonstrated to me what happens when the cops don't come, as well as the value of the Second Amendment not being infringed upon. I began testing for various departments around Southern California but couldn't get anywhere without a degree or special status. I had tried college as a philosophy major but just didn't have it in me to be a student.

When the Border Patrol offered me a job in 1995, Dave, my boss at the club, offered me a management position. He told me that I would be in charge of the bar staff, but with the opportunity to still pour drinks on busy nights. It sounded pretty good, so I took it and committed myself to the management slot. Two years later, with much gratitude to Dave, I told him that law enforcement was still something I had to try. He was very cool about it; I owe him a lot. My father-in-law had also been talking me into at least giving it a shot, and that made sense. I took a position with the USBP.

It was not easy to leave my hot young wife for four months. What made it a lot tougher was the fact that I asked for it and could quit and go home at any time. I might not have been much of a Marine, but had been a pretty good bar manager, and did not want to quit on anything good ever again.

Hiring Process

After the application is submitted and accepted, a Border Patrol candidate proceeds to the interview. In some cases, the physical was thrown in there, but I do not remember having to take one. The first time through, I withdrew before the physical, and the second time, I simply have no recollection. This process has changed considerably since I went through it in 1995 and 1996, so if you are interested, definitely don't take this to heart. In my experience, the process differed with the area of the country in which you tested, who arranged your test, etc. In my class, we all had different experiences.

When notified, I was instructed to drive out to the El Centro Border Patrol Station (ELC) for my interview and to be fingerprinted. My wife and I packed up and got a room the night before since we lived up in the LA area. Being in El Centro was a bit of an eye-opener. While I had lived in San Diego's North County from 1973 to 1984, we never did venture to El Centro; most family trips were to the north or to the mountains around Julian. The desert landscape was fairly new to me.

We went to sleep watching Heath Ledger in his old series Roar, then I got up early the next day to put on my suit and report to ELC. I remember waiting nervously with the other anxious candidates in the front reception area until called. Not having any friends in the Border Patrol, I did not specifically know what was going to happen, but some of the off-duty police and deputies who worked security at the nightclub had given me the gist of the questions that would constitute the graded portion of a law enforcement interview.

Always call it in. Never leave your partner. Use the least amount of force necessary to get the job done... These things made sense to me after my military service, a few temporary security guard gigs, and working several years in busy and sometimes violent bar businesses. They told me what was expected. The best advice came from Gus and Tony, a couple of LA County Marshals whom I had worked with since starting at my first club. They advised me that nobody expected the kind of answers that a cop would give; it was about the thought process, articulating facts. This might have been true for the "real police," but I didn't know if the Border Patrol would be the same.

Going into the interview, I entered and centered myself in front of the table where the board would sit and assumed the position of attention like a good Marine. Looking back, it seems stupid, but I was there to make an impression. They told me to sit in a chair facing a table with several agents in dress uniforms. There was one agent with Captain's bars on his collar: the only one with visible rank. I would learn later he was a supervisor. He was at least 100 lbs. overweight and I could hear him breathing hard just sitting there. That was a bit of a surprise. The other guys seemed squared away to me; physically fit with shiny boots and brass in their green dress uniforms.

They asked several questions. A situation is set up, and as they tell you what is happening, you reply when asked how you would respond. Whatever you reply, another obstacle is placed in the scenario, and it becomes what seems to be an unwinnable situation. What they want is to see how you articulate the reasoning behind your actions, which is a big part of making cases or justifying the use of force.

Looking back, I got a little frustrated because of their set-ups and roadblocks. But they all happened in the field all the time, as I would find out.

"I would call dispatch for backup," I would say.

"Your handheld doesn't work."

"I go in the vehicle and use that radio," I said.

"That one is broken too."

The suspect attacks me. "I use my baton."

"It doesn't work. He grabs a rock." And so on...

Every time (in the scenario) I said I would call something in, my radio "was broken." Every time I used intermediate force, like an arm lock or takedown, "it didn't work." Finally, one scenario deteriorated enough that I told them "I draw and shoot him."

"Where do you aim?"

"Center mass," I replied.

"How many times?"

"Until the threat stops." This one I knew from guard duty in the military, and from an armed guard class I took in California.

"What do you mean threat? He didn't threaten you, he is trying to kill your partner!" The giant supervisor exclaimed.

"No sir, you shoot to stop. I wouldn't let him shoot my partner."

He got very animated. We went back and forth as he tried to break me. It caught me off guard because I was pretty sure he was wrong, but maybe the Border Patrol shot to kill? I remembered what my friends Gus and Tony said and stayed calm, not changing my answer; no one expects you to know their policy. The big supervisor acted as if I had failed; the other agents seemed to be getting fidgety like they were over it.

"Is that your final answer? Are you sure?" He asked me again.

"Yes sir, shoot to stop the threat."

The interview ended, and several of us proceeded to get fingerprinted. The guys that failed out were already gone. After that was over, I bumped into a few of my interviewers, including the big supervisor. They were cool, and said I passed, but the big sup was emphatic that if I ever had to pull my gun, "you shoot to kill!"

One of the agents hung out with us for a little bit and pointed out a few things at the station. We watched as a van came into the sally port and unloaded some aliens. Then it was time to go. As years went by and I got to know some guys who were on Oral Hiring Boards, I learned that even though they had benchmarks, a lot of it was up to the discretion of the agents on the board. This has since changed, but back then I understood. If you go to pieces in front of the board, you should not be put in a position where you have to apprehend a group of aliens. Some candidates had all the answers but folded under pressure. It was the same later on for the Spanish boards and various other tests.

After the interview, you waited; some for months, some for a year or more. After two years, your application needed to be resubmitted. In my class, there were wide variations in how long it took to get an academy date. Granted, you never really know what other people have going on, but some of the guys who had only been to college and lived with Mom and Dad were taking a long time. I figured mine would take a while since I worked in bars and had lived in a lot of different places. Some of the people I had worked with in the bar business were into criminal activity of one kind or another, and I figured that would have an impact. Surprisingly, it did not; an OPM Special Investigator visited my home and interviewed me, as well as my wife (after asking me to leave). They came by the club and spoke with my boss and some of the employees. It took seven months before I got the call for my academy date; not bad at all.

Arrival – Charleston, South Carolina

It was late at night, some dull streetlamps giving off a dingy yellow hue. The bus pulled in front of a long building with lighted double doors, and a lone figure stood there in the familiar green Border Patrol Class-A uniform with his Smokey-the-Bear hat pulled low over his eyes. I sat in the rear seat of the bus observing this and nodded at the guy next to me, who was also a veteran.

"Here we go," someone said.

I inwardly grinned because many, if not most, of my fellow trainees in Class 357 had not been in the military and I figured they had no idea what was about to happen. I can't remember if this was addressed by R. Lee Ermey's character, Gunny Hartman, in the movie *Full Metal Jacket*, but it should have been. As I sat there, I flashed back to my own experience arriving in USMC Boot Camp at Parris Island and watched as our instructor slowly climbed the steps onto the bus. Adrenaline coursed through me as I mentally rehearsed sprinting right through the bodies of anyone in my way as soon as I heard: "GETTHEFUCKOFFMYFUCKINGBUSRIGHTNOW!" or something like that.

He stepped up, looking all squared away in his Ike jacket, Supervisory Border Patrol Agent Carl, with his big duty belt, shiny brass, smokey hat all low and bad-ass, looking like any drill instructor anywhere would have looked before lighting into a mob of sloppy, undisciplined recruits... he looked left, looked right, and sighed.

"Hi guys," said he, in a welcoming, almost soft, friendly voice. That didn't mean anything; it could be a trap! "Go ahead and get your stuff squared away, and meet me inside those double doors over there," he pointed, "bathrooms are straight in and coffee's on the right."

It was not a trap.

He stepped down off the bus and went inside. The guy next to me and I chuckled. What the..? Is this what it's like for officers?

Later, SBPA Carl did much of his instructing in the voice of the famous actor and political commentator Ben Stein (known mainly as the teacher calling for "Bueller" in *Ferris Bueller's Day Off*), and quizzes were in the style of the 90s game show *Win Ben Stein's Money*. Carl was quite a character.

It was the first inkling that this was not going to be Parris Island or anything like it. They even had cleaning ladies to take care of our rooms! Later, some of the Spanish instructors tried to act all

21

hard, coming in and yelling at us like military recruits, but by then it was too late. It didn't land.

Class 357 at the Academy

Charleston smelled really, really bad. I think it was a paper mill or something but whatever it was, it was good training for getting used to bad smells. The Border is a festival of bad smells; sewage coming north from Tijuana sometimes closed the San Diego beaches when I had lived there. The smell of trash and fires frequently waft over the fence. The T.J. River is a notorious biohazard. The aliens stink, and the agents don't smell much better after a few hours of chasing them! At any rate, the Federal Law Enforcement Training Center at Charleston did the job of training agents just fine, until the Border Patrol found a better place in Artesia, New Mexico. Some agents also went to the academy at Glynco, Georgia, but comparatively few.

"Get used to bad smells and smelling bad," SBPA Carl advised us. They would frequently not give us enough time to shower after physical training as a way to make us more uncomfortable. When one of the lawyers who taught the law classes complained about how bad we smelled, we reported this to SBPA Carl. He was unmoved. "You're going to smell bad."

We had two Law Instructors, one Supervisory Border Patrol Agent (SBPA), Carl, who was a permanent staff member at FLETC (Federal Law Enforcement Training Center), and the other a detailed BPA on loan from the Chula Vista station. They split Class 357 between them, Sections A and B. They were our shepherds throughout the process; points of contact for administrative and logistical problems as well as instructing us in Immigration, Statutory, and Constitutional Law, and Operations, among other subjects. Some of the law classes featured attorneys as instructors, but a lot of it was done by our BP instructors.

One of our law instructors summarized Immigration Law: "Tell them who you are. Ask them, 'US Citizen? No? Got papers? No? Get in the truck.'"

Having said that, he went on to explain that immigration law was the most difficult and ever-changing subject with numerous classifications, each with exceptions, and many of us would fail it. Many of us did.

There were several Spanish-speaking instructors; the fifty of us were divided into Groups One through Five. Group One was composed of fluent Spanish-speaking trainees with Group Five trainees being completely ignorant of the language. I could count and knew the alphabet in Spanish, so I got group Two. We didn't have many fluent Spanish speakers.

One of the most useful things I learned about tactics in the field was taught by one of the Spanish instructors. We had been in the academy for quite a while now, and some of us were curious as to why we weren't being taught how to handle large groups. This particular instructor did not blow us off; when pressed on how he got control of groups far outnumbering him, he went into a little more detail.

His suggestion was that when you have the group apprehended (how to do that, he did not elaborate), line them up seated on the ground "nuts to butts," then have everyone lie back onto the person behind them. This way, you could efficiently keep an eye on everyone from any position, and if they wanted to run, they would easily get too entangled to get up and run off. With multiple agents, you could search the alien in the front of the line, then handcuff or send him to the back to assume the position. When the time came for everyone to move out, it made it easy to flex-cuff their hands together as well. I have used this tactic many times in the field over the years and it never failed me.

We had two Physical Techniques instructors; one was a muscly weightlifter and the other one was, you guessed it, a skinny marathon man. "Muscles" was really funny with very few words, and always spoke in a monotone no matter what. "Marathon Man" was even less talkative. These guys were the most professional of all of the instructors, and they were responsible for getting us in shape (only about half of us were), teaching us arrest techniques, use of force continuum, and defensive tactics.

Early on, I re-injured my knee and had to favor it throughout the academy. Muscles took me aside at one point and asked me about it. There was no way I was going to quit; though I might fall behind on some of the runs, I assured him I would not drop out. As other "guest" instructors came and went, I really appreciated how squared away Muscles and Marathon Man were because a lot of the PT instructors had a chip on their shoulder and liked playing "The DI" and harassing their poor trainees. Harsh treatment is fine; law enforcement agents are often expected to make correct decisions and think clearly in tense situations, but at some point, it becomes pointless harassment. I saw some of this later when I became a Firearms Instructor.

Firearms was my favorite. I had an interest in guns, and one of the reasons I chose law enforcement was free ammo. We had one permanent staff Firearms Instructor, or Lead FI, and a bunch of Detailed Instructors who split themselves up amongst us when on the firing line. Our Lead FI was a really larger-than-life character with flaming red hair, a heroic mustache, and a very Texan accent. He had started his career as a Deputy US Marshal and transferred to the BP. Ten years later, when I came to FLETC as an instructor, Red was still there and beloved by his trainees.

The Driving Instructors were all very laid back; I can't remember much about them. Pursuit driving was a lot of fun. The off-road class was ridiculous, consisting of a few mud puddles. The instructors seemed more worried about getting their Broncos dirty than teaching us how to drive off-road. In pursuit driving, my roommate Jeremy and I tried really hard to push our Crown Victoria to the limits of gravity and friction, but if you stayed on the track it was almost impossible to roll.

Each class was divided into Sections A and B. Each section elected a Section Leader from amongst their own who was responsible for getting us to morning formation, marched around to class, chow, and afternoon formation if there was one. Our guy had been a Sergeant in the Marine Reserves and had actually been a Drill Instructor at the Marine Corps Recruit Depot in San Diego before coming to the BP. Damien was even-tempered and hilarious, could count cadence well and everyone liked him, so it was pretty much a unanimous vote if I remember correctly. He left the BP after a couple of years for a job with the "real police" in Escondido, CA. In a short time, Damien became a hero after ending a car chase through a residential neighborhood in a very short gunfight. Our loss was Escondido's gain; he is solid.

Every class chose a class motto. When we voted on the choices, my contribution to 357 was the Latin phrase, *"fidem scit."* While the literal translation is "faith knows," or "he knows the faith," I had always been told it was idiomatic for "keep the faith." The pronunciation, "feed 'em shit," ended up killing it though, so it was forbidden and we had to go with something else that I can't remember.

Class 357 had a psycho; he stared at everyone with crazy eyes and would ask the stupidest questions sometimes. Pasillo was laser-focused on the use-of-force part of the job. He stated at one point that, if necessary, he would screw over anyone in the class in order to graduate and become an agent. He could talk to you like everything was cool, and still say stuff like that. The BP, unfortunately, did not have a psych eval back then, or if they did, it failed us. Luckily for the taxpayers of the United States, the Border Patrol, and perhaps any number of illegal aliens, BPA(t) Pasillo never made it past the mid-term. He just couldn't get through the Spanish. Later, one of the firearms instructors expressed surprise that we were so happy to be rid of old Pasillo. The FIs thought he was just working hard to shoot well (he couldn't). When we explained his deal, it was agreed by all: It was good that he could not shoot any better than he could speak Spanish.

To summarize, the Border Patrol Academy was very thorough in its coverage of immigration, statutory, and constitutional law as applied to immigration law enforcement. The Spanish program was fantastic, especially when one considers that it was taught by Border Patrol Agents and not teachers or Spanish professors. Firearms was also excellent. Driving was slightly less exhaustive in its coverage, especially the off-road portion, but I am told it got much better later on at Artesia. In Charleston, driving was mainly focused on Non-Emergency Vehicle Operations and Pursuit Driving. There was not much coverage of Border Patrol Operations at the academy. This was probably because ops varied depending on where the trainees were going, and it is best to have the stations teach their way of doing things. After about five months (our class was there over the holiday season), Class 357 was definitely ready to get to work. I do not remember the exact numbers but believe our class attrition rate was right around 15%.

Trainees - At the El Cajon Station (ECJ)

After the Academy, we got about a week off to get packed up and move to wherever our stations were. Half of 357 went to San Diego Sector, the Temecula (TEM), and El Cajon Stations (ECJ); the rest went to other Sectors in El Centro, Yuma, and a few to Tucson. Back then, you went to the Academy only knowing what Sector you got, and then when you were a little more than halfway through, they would assign you a station. I got hired for San Diego Sector. This was a big one, from Imperial Beach on the coast to Boulevard in the mountains of East County. There was not much time to set up in our new area. Luckily, my sweet and lovely wife was more than happy to go out apartment hunting with her friend when I found out El Cajon was going to be my new station.

On our first day at the El Cajon Station, our main Field Training Officer had us in the training room. We all hushed up and leaned forward expectantly to hear what was going to happen.

"All women are whores," said he, and expounded upon this thesis at length, explaining what a bitch his ex-wife was, spending his money, cheating on him, and dumping him or whatever. I didn't hear much more of that shocking introductory lecture; I was stunned. Thoughts flooded in; about the pay cut I took to get here, if my old job would take me back, and whether or not the wife and I would be able to pay the bills... It was going to be a long, bumpy road hanging in there with the two main FTOs we had.

The other main FTO was a loud, large, fat, shaven-headed guy with a lot of time in service and a handlebar mustache that made him look like some kind of Mexican pirate. One of the first things this guy said was that he had "more time backing out of donut shops than you have in the Patrol!" This was one of the more believable things he relayed to us. It was also the first time (but not the last) that I would hear a senior agent try to belittle junior agents by telling us how much time he had in. I later observed that he was nothing special in the field. He would ruthlessly pick on one of my classmates, making him stand up in class and berating him for being, of all things, overweight.

In my opinion, our two main FTOs were unimpressive, and I wanted nothing to do with them. I had been promised a "highly mobile, elite law enforcement agency," and here we were, stuck with a pair of apparent losers. There were a few other FTOs who were squared away, such as "Captain America" and "Shotgun Tom", but it was clear that those were just the field guys. "The Pirate" and "Divorced" were the two primary ones doing our classes, administrative, and processing/casework instruction.

Class 357 at El Cajon Station stayed on the FTU until we had passed our 6-month and 10-month Spanish boards. There were law exams, but no one really worried about them. Spanish was the focus and most of us weren't great at that, with a few exceptions. Failing the Spanish board got you fired. It definitely consumed much of my spare time. We went to remedial classes given at Sector, and the more you went to, the better. After passing the 10-month exams, agents were allowed to ride on their own sometimes. Usually, this meant you got Checkpoint, Transport, or Hospital Watch; the assignments no one else wanted. Back then I preferred Transport since we could drive the roads and learn the area from there. Then, when someone "went 10-15 (apprehended aliens)," I was the guy to pick them up. If it was slow, I could do whatever and explore.

First Allegation

It so happened that after completing our six-month Spanish exam, my buddies Curtis, Tom, and I were eating lunch at a McDonald's near Sector Headquarters on Telegraph Canyon Road. We were wearing our summer dress uniforms, unarmed (because it was a do-or-die exam and nobody wanted to fire armed trainees if we failed). It was pretty crowded but we got our burgers and sat down near where people were lined up to be served, Tom with his back to the wall. On the wall was attached a plastic case with some kind of Happy Meal toys displayed inside, just behind and above his head. Some kid was all over it, trying to open it, touching it, bumping into, and jostling Tom. Tom took it well and continued eating while I chuckled, thoroughly amused at the spectacle of my friend trying to ignore this obnoxious kid whose mother was obviously ignoring him.

"You wanna get out of here?" I asked. He shook his head no, and we commenced devouring our Big Macs and fries, so we could leave to get back to the station.

Then, she appeared.

"What the hell are you doing?! Fuckin' Border Patrol, WHAT ARE YOU DOING?!!"

A very large Hispanic woman bore down on us, snatching up the kid. He might have been six or seven years old.

"Uh, nothing?"

"I saw you, I SAW YOU! How dare you push him! I saw you push my son! He has special needs!"

I remember putting up my hands, in the "whoa there, take it easy" type gesture, as we proceeded to leave. We said something like, "Hey, we don't know what you're talking about lady. Call the station if you want to complain." She continued berating us and accusing us of abusing her disabled boy in front of what must have been dozens of witnesses. We later presented ourselves to our FTO, (Divorced) and explained to him what happened. He told us with his wry smile that it was a good thing we came to him first, as word had preceded us and we would have been fired for sure if we hadn't come forward. Divorced made it seem like we passed some kind of test.

A few weeks after that, we had to get all dressed up to

"Stand Tall Before the Man." The Deputy Chief was "Doc" Beasley, a Vietnam Vet Navy Corpsman, and looked like it. I was pretty sure we were going to be fine, but you never knew. He smiled. "Welcome to the Border Patrol," was the only thing he said that I remember exactly. Apparently, the woman at McDonald's had called and spoken to him in the same none-too-charming way she had addressed us, that is, like a raving lunatic. The upshot of it was, that we had conducted ourselves well enough, and had reported it right away.

It was an early lesson that stood me in good stead the rest of my time in: if you're reasonably acting like a Border Patrol Agent, and you make a mistake or do something stupid, or are in the wrong place at the wrong time, getting in front of it is always the best play. If there is discipline, it will be relatively minor, or at least not as bad as if you get caught in a lie or try to "brush it out."

Shortly after this incident, one of the more senior guys summed it up in a way that I tried to pass on ever since: "If you're a hard-working PA, you are going to hurt feelings, break shit, and get in trouble. Be honest and it will all work itself out."

I wish I remembered the agent who told me that first, I would say "thanks" to him too.

First Group

I will say this: the first FTO, Divorced, whose name I am not using for obvious reasons, did later take us on our first "walk" whereupon we caught our first group. As I recall we drove out on Highway 94 to Marron Valley Road, went south, and took a right to just past the gun club to a place called Birdman. This is on the eastern side of Otay Mountain, where a trail dropped into Mine Canyon.

Mine Canyon got super-hot in the summer, and there were few places to get into or out of the canyon. It runs north from the Tijuana River and if memory serves, bends to the west a little bit towards the end near Birdman. Also, there were a lot of open holes in the rock, as the name suggests. This is where I discovered my new worst fear: falling alone into a very deep hole to be crippled and eaten on by animals until dead.

Divorced pointed to a piece of plywood laying on the ground near the trailhead. It covered a vent shaft for an ancient mine: "There are holes all over the place. Don't fall in." We started down the rocky trail. It was not too hot yet, but we were sweating our asses off in our clunky black boots, heavy polyester rough-duty trousers, heavy and unbending UNICOR body armor, belt gear, and Camelback hydration packs. The trail was well-worn but uneven; we had to pay attention.

Once down, we paused and drank some water while some of the others caught up. Divorced might have said a few words that we were expected to pass on to the stragglers. I can't remember what, but probably something like "there's a sensor over there; when it bangs off, you can park at Birdman and drop in here, or wait to see what they bang next," which would indicate if the group was coming out on the trail or staying in the canyon to further their illegal entry.

When everyone had gathered up, we continued into the creek bed behind Divorced. He went into some brush where the creek went around the corner, then popped back around with a grin, nodding towards the brush.

"Look guys - aliens!"

All thirteen or fourteen of us charged around the corner to confront a very surprised group of illegal aliens, equal in number, all squatting down next to the creek bed taking a break. I'm sure we spouted orders in our Academy Spanish "*Parense. Somos La Migra,*" etcetera. Our first walk had been a short one; we searched the aliens and walked back up to Birdman's to call for transport.

Later, we got to know Mine Canyon very well.

Riding With a Journeyman

Towards the end of the FTU, we had a period of time when we were assigned to ride with a "journeyman agent" who would work with and observe us and our deficiencies, and presumably report this to the FTU supervisor. I am not sure this ever happened, but we were convinced that until our probationary year was up, we could be fired at any time. My first journeyman was Marc, a guy who only had a few months on me, Class 336 or something. I called him "sir," and he laughed in my face. "Fuck that, I'm a nugget like you. Let's go learn the area."

There was another journeyman I rode with who was all about catching bodies at that time. Brad was a short stocky white guy from back east, spoke super-fast, and could talk shit like nobody's business; he was a real comedian. On the day I was assigned to ride with Brad, we drove out to a small collection of houses off of 94, near Dulzura, CA. This area was known as "Middle Earth." We drove out and met up with another guy, Haldo.

Haldo quickly became one of my favorite agents at El Cajon; he had a very infectious sense of humor and goodwill. Haldo wanted to help us new guys learn how to be productive, was really into the job, and was fast enough to chase down any runners. Also, being fluent in Spanish, he could calm down the aliens and even blend in with them in the dark if possible, which was very cool to me.

We met up at a spot near some houses in the shadow of Little Tecate Peak; the plan was for Haldo to get into the brush behind them where he thought a group was laid up, and flush them out. Brad and I were to stand by on foot close to the road so we could swoop in when the time came and make the arrest. Haldo disappeared.

A short time later, I heard "a whoopin' and a hollerin'" as a bunch of what appeared to be illegal aliens burst out of the brush between the houses near Brad and run down the road to the east. I was the westernmost guy and gave chase as Haldo came out following them, Brad grabbing a few. In the tight UNICOR body armor with all my shit on like a good trainee, I was huffing and puffing by the time I got to them. "Grab these guys," Brad told me and took off after Haldo and the rest of the group. They sprinted down towards the group, laughing and yelling the whole way.

Later we got all of them together, searched, and were driving to meet the transport van. Brad and I loaded quite a few in the back of his 1997 Chevy Tahoe; at the time, it was the latest two-door 4x4 patrol vehicle and had a rearward-facing caged off bench seat for three detainees. (We often loaded up a few more for short trips.) One of the IAs said something through the cage to Brad, to which he replied, "*y ahorita, tu no vale verga*!"

"What did he say to you?" I asked.

"He's the foot guide; he says always gets his chickens through," Brad cackled in his high-pitched, back east way, "and never gets caught. I told him he ain't worth dick now."

After dropping off the aliens with transport, it was getting dark. Brad drove back up the hill past the houses to a spot where a pullout ended in a steep upward grade.

"Now, I will demonstrate the shuttle-launch position," he said as he gunned it until we were facing Little Tecate Peak at about a 45-degree angle. Out of his trique bag, he pulled a mini-mag flashlight with two flex-cuffs attached so that he could loop it over the sun visor and shine the light onto a book, while he sat reading comfortably. Obviously, this is way before smartphones, and just as unsafe to sit there in the dark with a light on the inside of the ride.

Brad must have been reading the look of concern on my face. "Dude, nobody's gonna fuck with us... I'm sure you have Spanish or something to study. I don't give a fuck what you do. We caught bodies, now we're going to take a break. This job is a fucking joke. You'll see."

It was a long time ago, but it made an impression. At the end of our shift, we drove to a 7-11, backed right up to the front door, and he went in and bought a couple of cases of beer for "choir practice." This is a now-dated ritual in law enforcement, wherein the guys drink beers at the end of shift and talk about their day before going home.

I was invited, but uncomfortable with this. As a probationary trainee, I could be fired for just about anything, and a "deuce," or DUI, was a one-way ticket to unemployment. Also, it wasn't really my place to talk shit with the boys after work, being a nug. It was nice of him though, asking me to stay.

III. PAs-Out in the Field

Journeyman Agent, ECJ

Once released from the Field Training Unit, new agents, or "PAs," as we call ourselves, are doled out to the Patrol Groups, depending on the needs of the service. Most are pretty eager to prove themselves, as were the agents of Class 357. While the first part of the book is from mainly the author's point of view, multiple agents (author included) have contributed their recollections to the balance of this book. Again, names have been changed or omitted when necessary or requested.

First Felony Stop

After your probationary year was up, you were on your own. As I recall, times were lean in the INS years, and there were only enough vehicles for the most senior guys to have one assigned. The rest of us got what we got; usually, a beat-up old Dodge van or one of the already "well used" 1994 Bronco 4x4s, if we were lucky. Typically, we rode with a partner. Since the senior agents didn't want to ride with a trainee, our partners were usually other agents who were just off the training unit.

One afternoon, my buddy Marty and I were driving Highway 94 eastbound to wherever we were assigned that day when Dispatch put out info regarding the burglary of a barn in Dulzura. Apparently, the people who did the burglary made their getaway in a U-Haul-type box truck. I am sure Marty made one of his typically funny remarks in an under-his-breath, mumbly voice, and as we commenced talking shit about using a U-Haul as a getaway vehicle, a U-Haul drove by us going the other way. The occupants matched the description that had just been put out by Dispatch.

"What the hell? Was that it?!"

"Let's get 'em!"

I flipped around while Marty called it in. We caught up to the suspects near the "35 mile-an-hour-curve" and, in our excitement, initiated a felony traffic stop with lights and sirens. Could this be the big case that cements our reputation? I remember the box truck pulling over into a dirt pull-out as Marty fumbled for the public address mic which was, predictably, broken. As Primary Contact officer, I began the spiel:

"DRIVER! SHOW ME YOUR HANDS!" I shouted, following the script we had all memorized in the academy for a high-risk vehicle stop. In the hubbub, I was completely tunneled in on the driver, concentrating on my script, hand on my gun behind my open door. Then all of a sudden, another PA was right in front of me. Sauntering up to the suspect vehicle with what looked to me to be supreme nonchalance, was Big Ed.

"Baah," he growled. Big Ed was an old-time Senior Patrol

Agent who had come from El Centro. He spoke with the driver while Marty and I kind of looked at each other, wondering "WTF?" Then the truck drove away and Ed came over. Apparently, it was all some type of misunderstanding. Deflated and dismissed, we went back east to our area. Later on, I got to know Ed as a very squared away, low-profile agent who was not shy about taking charge but didn't make a big deal out of it. Classic old-school GS-11. He would be one of my supervisors a few years later.

First Big Group

Around that period of time, Marty and I were often paired up. Though it is not great to put academy classmates together when they are just off the training unit, the supervisors on our shift didn't seem to mind, and the senior agents wanted to do their own thing. One evening, Marty and I heard about a big group in a place called Sycamore Canyon, which came out of the Otay Mountain Wilderness and opened up on its way to Highway 94. We could hear on the radio that multiple agents were working a group of thirty or so with a helicopter, which was called "Foxtrot" back then.

"Should we get in there?"

"Fuck it, let's go!"

We went in through "Pink Gate," the entrance to Sycamore Canyon, and drove south on the dirt road about half a kilometer while listening to the radio traffic and paying attention to where Foxtrot was. The ritual of going in with lights out and getting out on foot with Maglite in hand, Camelbak on, and gloves on was still new to us. We weren't exactly sure where the group was but had a good idea. We bumped into another agent in the dark as we made our way up a hill for a better view.

We didn't know the other agent and I don't think I ever discovered who he was, but we were learning that in the dark when working traffic, you pick up instantly on things that are not necessarily conscious. Aliens look and act a certain way. Agents look and act a certain way. Animals look and act a certain way. All you can see is maybe the silhouette or part of it, but there are little mannerisms, noises, smells, etc., that are instantly recognizable in the moment.

Our mystery agent had an idea: the aliens were on the other side of the hill, brushed up. His plan was to get in behind them and get as close as possible since there were guys from the FTU up ahead laid in for them. If the group got busted, we would be right there in their faces when they turned around.

He sounded like he knew what he was doing, so we fell in with him and worked our way around the hill going southbound on

37

the east side of the slope. We made out the trail they were following in the starlight (there was no moon if I remember correctly), then followed it north. In a few minutes, we could see them all crouched down in a line. We heard the Mystery Agent say something to them in Spanish like "It's us, let's go," or words to that effect, and everyone got up and continued their walk north on the trail. We were behind them on the trail, descending the hill now, when from a brush line up ahead, a bunch of flashlights turned on. The conga line of aliens froze with that "should I stay or should I go" kind of crouched, rocking back and forth stance. Mystery Agent identified us as agents to them, and they all crouched down and chilled; when he hit his light, we hit ours too, then we moved up on either side of the trail and that was it. They were caught.

It was really very cool for Marty and me. We ended up with twenty-something aliens; a few up in front took off and Mystery Agent ran to get them with some of the FTU guys. We were instantly surrounded by the rest of the Training Unit, a bunch of wide-eyed new guys yelling *"Parense!"* a little too late. According to their FTO, they had brought a couple of transport vans, so if we would help walk out the group, we could take off after that. The trainees would write them up.

A Surprise Near the Station Wagon

Hanging out near the end of the IBF, west of Tecate, I sat in my Bronco munching on some chips and looking over the fence into Tecate. There is a house there right next to the fence where a creek bed went south into Mexico. It is called Pilgrim's Grove. This is where, years before, an on-duty Border Patrol Agent had been caught by his supervisor loading bags full of dope into his marked service vehicle. The guy had been suspected of doing that for a long time.

That was before I got there in 1998. Whenever I was assigned to this area, it was my habit to cut along the line to the end of the fence, just in case. If you continue to walk west, uphill, you end up south of a landmark called Lizard Rock. Lots of groups crossed in this area at the time.

From my spot at the Grove, I could go east towards the POE, or west up to Tecate Peak if necessary.

A sensor banged off north of me, so I answered up and started towards a dirt cul-de-sac called the Station Wagon. There was a shell of an old wrecked 1960s station wagon there, slowly becoming part of the earth. It was a Border Patrol parking spot for working a number of trails that descended down the mountain towards Highway 94, and points north.

A typical sensor response sounds something like this:

"7503, for three," calls dispatch (call sign 820), "seven-five-zero-three, good for three."

"10-4 820, E-368 will check that 7503." (E-368 was my call sign. The E (Echo) meant El Cajon Station; 368 was my 'star number,' or designation, at El Cajon.)

"10-4, E-368 responding to 7503."

I'm making up the sensor number, but that's how it goes.

There was one gate to unlock, then it was north through "Stonehenge," a place with weird tall rock formations that reminded me more of the big faces on Easter Island than the prehistoric stone circle in the UK. From there, it was a straight line to the Station

Wagon. I thought if I hurried, I would be in front of the group instead of chasing them downhill.

The sun was going down as I got out on foot, with my Camelbak on and Maglite in hand, to go get some aliens. The trail was west; the sign would be easier to cut into the sun. There was a large area of cap rock at one point, and a couple of trails that came out over there. I picked one and started checking the dirt for sign.

It wasn't long before I picked up foot sign and began following it. It wasn't dark yet, but the trail was worn through thick manzanita, so I used the flashlight to periodically confirm I was still on it. This was before shoe booties became common for the aliens, who used them to obscure their tracks with varying degrees of success. I can't remember what kind of foot sign it was, but it took me straight towards the cap rock which I had just traversed.

So I was late, I thought. With the large area of rock without a lot of dirt on it, it was going to be pretty hard to cut it. Some guys are geniuses at sign cutting, but I am not one of them. Tom Johnson used to snarl in his smoker's voice, "Persistence!" This, according to him, was the best indicator of good sign cutting.

My plan was to go to the edge of the cap rock and circle the entire formation where it met a trail or any likely dirt and cut from there. Eventually, something would reveal itself. Even as a young guy, my right knee gave me a lot of problems, so I steeled myself for a long walk downhill to 94.

Before long, I was almost out of options on the cap rock. Maybe they were already heading down, but none of the bugs on known trails had banged off. Either they were off-trail or laid up somewhere nearby. One more big rock...

There was a crevice between the rock I was on and the one I wanted to get to, so I hopped over it like I had a million times before. The problem with cap rock though, is that it shears off from time to time. This is what happened. The sandstone sheared, and I fell ass over teakettle, backward into the crevice.

Whenever I lose my footing or take a spill by surprise like

that, it always takes my breath away. There wasn't even enough time to be terrified of my worst fear, falling into a hole at night. I fell down about ten to fifteen feet, landing partially on top of one alien and his adult son.

The Camelbak was still pretty full, which served as a cushion for my back. I scrambled to my feet between the startled, and luckily uninjured, Mexicans. Before I could catch my breath, the older guy had his hands up, "It's OK *oficial*, OK," he said.

It was OK. Lucky for me, they were just normal folks crossing illegally, like most of the IAs at that time. We did not get a vast number of criminal dirtbags at that time, at least not that I recall, with about nine out of ten being regular working people. If they had wanted to, they could've given me a pretty hard time in between those rocks there.

We spoke as I patted them down. Both were Mexican, coming to work the fields. They had been sitting on the rock when they heard my vehicle coming and got down into the crevice to hide. It opened up towards the north, so we went out that way, picking up a trail back to the Station Wagon and my Bronco.

It was the last time I ever jumped around on cap rock, but not the last time I took a fall.

Weird Place Names and Nicknames

Some of the landmarks BP Agents refer to have strange names. Some are named after an agent who crashed or got stuck there, shot a cow, or otherwise earned it, like Wolter's Wash, or Scott's Hill. Some are more banal like "The 35 Mile an Hour Curve." There are 35-mile-an-hour curves everywhere, but when you said those words at the El Cajon Station at the end of the last century, everyone knew which one you meant. Another 35-mile-an-hour curve was called Murphy's Curve. At one point I knew why, but it has since slipped away. When unusual names are mentioned, they are probably just weird place names that someone came up with. There is Pink Gate, Patty's House, Dinosaur Eggs, Moon Rock, Spooky Forest, Parking Lot, Ant Hill, Castle Rock, Eagle's Nest, The Phone Booth, The Hiltons, Burning Bush, Refrigerator Canyon, Scootville, Last Chance Cafe, Turd Farm, Dead Cow (turns out pretty much every station has a Dead Cow. Even though the border area is littered with desiccated bovine remains, it seems like agents always have a certain place by this name). The names change over the years as agents who know their origin leave and are then replaced with a new group of agents that will assign their own names, and so on.

Although it might have been more common in years past, some of today's more distinctive agents still acquire nicknames. Not all are complimentary or embraced by their bearer. Some nicknames that I assign to people are NOT what they were called at the time and should not be used to try to identify them.

Jargon, Tonks, Maglites

A few things. In normal life or on TV, when one hears the word "bodies," it is assumed to mean dead ones. For BP Agents, it is another word for a contact. If you are calling out a group from a scope truck, or encounter a group on patrol, it is commonly accepted to radio "I've got bodies," or "we have 150 bodies in processing." So, throughout the book, this term is interchangeable with aliens, illegal aliens, IAs, apprehensions, apps, etc. One can argue that it is insensitive or dehumanizing, sure. Behind every alien's eyes is a story, some worse than others. Whether you are arresting a group of two to ten in one encounter or hundreds to thousands in a 20 to 30-year career, you don't have room for all of them in your head.

It is definitely tragic that huge numbers of people flee the countries beyond our southern border. Cartels are taking over Mexico, which has been verging on "failed state" status for years now. This has been taken full advantage of by elites within the United States, as has been the case for as long as anyone can remember. Importing a vast underclass that will need services and representation on one side and cheap labor for the greedy bloodsuckers on the other. Agents can know this and still do their jobs to the extent possible. One of the first things we were told at the academy is "you will not make a difference in the illegal immigration problem."

Fact check: True! The Patrol is approximately three times larger now than it was when I joined up. Illegal immigration is worse now than ever. Drugs? Worse now than ever. Agents doing the right thing, when it counts, means more to me than all of those things I cannot control. We are always trying to balance the spirit in which we joined up and swore the oath with the reality that, in the grand scheme of things, we and our actions mean next to nothing.

Agents must also balance empathy and officer safety all the time. That is why there are procedures to follow, accepted ways to recognize reasonable suspicion/probable cause, make an arrest, and prevent an escape. You can't be feeling everyone's feelings all the time, but you can recognize people *in* trouble who need help, and people who *are* trouble, and need restraint. As the police phrase goes: be professional with the perps, compassionate with the victims.

After climbing up a mountain in the dark to pursue a group of aliens, we busted a group. The bodies ran in different directions, one trio right in front of me, but I couldn't reach them due to a drop-off in between us. The agent behind them tried to run after them and everyone fell ass over teakettle. The three got away; the agent following picked himself up and got the rest of the group a few minutes later. We took many breaks and spent a long time helping the young Guatemalans remove the cholla spines from their feet before we walked them down the mountain. This illustrates the dichotomy of the Border Patrol and law enforcement in general. Had he caught up to those three guys, the fight would have been on, on the side of a mountain, three against one until I got around the ravine to help him out. Instead, we ended up playing medic and helping the others down the hill.

The Border Patrol, as well as some BP jargon, is (incorrectly, in my opinion) viewed today as racist. Racism is a belief that race is a fundamental determinant of human traits and capacities, and that racial differences produce an inherent superiority of a particular race. As noted before, Border Patrol does not care what race the aliens are. They are legal or illegal. The Border Patrol is not immune to the PC language police. One example is the word "tonc" or "tonk." The origin of this term, as far as I have been able to figure out, can come from one of three places (at least in this country. In the UK, tonk means fit or hot, as in "that bloke/bird is tonk!").

Chinese laborers who, in the 19th century, were imported to help build the railroads, were oftentimes trafficked to the United States as virtual slaves by Chinese Transnational Criminal Organizations known as "tongs." Thus, the word may have evolved from this.

As another story goes, the use of the word "tonk" is an onomatopoeia that began with railroad police in the Great Depression era who reportedly used their flashlights as an impact weapon upon the skulls of hobos "riding the rails," which made the corresponding "tonk" sound. As another agent once pointed out to me, "that Maglite makes the same noise on my head, too."

According to the definition I was taught in the training unit by the Field Training Officer (the one whom I call "Divorced"), TONC is actually an acronym for Traveler Out of Native Country. It was a word used for decades. In the early 2000s, a Chief Patrol Agent decided it was based on race and banned it. Some ignored the ban. We all have heads.

Only the first example, tong, could be construed as singling out a specific ethnic group; the second and third are not even close. If the word tonk is used here, it refers to all illegal aliens from everywhere. As an agent, I have strayed into Mexico more than once by accident. In those instances, I would have been the tonk. Generally, agents call their apprehensions bodies, apps, EWIs (Entered Without Inspection), 10-15s, subjects, aliens, or illegal aliens (still the legal term), because that is what they are.

To belabor the point, people sneaking around into our country without permission, between the land ports of entry, in the dark, through the desert or mountains, from another country, are illegal aliens. That is a fact under Title 8 of the United States Code. It is a legal term and it has nothing to do with ethnicity or race. It refers to people who have entered without possessing legal documents from the Secretary of Homeland Security to enter, pass through, or remain in the United States consistent with US law.

One recent Chief of the Border Patrol was forced to retire after refusing to call illegal aliens "Undocumented Non-Citizens," an invented term that the then-Secretary of Homeland Security deemed to be "more inclusive." It was ordered that all personnel use the term "Undocumented Non-Citizens" in all correspondence and reports, but to still use the legally correct "illegal alien" in charging documents, since the law has not been changed. This should give the clear-thinking reader a glimpse into the world of the Border Patrol, an agency tasked to enforce Immigration Law but also tasked to be "more inclusive."

Back to the word *tonk.* It can refer to the sound of a flashlight striking the human head. Before you ask, I have never witnessed anyone hit with a Maglite. If you wish to judge a Border Patrol Agent (or any police officer) who did such a thing, I ask you to view the totality of the circumstances surrounding the event.

Envision this: You're by yourself or with another agent when you come upon a group of figures in the dark who are hell-bent on getting around or through you to get into this country. Unless you know they are carrying weapons or dope, you are probably not justified in drawing your handgun unless you are attacked. If an attack happens, you are already carrying a Maglite in one hand and if you lose it, it might be used against you. With your other hand, you might be fending off blows, or perhaps keying the mic on your radio to summon help. Maybe now you can imagine how someone might get hit with a flashlight when trying to run through or over a Border Patrol Agent.

Another problematic term is a legal term that was taught in the Border Patrol Academy when I was there, called "wetting them down." This expression is thought by some to be racist, as it comes from the fact that illegal aliens crossing the Rio Grande River back in the old days were referred to as "wetbacks." An early attempt to deport what was considered to be a surplus of illegal aliens back in the 1950s was actually officially called "Operation Wetback." This has become pejorative in modern times and I do not use it, even though my back would be wet, too, if I tried to apprehend an illegal alien in a river, and I am not of Hispanic or Latino heritage. Nonetheless, this expression was taught in the FLETC Border Patrol Academy and refers to the process of determining alienage.

I am sure there are other examples, which we will address if they come up.

Checkpoint Operations

Next to processing, the checkpoint has always been my least favorite place to be. You are completely exposed to traffic and the orange plastic barricades are often not filled with anything (i.e., sand or water) and are of zero protective value. Also, although the Supreme Court Case Martinez vs. Fuerte established that immigration checkpoints are constitutional, there isn't anything in the law that requires drivers to do anything other than stop at the stop sign and be questioned as to their citizenship. Uncooperative motorists have only to sit there until you run checks on their vehicle or run the K9 in an open-air sniff around the vehicle, and then you pretty much have to release them if you have no further suspicion of illegal alienage. If the dog alerts to an odor it has been trained to detect (i.e., dope, bodies), that equals probable cause, and the driver must then be detained while agents investigate the alert.

Many people, especially those who reside or spend a lot of time on Indian Reservations, greatly and understandably resent Border Patrol Immigration checkpoints on their land, and some of these people are most unpleasant to deal with. If I lived on a reservation and had to stop and answer the same stupid questions day in and day out just to carry on my daily business, I would not appreciate it either.

There are BP agents who enjoy the checkpoint, embrace it, and make great cases. There is always stuff coming through the checkpoint, and agents who pay attention and spot the little things can often discover big things, which turn into cases. Also, most smugglers are idiots and talk themselves right into handcuffs.

I have never worked at a main multi-lane checkpoint station like the San Clemente, CA, Murrietta, CA, or Wilcox, AZ, checkpoint stations. These stations exist to service major interstate highways, as well as minor supporting checkpoints in the surrounding areas. In practice, due to the sheer volume of traffic, lack of available manpower, or ability to conduct effective enforcement operations, these checkpoints were usually "down" when I have driven by. At the stations where I have worked, a checkpoint is a two-lane affair, one lane going in each direction, and we only stop traffic going one way. There are usually limited lighting and safety features, and the agents at the point need to maintain situational awareness at all times. There is either a single-wide trailer for offices and cells or a crudely modified "Connex box" with a refrigerator, a desk, and maybe a three-man cell. In "Primary," standing in the middle of the road, you have to have eyes in the back of your head. Inattentive or impaired drivers are very dangerous to anyone standing near or in the middle of the road, as checkpoint agents must.

At small checkpoints, there is usually an agent in "Primary," an agent in "Secondary," and another agent; a K9 agent if available, and a supervisor if available. It is best to run with five agents in these situations, but we have done it with two or three in a pinch. Ideally, you want to have someone to watch your back at all times, especially when inspecting a vehicle in the secondary inspection lane.

Vehicles drive up to Primary and are greeted by the agent there. If he has any suspicion of illegal alienage, he indicates the driver to pull over to the side lane, or Secondary. Both he and the secondary agent accompany the vehicle to the side, ready to throw spikes or a "Controlled Tire Deflation Device," in case the driver decides to bolt. While they are doing this, a third agent is watching or taking over Primary. If they are lucky, they have a supervisor or a fourth agent to oversee all of this, and/or run the radio.

If all goes well, the driver is released. If criminal activity is detected, agents hold the suspects and call the relevant agency. If illegal aliens or narcotics are discovered, then agents arrest the principals, seize the vehicle and/or contraband, and take everything to the station to process the case.

It is not advisable to run an immigration checkpoint with fewer than three agents, and an internet search for "Newton-Azrak Incident" explains why. Two agents, Theodore Newton and George Azrak, were tragically abducted and murdered by drug smugglers from their assigned small checkpoint in 1967. Every Border Patrol Agent knows the story: the two Border Patrol Agents (called "Inspectors" back then) became suspicious of an old military-surplus ambulance that seemed excessively loaded down for what the driver claimed to be doing, camping. When commanded to stop, the driver of the ambulance took off. The agents hopped into their patrol car in pursuit. They eventually caught up to and stopped the ambulance. They arrested two drug smugglers, Bone and Mationg, and seized 800 lbs. of marijuana. As they were doing this, however, Bone's and Mationg's accomplices, the Montoya brothers, approached from behind. The Montoyas snuck up and overpowered the agents. After freeing Bone and Mationg, agents Newton and Azrak were placed in the trunk of their vehicle, taken to an old mining shack, and executed with their own weapons.

The Border Patrol's highest award for bravery was named after these two agents; the official version of this story is on cbp.gov.

Processing

As the processing agent, you receive the van loads of aliens that are brought in from the field, each of which is supposed to come with a sheet of paper called a Field Processing Form, or 826, which contains the bare-bones biographical information for the individual, as well as the basic circumstances of the apprehension.

The bodies are matched up with their 826s, bags if they have them (also called "mochilas"), searched, and placed in a cell. Then, one by one, you remove them from their cell and question, photograph, and fingerprint them. They are then placed into another cell until you get a return on their biometrics. Sometimes they are a "first-timer," and therefore amenable to basically getting kicked back to Mexico, until a few years ago. Repeat offenders, or aliens from countries Other Than Mexico (OTMs), and convicted criminals are considered "an A-file." For the last several years, a so-called "Consequence Delivery System" has been in force, which supposedly accomplishes the same thing (but with way more man-hours and paperwork). Field agents might disagree with the "Consequence Delivery" part of this system, but that is for another book.

Completing a file, or an A-File (the "A" is for Alien), is basic BP 101 stuff: completing various forms to the satisfaction of the Duty Supervisor, putting them in a folder in a specific order, and submitting them to the FOS or Watch Commander. At some point, a bus comes and takes the body and his or her file to Sector and from there they get either Deported (a formal legal proceeding with attorneys and rights), Excluded (a less formal proceeding for certain aliens; basically, a quickie deportation sans attorneys and rights), or in the case of criminals, turned over to the US Marshals or held until extradition to whatever state they are wanted in.

I do not like processing because it smells in there; these people have been on foot in the desert or mountains for days or weeks without a wash. Aliens are hacking and sneezing and picking their noses, relieving their bowels in the little toilets to the rear of the cells (often explosively since they have sometimes been drinking water from cattle tanks). Mostly though because I would rather be catching my own groups instead of processing everyone else's. Many agents feel this way, but everyone takes their turn.

Every once in a while, you get a good story. The aliens are just people, like people everywhere else. The percentage of illegal aliens who are criminals fluctuates, but most of the people illegally crossing are just trying to get here for a job, education, or health care for themselves or their families, etc. They have not had the unbelievable good fortune to be born in the USA, and their home countries are almost universally hard places to live for most of the normal folks from there. If you're in the top 1%, you are living large just about anywhere, but these are not the people we encounter running through the brush at night.

Sonoita Station agents brought a guy in once from Belize. This immediately piqued my interest, as we do not normally see EWIs (Entry Without Inspection) from this country, at least never in the stations where I have been assigned. This guy was fairly squared away, dressed pretty well with good shoes as I recall. He spoke perfect English, their official language, which also made it easier to understand him for those of us whose Spanish was not so great.

According to this alien, whom I will call William, he was a working-class young guy with a decent job and a pretty girlfriend. This young lady caught the attention of a local gangster named Satan. Apparently, she was not the kind of girl who would date Satan, and he took offense when she rejected his attempts to woo her. After a time, as you might imagine, Satan ran out of patience and abducted, mistreated, and either killed the girl or "put her to work."

Young William was fairly matter-of-fact and kept his composure as he relayed his story, who knows how true it was. He continued on, stating that he went to Satan's place to find his girl, only to learn that she was either dead or turned out (I can't remember which). He freely admitted to murdering Satan and then fleeing his gang. Soon thereafter, he crossed into Mexico and continued north to the United States.

He wanted to claim Credible Fear, a legal term for a person who allegedly cannot return to his or her country of origin due to fear of violence or imprisonment. This is supposed to apply to persons who fear their government but is often claimed as fear of gang violence by those from places like Mexico and Central America. William told a great story, but he had crossed illegally and we processed him accordingly, albeit with his Credible Fear claim, which was not ours to adjudicate. Asylum Officers and Immigration Judges are notoriously lenient though, and according to everyone I have spoken to, they tend to err on the side of not deporting people.

Transport

The third of the most unappealing assignments for new Border Patrol Agents is transport. Nobody wants to do it, but when you're out in the desert with a bunch of aliens, you definitely want the transport guy to get there fast and take them off your hands. Most agents get it and do their best, sometimes to the point of recklessness.

When I got started, the transport vans were stinking two-wheel-drive jalopies that were barely roadworthy from hard use. There were not many supervisors and we were kind of busy, so the transport agents made lots of runs between agents in the field, Tecate Processing Center, and our small 94 checkpoint where most of our aliens were then picked up by the Detention Enforcement Officers who took them away on the bus for V/R, or to *El Corralon* in El Centro to await their Deportation Hearing.

The transport agent was to listen up for radio calls, go to where the apprehended aliens were being held, and pick them up from the field agents. You had to have a lot of 826 forms, (Field Processing Forms), pens, and nitrile gloves because the guys in the field might not be anywhere near their vehicles after a long hike to catch the groups. Also, it was a good idea to search the aliens going into your van yourself, because tired agents might miss something, and once they are in *your* vehicle, they are *your responsibility*.

There were frequent angry muster briefs about things that were missed in alien searches; usually mirrors and safety razors, but too often, tools, blades, and even a firearm or two. Things like inspecting one's vehicle (especially the alien compartment) and thoroughly searching one's aliens, were impressed upon us with great emphasis.

As a newer agent, I liked this assignment. It wasn't processing, or checkpoint; the real reason was that it was a good way to learn the area. The first rule of learning an area was to drive the roads and learn the landmarks. Also, it was a good way to learn who the agents were that caught all the bodies. These were the guys you would pay more attention to in the field and try to accompany on walks to learn more about the business of looking at the dirt and getting apprehensions. This served me well when I transferred to a new station as an agent, and especially as a supervisor at yet other stations. The guys always needing transport for dope and bodies were the guys to watch.

The best transport vehicles ever were the rare 2008-12 Quigley-modified Ford vans. They were lifted 4x4 behemoths that were narrow enough to get through the mountain roads and lifted enough to not bottom out with a full load. I never saw one get stuck. The downside was they only got about 8 MPG and were not at all comfortable to drive. No such thing as a free lunch.

Some of the older field agents used transport as a way to contribute when their knees and backs began to fail them. Also, the agents out of quarantine, recovering from COVID-19 but not quite 100%, might not be able to climb a mountain, but were perfectly capable of searching and shackling your apprehensions.

Vans became less important for several years when the Border Patrol began buying ¾-ton 4x4 pickups with "dog catcher" boxes in the beds. They could fit two agents and eight bodies with plenty of room for baggage, and still go wherever agents needed to go within reason. Around 2012, however, somebody in D.C. noticed that we spent a lot on gas, and they went to ½-ton trucks with no box in the back.

Rescue Near Barrett Junction

In the summer of 1998, on a very hot afternoon, I was riding with BPA Angel. Angel had a good reputation and I was happy to ride with him. When we received a report via radio of an agent who was suffering heat exhaustion and had cramped up, he abruptly changed direction and answered up. The location of the stricken agent was somewhere up a mountain, off of the Tecate Truck Trail, south of Barrett Junction. Some of the canyons in East San Diego County in the summertime could easily get up over 100F in the afternoon, and heat injuries are very common among agents as well as illegal aliens.

Other agents were coming in from another direction as BPA Angel started up the mountain. The other guys found the agent in distress, and a Foxtrot helicopter unit that was in the area dropped some extra water for him. The agent, who was eventually able to walk himself out with the help of the other agents, reported that he had been pushing a group of seven on that particular trail and that they were likely also in bad shape.

This was put out over the radio, so we began looking for the group. Foxtrot flew up the canyons from bottom to top all along the reported route of travel and finally spotted them. We were not far off. Angel headed up the switchbacks until we saw the group on a rocky outcropping halfway down the canyon, one laid out on the rock. It was only a short distance away, but the canyon was pretty deep and it would take us a while to get over there on foot.

"Wait there!" we shouted and pulled up to a turnout where we could park without blocking the road. We grabbed a few extra one-gallon water jugs, as well as our own Camelbak packs, and got to it. Angel, a former Marine and about 6'6", set a pretty good pace. It only took about a minute before we were sweating like crazy. To cover a few dozen yards straight-line distance, it took us a long time as we descended into the canyon, rock-hopped through it, and then came out the other side at the same elevation as the group. Since the mountain was so steep in this area, we mostly side-hilled into the canyon, picked through the rocks, and side-hilled out. Not spraining anything on loose rocks was the primary point of concern, as well as avoiding any rattlesnakes that lived in and around them.

The aliens were pretty happy to see us. We passed out the extra water and advised them to drink slowly. If you have heat exhaustion, you don't want to guzzle water and risk throwing it all up. This just takes more moisture out of you than you started with. Angel looked at the one that was barely conscious - a young kid. No way was he going to be able to walk out.

"Foxtrot, can you take this kid? He's out of it."

No dice. The small Border Patrol helicopter had nowhere to put another person, plus there was nowhere to land. The pilot got on an air channel and requested a Sheriff's Department bird to help us out.

Before long we had two helicopters circling. The San Diego Sheriff's Department (SDSO) chopper was looking for a place to put down while the BP chopper was taking care of communications. It was decided that there was nowhere to land and no possibility of getting the kid out on foot to the nearest landing zone. The weather was hot and only getting hotter.

Finally, after a lot of back-and-forth discussion between Angel and the helicopter pilots, the agreed-upon plan was for the SDSO helicopter to come in on the big flat rock we were standing on and Angel would bring the kid to them. It was only big enough for one skid of the SDSO bird to set down on it, so this was going to be tricky. We cleared the rest of the group over to the side of the canyon and the bird came in. As soon as the skid hit the rock, Angel had that kid in his arms. Carrying him like a baby, he took two giant steps over to the side of the rock, where the helicopter half-hovered with the crew chief leaning out, and just handed him over. They flew straight out of there to medical.

It doesn't sound as dramatic as it actually was, to me, at the time anyway. The helo was moving, the rock we were on was moving under our shifting weight, there was brush everywhere, and debris flying through the air. What the pilots agreed to do was highly unusual. I only saw similar flying feats a few times after that and it always looked pretty heroic to me. Not to mention if anything were to go wrong, BPA Angel probably would have been the first to get hurt or killed. In any case, the teenager was clearly in great distress, so they went for it, and it worked.

The kid ended up surviving. Later, the San Diego Union-Tribune had a small article about the rescue, and we got Employees of the Month. That was nice, but if there had been some kind of lifesaving medal, BPA Angel deserved one for handing a semi-conscious kid over to a hovering helicopter, on the edge of a rock outcropping, on the side of a steep canyon.

OTMs

In the news today, there is much discussion about OTMs (Other Than Mexican). Back in the late 90s and early 2000s, catching some OTMs could mean either a one or two-hour delay at the end of shift, or up to a 10 to 12-hour marathon of casework. If I remember correctly, the Central Americans were not too bad to process once you had done it a few times. It was the Chinese, Brazilians, and Eastern Europeans that could be a mess to process unless you had agents who spoke their language.

At the El Cajon Station, we had one agent who was fluent in Portuguese. We got a lot of Brazilians, so this was great for us, as he was willing to be called in for overtime to help us interview these aliens. I remember that he was a very experienced, competent agent, and very patient with teaching us new guys how to process and interview.

Another guy, Ski, was and is an absolute American hero to me. We all called him Ski because his last name ended in "ski." He had escaped from behind the Iron Curtain in the 80s when that was still a thing. At great risk, he arranged to have his family smuggled out as well. After years in a concentration camp in Italy, he earned a place in the United States as a refugee. A Lawfully Admitted Permanent Resident, with $500 and a one-bedroom apartment, he got to work building a life. Ski did not have the advantage of today's so-called "refugees." There were no public benefits for him. He served in the United States Army. He busted his ass on a fishing boat while going to college. He graduated and joined the USBP, much to our benefit. The guy spoke at least five languages and was 100% true-blue, dedicated to the USA and the Border Patrol Mission. When processing the OTMs from the former Warsaw Pact nations, he was able to interview most of them. They would relax a little when he gave them the spiel in a language they could understand, but he soon made it clear that he was NOT their friend. He would explain that he came here the hard way, the legal way, and that they had broken the law and would be treated accordingly.

I worked with Ski whenever possible because of the breadth and depth of his experience. Once he told me that his uncle had been Border Police in East Germany. His uncle had explained to him the mission of the East German *Grenztruppen* (Border Troops): "They gave me a Kalashnikov and a dog. Anyone trying to leave was a traitor and must be stopped. Anyone coming in was a spy and must be stopped."

While this is nothing close to what was expected of us, Ski definitely was in it to win it. He never coasted. Later he transferred to another station, and I never heard anything further. I hope he and his family are well.

At the Tucson Station, there were two Mandarin speakers. One guy was a blond-haired, blue-eyed *huero* with extensive experience in Chinese martial arts, which included traveling to the far east to study. The other guy was 2nd generation American of Asian descent. Their approach to interviewing the aliens from China was different. One guy would be all friendly and try to achieve rapport with the aliens, which met with limited success. The other guy claimed he understood Chinese culture a little more and spoke very harshly to the aliens, supposedly getting more information and cooperation out of them. I couldn't tell. He told me that the Chinese OTMs would not respond to "good cop" because that did not exist in China.

Nowadays, OTMs are processed in very specific ways according to where they come from and it does not take as long. Most PAs that speak exotic languages seem to have been snatched up by special details or other agencies so, in processing, the agents must rely on AT&T operators with special language skills. This can be a problem as a few AT&T operators have been caught advocating for the aliens, which they are specifically not supposed to do. Sadly, unless someone else in processing speaks the lingo, this will probably continue to happen.

Mystery Girl

Around 1999 or 2000, there was one instance that may or may not involve an OTM, which troubles me to this day. I was assigned to the POE area in Tecate with my partner Andy. Andy and I ended up catching a group in which there was a young girl about fourteen years of age who spoke a dialect that almost sounded like Spanish but wasn't. She had no family in the group, so we processed her as an unaccompanied juvenile. Andy was another of many outstanding agents coming out of the El Cajon Station and was later a Physical Techniques Instructor at the Academy in Artesia. A Naturalized USC himself, Spanish had been his first language. He was able to get her name and age, and that she claimed to be Mexican, but could not tell for sure where this girl was from.

We took her down to the POE where Andy asked one of the Mexican *Aduaneros* (The Mexican Customs Officers) to talk to her. We did this often, as they were adept at "breaking" OTMs who falsely claimed to be Mexicans. The *Aduanero* spoke to her for a while but it was clear to us that he wasn't getting very far. He told us that she was either a Guatemalan from the mountains or one of the Indians from Southern Mexico that spoke a dialect he could not understand. We took her back to the processing center and were instructed to complete an entire A-File on her; many blanks were marked "unknown." Later, she was sent off on a bus and released to some guy in Los Angeles whose first name and phone number were found in her pocket trash.

Andy and I were commended for our efforts, but to this day I do not feel great about the possible fate of this fourteen-year-old girl. She should have been kept in custody until we could find a legitimate way to get her back to her family in her home country, not released to some random dude in LA who had God knows what in mind for her.

Angel of 1000 Trails

East of San Diego in the 1990s: it was a cool, clear, early-morning around 3:00-4:00 AM. Border Patrol Agent "PJ" responded to a sensor activation near the 1000 Trails RV Park just off of Telegraph Canyon Road. At this time, there were very few agents assigned to the El Cajon Station, and PJ was riding solo down Highway 94, which was close by. He keyed the mic and answered up before turning southbound on Telegraph Canyon.

PJ passed the RV Park and kept going for a bit before pulling off the side of the road, parking his Bronco under some trees. He put on a rough-duty jacket against the chill and his 2-quart canteen on a sling. The canteen pouch, besides his canteen, also had a bunch of the new flex-ties for securing the hands of any apprehensions. It was lighter, and quieter, to carry the flex-ties as opposed to several sets of hard cuffs. Lastly, he grabbed his battered but trusty Maglite out of the map pocket in the door, his companion since the old days when he had been a young police officer in New Mexico.

PJ walked in towards where he knew the trail was. He took his time in the dark, letting his night vision strengthen and other senses become attuned to the sights and smells of the hills of East County. After a while, he picked up the pace and hit the trail that led into a ravine. An old mine camp, long since abandoned, with a broken windmill standing sentry nearby, was at the end of the ravine, but he had a way to go yet.

He was expecting to see people, even at this odd hour. In the past, some elderly folks had been known to be on the trails around the RV Park on their morning nature walks, and in some of the canyons as well. They shared the trails with animals, nature lovers, illegal aliens, and Border Patrol Agents.

PJ halted; he thought he heard something. He quietly stepped off the trail and into the shadows, which were pretty dark at this point. The moon was obscured by trees, brush, and the sides of the ravine. In his dark green BP uniform, it was easy to disappear.

After walking for about a half an hour, PJ's eyes had

completely adjusted to the dark. A lone figure came around a bend in the trail, with long hair, walking casually. PJ had been an agent long enough to be pretty sure that this was no illegal alien. He stepped out on the trail, hitting the light at the same time, and announced himself.

"Border Patrol."

"Oh," said the man. He was an older guy in overalls over a white collared shirt, sleeves rolled up just below the elbows. His long hair was white, eyes very bright blue, and he wore Dingo boots on his feet. "How ya doin,' young fella?" He asked.

"Fine, you?" PJ replied, turning off the light. "You probably shouldn't be walking out here without a flashlight."

The man grunted. "I'm doin' fine... When you get out over the hill by the mine, you better be careful. You by yourself?"

"Yeah, I'm by myself." PJ stepped aside and nodded, "You be safe now."

With a nod, the old-timer went along. PJ waited a minute, watching him go, then moved off towards the mining camp. If a group had activated the sensor in question, they should be along any time now. He moved cautiously but with a purpose, traversing the little hill and keeping on towards the broken windmill. There was a mine shaft beyond that had filled with rancid water and who knows what else over the years.

Before long, PJ was almost to the camp. Suddenly the hair on his neck went up; out of the corner of his eye, off to the right, there was something. Everybody has this "sixth sense," but cops, soldiers, and criminals are more likely than not to listen to it. Simultaneously, there wafted the faint odor of wood smoke and dirty ass. It stood out in the otherwise fresh air. PJ turned, Maglite in his left hand, and hit the button. Four aliens crouched along the brush line.

"No te mueva. Soy la Migra. Ensenen las manos." Don't move. Immigration. Show me your hands." The orders were quiet but firm. No need to escalate by shouting and fussing. They raised their hands and stayed put. Keeping the light on them, PJ had a

quick scan around, killing the light and then moving a little off to the side.

Then the "wet-down:" "Of what country are you a citizen? Do you have permission to enter the United States?" Mexico. No.

He quickly removed some flex-ties and secured their hands, then patted them down for any possible weapons. This is the most dangerous time in any arrest; the suspects know at this point it's do-or-die. An agent has to make a determination whether or not to use the hard cuffs, or "flexies," based on the vibe he gets from the aliens. The resistant get the handcuffs; if you're cool, we'll use the flexies or nothing at all.

Because agents often have to walk out their apprehensions, sometimes over a long distance in rugged terrain, it is best to use as little restraint as necessary. Once you cuff them, they are your responsibility. If an alien falls and breaks his face because he or she could not break a fall, it's on the agent.

In this case, everyone was cool, and PJ flex-tied them to each other. He then checked more thoroughly around the immediate vicinity for other persons or any discarded evidence. There was none. Next was collecting any ID documents, such as birth certificates or the ubiquitous Mexican Voter ID Card. In the United States, the state-issued driver's license and ID card are the most common forms of identification; for Mexicans who illegally cross the border, it is the *Tarjeta Para Votar.*

PJ then sent them ahead on the trail, using the Maglite to indicate direction. For his safety, PJ walked just off the trail and to the side, when possible, to observe as much of the group as he could. He admonished them to keep quiet and move quickly. *"Callase. Pasen mas adelante."*

Back at the truck, he searched them again, more thoroughly this time, went through their *mochilas,* and packed them in the rear compartment of the Bronco. Again, everyone was very cooperative. There was no hassle, as commonly happens with people who have been walking for days through the mountains, only to end up arrested so close to their objective.

It was about a 45-minute drive back to the station. On an impulse, PJ decided to run their names and dates of birth for wants and warrants, and a criminal history, if any. He hit the dome light and laid out the ID documents on the seat while standing outside the door, grabbing the mic. He read all of their names and birthdates out over the radio and waited a minute for dispatch to come back.

Each one of the four aliens was an aggravated felon. Armed robbery. Burglary. Assault. Two of them had done prison time in the US. It didn't square with him; they had been so docile in the course of the arrest. Through the cage, he confirmed the histories with them.

"Why didn't you guys try to run, or jump me?" He couldn't help but ask.

"The big white guy behind you," said one. *"El gringo grande."*

"No," PJ said. I'm alone. *"Yo solo."*

"No oficial, el gabacho grande atrás de usted."

Every agent has heard strange stories about being out in the brush. But even today, it gives PJ a little chill to tell this one. "Maybe it was an angel?"

Kind of a Boring Day

It was a cool winter day in South Texas, and two Border Patrol Agents were driving eastbound on the stretch of I-10 between Van Horn and Sierra Blanca. It was a slow day, and they were taking the opportunity to explore a little. "PJ" was new to the area, and his partner, "Gus," was behind the wheel, showing him around.

They exited on 90 heading towards Marfa, chatting about the difference between San Diego Sector, Yuma, and Marfa. As they were shooting the shit, getting way out of their area, a lone store on the side of the road - the Prada Marfa.

"You gotta be kidding me!" exclaimed PJ.

Nowadays, it is the subject of many Instagram photos and trendy hipsters stopping to take photos. The store featured actual Prada products in the display window, but is never open, and serves as more of a work of art rather than a retail outlet. On this day in the early 2000s, PJ was no different, fishing through his tricky bag for a camera, this being before affordable camera phones. They pulled over and got out. Gus snapped a photo for his partner.

"We better go back, we're getting pretty far out of the way," he said. Soon they were back on the road, heading back towards Van Horn. He tossed PJ the keys. Usually, agents ride solo, but when paired up, it's polite to switch out driving at the halfway point among BP Agents. One guy drives south, the other takes it north.

"Kind of a boring day," observed Gus. "You know what would be great?"

"What?"

"A load."

An old truck, a 1970s vintage pickup, entered the highway ahead of them in a cloud of dust. It wasn't going too fast, and soon, without effort, they caught up to it. The pickup had seen better days, and the frayed tonneau cover, snaps missing, flapped around wildly in the wind at the corner.

Not being in any kind of hurry, PJ stayed behind at a distance. Gus went on, saying how they got aliens off of buses, trailers, and trains, but not necessarily passenger vehicles. PJ relayed a story of a load vehicle from his El Cajon days.

"We don't get that around here," Gus commented.

"Why doesn't he get that fixed?" PJ asked, pointing his chin at the flapping cover on the truck.

"He's Mexican," chuckled Gus, an American of Mexican descent.

As if on cue, a hand appeared from the darkness in the bed of the pickup, grabbing the corner of the tonneau cover from the inside, and pulling it down. The two PAs following looked at each other; Gus keyed the mic. The day just got interesting.

"Dispatch, 10-28/29 on a Texas plate..." Gus called in the plate number for a return. A person riding in the bed of a pickup is not necessarily reasonable suspicion for a traffic stop, but it's a start if they are hiding under a piece of plywood or a tonneau cover. In a moment, the return on the plate came back... to a completely different kind of vehicle. That, dear reader, is reasonable suspicion. While it is possible that a mistake has been made, either by the agent or the dispatcher, a quick confirmation is all it takes to make it official, and grounds for a stop.

"Dispatch, we'll be 10-32 on that vehicle." PJ hit the emergency lights and chirped the siren to initiate a traffic stop.

"You want contact or cover?" Gus asked. The contact agent actually conducts the stop, while the cover agent watches his back and handles the radio traffic.

"I'll cover you."

Gus walked up on the driver's side, PJ a little behind, on the passenger side.

Gus stopped short, grunting, "Oh, shit!"

"You OK? What's up?"

"Come look."

In the cab of the pickup on the filthy floorboard, were four women. It was a load. PJ opened up the back, peeling back the cover to reveal another 14 bodies looking up at him, shivering in the bed.

Gus, having secured the driver, chuckled. He addressed the people in the back of the truck in Spanish:

"Who pulled down the cover?"

One of the aliens, a young male, hesitantly raised his hand.

"Why?"

"It was a little cold."

"I've Never Fallen Asleep on Duty"

When things were calmer, there was time for practical jokes.

There were five of us on the midnight shift, 11:00 PM to 9:00 AM. Dan, G, Mags, and me. Our Acting Supervisor was a PA we called Skat. One cool night we headed down to the POE. Dan and I had a van.

We headed over to West High Point, a hill north of the Port of Entry, where we could hang out with a view, and respond east or west as needed. It was about a quarter of a mile north of town, with a good view for glassing. It was a tiny town, basically, a two-lane road leading into Mexico with some buildings on either side. Dwarfed by its sister city in Mexico, there weren't more than a few hundred people on the US side if that. It was easy to keep tabs from West High Point, or from Customs High Point on the east side.

Skat had told us once, "I have never fallen asleep on midnights! If I ever catch anyone..."

Being a regular PA, he was only temporarily detailed as a supervisor, an "Acting" or "Temp Sup." Predictably, some of the senior guys were unimpressed. When he rolled up behind us on West High Point, we thought nothing of it.

"You guys can take off, I got it."

He was at least, nominally, our supervisor so we shoved off. When we got down low, we ran into Mags and G.

"We thought you guys were up on the hill," G said when we pulled up to them.

"Nah, Skat is up there."

We sat there, parked next to each other, bullshitting for a while. It was common in the winter to have some old Army blankets on hand for the aliens, who were frequently caught shivering and in danger of hypothermia. In the back of the van, we had a bunch of blankets.

"Hey," said Mags, "those are some nice blankets." He had a mischievous streak and was not shy about using it.

We snuck up the hill towards Skat's ride; it was one of those old snot-green Chevy Caprice pursuit vehicles prior to the BP painting all the vehicles white. The engine idled quietly; we could tell as we approached that the windows were fogged. Sleeping!

As quickly and quietly as we could, we turned and headed back down. The loose rocks on the dirt rolled beneath our feet and we flailed our arms to keep from falling. Back down at the van, the four of us collected all the blankets and headed back up. Just so you know, we were never far. We would never leave a buddy in a helpless situation, jackass or not.

In a short time, we had covered every window on the Skat's sedan with the thick woolen Army blankets. Hopefully, he wouldn't wake up to take a piss. But, either way, the point was made.

The sun eventually came up, but Skat did not stir. We waited and waited, but I guess due to the pitch blackness within, he snored away soundly. Finally, Mags couldn't wait any longer; it was almost shift-change.

We shook the car from side to side. "Hey, Skat! You OK?" Mags called.

There was a little thrashing around in there. "Huh, what?!" Then, "You motherfuckers!"

He burst out of the car; verily, he was pissed. "You motherfuckers! I..."

Mags nodded to Dan and me. "You guys can take off."

Apparently, there was a heart-to-heart. Skat learned a valuable lesson that evening that Karma can be a bitch! When we saw him again, Skat had nothing to say. We (PAs) are the type of people who are relentless with practical jokes and other things; a little humility goes a long way.

Shooting on the Line

In the summer of 2000, one of our Border Patrol Agents, "D," was assigned to an "X" near a small port of entry in Arizona. An X is a static position, to which agents are assigned in order to deter and/or respond to traffic in an area where there is limited reaction time. Cities like Imperial Beach and El Centro, California, Nogales, Arizona, and El Paso, Texas have many such static positions.

The highway here was a two-lane paved road at the center of the small desert border town, and the gas station/market was the largest business besides the US Customs Port of Entry. Enveloping the town was a National Monument and an Indian Reservation lay further to the east. Just about a mile north of the town, a dirt road went west onto the National Monument. The purpose of this X, where Agent D was parked, was to deter drive-through traffic and respond to the Inspectors at the Port of Entry, as well as Park Service officers. As he tells it:

"I was sitting on an X that day and thinking how sick and tired I was of sitting on that X... never getting to play because I was a junior guy.

"We heard on the radio that the Sheriff's Department was chasing a vehicle through Ajo, coming southbound. Now, the reason they were chasing this vehicle was that the day prior, they had also pursued this vehicle, and lost it." At that time, it must have been loaded with either dope or bodies; they would have driven around to make sure they lost the deputies or brushed up the vehicle and hid out before dropping off their load somewhere. There are plenty of places to hide out in this high desert area.

"It [the suspect vehicle] must have made it north because this time it was on the way south. So, they're chasing this vehicle south and the Park Rangers are out there, the law enforcement guys. They tried to spike the load vehicle but spiked the [Sheriff's Department] two rear vehicles right there at milepost 74. The road I was on was at milepost 79."

It is not unheard of when deploying a spike strip or other vehicle immobilization device to miss the bad guys and get the good guys. These are rapidly evolving dynamic situations. Especially if the pursuing units do not back off sufficiently before the spike zone, or if the deploying officer does not pull the spikes back in time. In this case, the park rangers took out both of the pursuing deputies' vehicles. They completely missed the bad guys and left our agent solo down south awaiting the oncoming suspect. D continues:

"So instead of three-on-one, now it was just a one-on-one. There was this other agent who [had gone] down to the Port of Entry and asked one of the Customs Inspectors there to deploy spikes. Remember, this is back in July of 2000; we [Border Patrol] were not allowed to spike. So, we went and got this Port guy to spike it for us." Before DHS was created, the land Ports of Entry were staffed by combined teams of Immigration Inspectors (I.I.s) and Customs Inspectors (C.I.s), who worked for the Justice Department and Treasury Department, respectively. In the immediate area of the Ports, they had supreme authority. In between the Ports, it was the Border Patrol. We tried to help each other out whenever possible.

"He [the Customs Inspector] sets up, and I am set up across the road." On another dirt road that could be used to bypass the spikes, and the entire Port of Entry as well. "I'm giving him room to get south, not blocking him in."

"The vehicle rounds the corner around milepost 78.5. He's coming down, and it's a green Ford Taurus; I'll never forget." The speeding vehicle came around the curve, saw the law enforcement vehicles there, and "this Customs Officer goes into the middle of the road, and throws the spikes. Well, this vehicle swerved and hit him. I remember everything was in slow motion from this point where he hit that guy, the Inspector... "

This is the stress response; while it can differ, the sense of time slowing down is because the brain actually speeds up, focusing on the source of danger, and blood flows to it and the large muscle groups. Tunnel vision, rapid heartbeat, loss of fine motor skills, and auditory exclusion can also happen. Any, all, some, or none of these phenomena can be experienced in one event.

"In my peripheral vision, I can see this vehicle try to turn onto the dirt road," says D, who was waiting for him. As the green Taurus turned to face him, it got stuck in a drainage ditch dug alongside the dirt road. D moved up in his vehicle, cutting off the smuggler. "As soon as he got out of that little ditch, he got out of the vehicle and reached inside his waistband."

This is known as a "deadly force movement." While each situation must be judged by the totality of the circumstances, it is a commonly recognized movement, and in an incident such as this, likely to result in someone being shot. In this situation, the driver of the vehicle had just struck a Federal Officer with his vehicle, advanced on another agent, and reached for his waistband. An agent is not required to wait to be shot and is completely justified in defending himself or another person.

"That's when I drew my [.40 Beretta 96] pistol and shot him. I actually hit him one time. The bullet went in through his arm, his bicep muscle on the left side, went all the way through, traveled between the skin and the muscle on the ribcage, didn't hit anything vital, and came out the other side. "

"He ran another 100 yards, and finally, kind of gave up. He didn't collapse, he was kind of in shock. He survived, and he did 13 years in prison for hitting that inspector. I had not been in even two years yet. It would have been two years in December, but this was July." After being a US Army Soldier, a Detention Officer, and now a Border Patrol Agent, this was D's first shooting. It was not without consequence.

"I remember that it was pretty horrible. That was a bad time for about a month or two. My wife said that from that day forward, that's when I changed completely, into the man I am today, angry all the time." This is also a common post-shooting response, though people can experience such things differently. In spite of all the violence on TV, in the movies, and in popular culture, the vast majority of people still are very reluctant to try to kill each other.

"Maybe [it's] PTSD," says D. "I never went to get tested for that, but yeah, that was the day that I ended up in my first shooting."

There was also a passenger in the car, the brother of the driver. They were nephews to a cartel leader in a nearby Mexican city. It was a well-known smuggling outfit at the time.

A little more from Agent D: "His brother was in the car with him. They were nephews of the [cartel] boss. By the way he reached into his pants, I thought he had a gun. The other officer, the Sheriff's Deputy, also thought he had a gun, and shot as well. It turned out to be a money belt with $55,000.00 in it. I guess that was the proceeds of their delivering the dope from the day before, and they were bringing those proceeds back."

"I guess, all in all, we got some money and got two bad guys. He did 13 of the 17 years he was sentenced."

Signcutting Op

Signcutting is tracking, or "cutting" signs of passage, either foot, hoof, or tire. In my first station, El Cajon, I daresay it was pretty simple, a matter of persistence and patience. Due to the soil, terrain, and routes used through our area, there was time to follow groups out, leave after your shift, and either turn it over to your buddies on the next shift or pick it up the next day. No one was wearing shoe booties back then, so identifying a group through their foot sign was doable. Never much better than average, I still got the hang of it and was able to acquit myself well in this department. However, if I was ever with someone really good, I would let them take the lead.

You're always looking for shape, shadow, shine, contrast, and color. Straight lines rarely occur in nature. Perfect circles as well. Little things like that. Even if the group is wearing shoe booties, the normal appearance of the dirt and weeds is mashed down where a bunch of bootied feet have tramped. Rocks may have been turned over, grass or weeds pressed or crunched, or maybe someone blew a snot rocket onto the ground or spat some goo on a rock, squished a bug, or left a tuft of fiber on a branch as they brushed past it. It sounds impossible, I know, but these are the things that agents look for.

On one pleasant evening, the weather was nice and I was riding solo on the swing shift. It was probably around five or six o'clock. I bumped into the other guy in my area while going up the Tecate Truck Trail (TTT) towards the 3-7 water tank. He was already going up that way. Speedy was a smallish, quiet guy with a huge heart, and was actually very speedy; his sobriquet was not sarcasm. Since he was already headed up to the 3-7, we chatted for a moment and I turned back the way I came to cut the road.

Keeping my crappy 94 Bronco in 4x4 "low" so as to move at a walking pace without me having to brake, I carefully watched the side of the road where rocks were kind of lined up from the BP vehicles constantly driving the road, sometimes pulling tire drags. After a while, I saw sign for a group on the road. The footprints were easily distinguishable. I don't remember the sign types but there must have been enough moisture in the soil that I was able to stay on it. There were no toe digs, so they were not running, and where the dirt was good enough, I could make out five or six different prints. If you ever wondered why people in movies and on TV always squat down and touch the prints, I am pretty sure it is to test how "crispy" the sign is. At least, that's why I do it. If you can feel sharp edges, it's probably older than it looks; if you can leave a fingerprint right in the sign, maybe it's pretty recent. Of course, the area and type of soil have something to do with it. If you are in the desert and the wind is blowing, then it might be more recent than it looks.

This particular sign had been hit a couple of times, meaning that two vehicles had driven over the footprints: Speedy and I. It was what is called "good," or workable, likely alien traffic. I got out and followed it for a little while until it hit the road again. The Tecate Truck Trail is a series of switchbacks climbing up the north side of Tecate Peak. This group was obviously heading downhill, towards highway 94, most likely between Cottonwood Creek and the 14 Canyon. Here there was an occupied property we called Harvey Dennis' Place. The aliens generally went around Dennis' place. A few miles north was The Flume scope site where sometimes we had a FLIR type scope truck set up, but not today. I marked the road and went back to the truck.

Because I was still kind of a new guy and didn't want to lose the sign, I repeated this process several times, all the way to just short of 94. Also, there was an off chance it could be hikers; it was doubtful but possible, so I didn't call it in. There were various places to cut the spot where they crossed Highway 94 and headed up towards the Barrett Lake area. I walked back and forth along fence lines and brush lines south of 94, looking for anything of use, but came up empty. Walking back up towards my ride along Cottonwood Creek, I began cutting closer to the brushy, reedy, nasty shit that grows along the water. I think it was mostly dry at this time. Before long, I cut a grass trail that came from the TTT. Outstanding! It was definitely good; no normal person would walk into the nasty Cottonwood Creek.

I thought that it was probably still light out when the group got this far, the tracks were pretty straight and they weren't "bouncing off" of thickets or rocks, so they must have crossed under the bridge. 94 is a relatively well-used, rural two-lane highway, winding its way through the low mountains of East County from San Diego to where it terminates near Campo, CA. Any illegal aliens furthering their entry would be trying to avoid detection, especially at this time of day when commuters are trying to get back to Campo or the Tecate Port of Entry after work.

I worked my way through the rocks, weeds, and stagnant water in and out of the creek, keeping my eyes open for poison oak. That stuff really does a number on me. It was still light enough to navigate, but I used my Maglite to periodically check good pieces of dirt for sign to confirm I was still on it. The bugs weren't too bad, and I didn't see too many cows or deer that might have destroyed the sign. After an hour I could smell it: wood smoke, manzanita, and body odor. As my friend PJ calls it: *"eau de extranjero."*

They were sleeping, shoes off, one guy gently snoring. This is a tricky time; if you startle them, they might freak out and want to fight, or bombshell in every direction in which case I might only get one or two. I sat there for a minute to calm down; as a fairly new guy, I hadn't busted too many groups on my own yet, and I figured to play it cool. If I only got one, nobody would know I fucked up unless I told them.

"Chapo..." I called out in a stage whisper, *"Chapo...Michoacano..."* I had heard that in the past, when a lost alien came down a trail one night, trying to find his little buddy. He found us instead, and I used his call from that night forward. It usually didn't work.

An older guy in a kind of gray pea coat woke up and looked around. *"Calmase viejo,* it's the Border Patrol. *No le corre,"* I said in my crappy white guy Spanish. "Do not run," I added in English, for emphasis.

They were cool. I tied them together with flexies *"for mi seguridad"* and we walked back to an open spot near 94 where I called for transport. They were all repeat customers and knew they had another shot in a few days. They chatted with each other while I searched them and their bags.

Back then, the conventional wisdom amongst the aliens (at least the experienced ones who came north and went south many times to work the fields, then go home for the holidays or whatever) was that if you don't run, you don't get hit. It was even the title of a "hit piece" in the local free paper in San Diego. We had all heard stories, even in the Academy, of such things, but in my experience very few aliens got hit at all, much less for simply running away. This may have happened before my time, but extremely rarely in my personal experience. Few aliens ever became actively resistant or assaultive, and of those even fewer still were stricken; it happened, but not very often if things were handled correctly. That brings me to Officer Presence.

Officer Presence

According to the Use of Force Continuum, your Officer Presence is the lowest level of force. The sociological term is "posturing." The general idea is that if you project professionalism, self-confidence, and reasonableness with a commanding voice and a smidge of controlled aggression, you win the fight that never happens. Some agents take it too far and get in a lot of scuffles. Some agents don't take it far enough, get in a lot of scuffles, and maybe get their ass kicked, or worse.

Any person who has driven a car for a while understands at some level that on any given day you can do everything right, and still get in an accident. Your experience and reactions in the moment can help determine how bad the accident will be for you and the other drivers on the road. Sometimes, it doesn't matter and drivers get killed or wounded. It is the same for law enforcement when they encounter someone. They have no idea who the suspects are or who the innocents are, and they are not there to be a friend; they need to find out what is going on and react properly and professionally every time, or the Department will surely have their ass, the suspect will, or both.

The internet is full of videos of all kinds of law enforcement officers getting in all kinds of trouble. Luckily for Border Patrol Agents, most of them are not in the public eye as much as the "real police," except at immigration checkpoints, God help us.

Unluckily for Border Patrol Agents, they are usually arresting people in groups, and sometimes large ones. They need to make an impression.

At the stations where I worked, it was deserts and mountains, mostly far away from homes and businesses, at night with little to no artificial light. The aliens moved in groups from a pair to a mass of 100. Nowadays, the big groups break up into pairs and trios and make for rendezvous points at recognizable landmarks. Either way, the agents are almost always outnumbered in these situations, and it behooves them to posture aggressively, but not too aggressively, and control their apprehended aliens to prevent violence or escape.

I have referred to the maxim "if you don't run, you won't get hit," because it was the title of the cover story in the local San Diego free paper one week back in the 90s. The article was an anti-Border Patrol hit piece about how we were all a bunch of racist thugs picking on the poor migrants, etc., etc. Agents read this with amusement. Sure, there were fights, and some agents were more "badge heavy" than others, but for the most part, things were pretty calm at the time. Before the cartels really took over the people-smuggling business, it was mostly working folks crossing illegally, in my area anyway. A minority were dirtbags with felonious histories, and most of those didn't cause a stir after walking through the mountains for a few days. Most of our apprehensions went calmly and without incident, like hide-and-seek; once you found them, they might sometimes passively resist by holding onto a bush or something, but we could usually talk them out of it. Any kind of violence, while not unknown, was rare. In places near cities like Imperial Beach, CA, or Nogales, AZ, where the prison bus let the convicts out and the Detention/Deportation Officers sent them south, that was a different story.

There were a couple of agents I knew. One of whom was fired or resigned in lieu of termination when his aliens made an allegation that he beat them while they were handcuffed. The other got fired for fighting another BP Agent, but he got his job back after a while (I knew his opponent and he probably had it coming). Both of these guys were known to be a little hard on the aliens, but I never saw them cross the line. However, no one was surprised when they got in trouble.

Most of the rest of us just tried to be reasonable. Most of the aliens, as I said before, were just regular people trying to get to the good ol' USA, and they were reasonable, too. But the one or two dirtbags in a group might need to know or believe that you will absolutely assert control over them if they tried to mess with you. There is a fine line, a dichotomy that must be respected, to keep an agent out of the hospital, or prison.

So, whilst being reasonable with a group of 20 or 30 that

my partner and I had just apprehended near a place called Charco on an Indian reservation, my partner was riding off on his ATV chasing after a runner. I calmly but clearly addressed the group and ordered everyone to sit down.

"*Sientese.*" Sit. Some of them just squatted down, like they were preparing to throw dice back in the yard at Pelican Bay or something. These are the guys who require a higher level of attention. *"On las nalgas."* On your ass. I bladed my body a little bit, met their eyes, and pointed. Usually, that is enough. In this case, one guy just stood there, his back to me. My rule was to ask them twice, then help them. If there are too many to help, pick one guy and make an example, then hope for the best. I walked up behind him thinking to myself, every one of these people can run, but this guy is not going anywhere and will sit.

Again, it's not about being a tough guy. It's about asserting control over a crowd to avoid a fight. When you are far outnumbered, a fight will not end well.

Right before I grabbed him, one of the older aliens in the group said something that made him sigh and sit down. Thanks, *viejo*, I thought. I put the hard cuffs on the guy and continued with my post-arrest procedures. No more problems.

What if he didn't sit? I wasn't about to just beat the crap out of him; the next level is contact controls, then takedowns, followed by open-hand techniques. If he took a swing, he would get the baton. If he picked up a rock, or if anyone else wanted to join in on his behalf, it is now a deadly force situation. You don't have to advance sequentially. The severity of the crime, the immediacy of the threat to the agent, and the subject's level of resistance dictate a reasonable agent's response at all times. If he stops resisting, your use of force must also stop. If you are approaching exhaustion and he is going to beat you senseless as opposed to just running away, that is also a deadly force situation to be handled accordingly.

Good officer presence prevents this kind of thing, most of the time.

Scope Truck

At the El Cajon Station Scope Unit, at the turn of the century, there were about a dozen agents assigned. They would be agents who either wanted a break from running around on foot, wanted to sleep on duty, or were recovering from injuries. Any other agents were the new guys who were off probation and were "mandated" to do a three-month tour on scopes.

We used these old 1980s vintage Chevy K5 Blazers with diesel engines that had been surplussed from the military, called "CUCVs," pronounced "cuck-vees." They were still painted in their camouflage schemes of green, brown, and black; they really blended in well, especially in the dark. They had been modified with Pelican cases bolted to the floor of the cargo compartment which contained tripod-mounted infrared scopes, disassembled into several component parts. The front passenger seat had been turned to face rearward, and there was a control panel and a small screen there for the operator, who on a good night, with a good scope, could see groups of aliens pretty far away by their heat signature.

We would drive the Blazer to our scope spot and back in. Then you had to take out the parts, set up the tripod, and place the scope on top where it was secured with four wing nuts. A cable, attached to the back of the scope, was permanently affixed to the truck. The engine was left running, mostly to keep the bank of batteries charged up.

The best camera went to Tecate Peak. This 3800-foot-high mountain stands west of Tecate, CA, and dominates the area. Groups could be spotted as far north as Barrett Junction, west to the south end of Bee Canyon, and parts of Middle Earth Ranch, east past the port of Tecate, before the hills made it worthless to look much past Crutches Pond on the line. At that distance, you couldn't do much besides call out the group and hope someone was close enough to get on them quickly.

The Tecate Peak Scope Site was always assigned a second agent, for "scope back-up." Some jaded agents called it "sleep back-up," for obvious reasons. It was a good idea to have a second agent with a caged unit in case you ran into groups on the way up. The scope truck was not configured for transporting aliens or even much more than the one guy who operated it. Scope back-up was supposed to stay on the mountain and respond to anything close by since there were a couple of gates on the switch-back road that went up to the top, and response times from other agents on the patrol group were extended. You didn't want to ever drive too fast on the road to Tecate Peak; it was a gnarly road and there were no guard rails. Once, they graded it and that made it easier to drive on, but it also made it easier to drive off the side, so a prudent agent took his or her time.

Once I went up in the scope truck and was assigned a back-up agent, Herb. He was a newer guy than me, but very motivated. When he got up there, he was looking over my shoulder as I panned the scope back and forth, checking various "good" spots as it got darker and the ground cooled off, which increased the contrast between black and white (hot and cold) on the screen.

"I hope you find something," Herb said. "I need some trophies!"

I didn't know what he meant by "trophies," other than catching bodies, but didn't question it.

"There's some," I said, zooming in. They were dropping down one of the canyons towards Highway 94. "You gonna go for it?"

He did, packing up and heading down the hill. This was far out of the way for him, but he really wanted to get a group, and this was it. He drove an hour down the mountain and out to 94 to the "Last Chance Cafe," a solitary country home where the owners always left a cooler with cans of pop and tins of cookies for the Border Patrol. I almost never saw the homeowners (I worked nights), but they were very nice, and sometimes a Coke really hit the spot. We really appreciated those folks.

By the time Herb hit 94, I had picked up the group hoofing it across the highway and dumping into Grapevine Creek. I hated the Grapevine because it had so much poison oak in there; it messed me up but good every time I went in. The group disappeared in there, but they had to cross the next road north, Barrett Smith Road, on their way northbound. Herb knew where to go, and he hauled ass all the way to Barrett Junction, turning north and back east on Barrett Smith, just as the group emerged and headed for the next range of hills north of there. They were headed to Barrett Lake further up, and from there to Lyons Valley/Japatul Road.

"Stop, stop," I called out when Herb finally got to the spot where the aliens crossed the dirt on Barrett Smith. He picked up the sign immediately. He got out and actually ran as I called out the group's location and direction of travel. He didn't waste time with the sign since I had the group sighted. They went up the hill and Herb was gaining on them the whole time, really moving out. Finally, I couldn't see any more and he was on his own.

Herb topped out on the hills from where he could see north to Shady Lane, an RV park nestled in the next valley. He cut around for a while and I heard him go 10-15 (subjects apprehended) on the radio much later, calling for transport to meet him at Barrett Junction.

Herb got six or seven. I met up with him waiting for transport after I got relieved on the mountain. On the side of his Bronco, where there were bars to keep the aliens from escaping out the back window, he had six or seven ball caps fastened by their little plastic fitting straps.

"I got my trophies!" he said, grinning.

Easy Apps

It was one fine autumn afternoon. My partner was B.D., a big guy with a flat-top and the classic cop mustache. We were heading eastbound on 94 after loading up with snacks from 824-Bravo, the last 7-11 on our way out to the field. I got my usual Pop-Tarts and Mountain Dew, as well as some delicious (and also somehow gross) Cool Ranch Doritos. By the time we hit the downslope heading towards our crappy two-lane Highway 94 checkpoint, I was not feeling so great. There is a downside to eating like a garbage disposal.

There was a call on the radio regarding a group on one of the ranches right off the road to our north. We answered up and turned into the driveway leading to the ranch house when in the distance we spotted a group running up a hill. Driving right past the ranch house, we got close to the foot of the hill.

I couldn't remember the Spanish for "Don't make me run up that hill!" so I just yelled it in English into our PA system, which miraculously functioned. *"Venga p'aca!"* I shouted, commanding them to come over here.

B.D. followed up with his Spanish, which was very good. He was married to a Mexican-born woman; I knew this because she called him frequently when we rode together.

They had made it to the top and were on the verge of heading over.

"Shit. I am gonna throw up if we have to chase them." My dog-like eating habits had struck again.

B.D. laughed. I was the junior guy, so any chasing came down to me. I threw on my Camelback and was almost ready to go when the group turned about and came back. We met up at the foot of the hill.

One of the aliens grinned sheepishly. "Sorry," he said in accented but excellent English, "they are shooting over there!" He pointed over the hill.

"Yeah, welcome to America," I replied. "We do that here."

The shouted commands rarely worked, but when they did it was nice. We got all seven of them that time.

There was only one other time when verbal commands got me a group. On detail to the Ajo, Arizona station from El Cajon, I was coming back in at the end of an evening shift. It was September and still very hot at midnight. As I drove north on State Route 85 from Lukeville to Why (the Ajo Station is in the small town of Why, AZ), this vehicle in front of me kept veering to the left, then snapping back into its lane. This behavior, to me, is an indicator of someone who is paying too much attention to watching me through their side-view mirror and not enough to the road in front of them. I tried to get closer in order to read the plate and called it in.

Before the return came back, the car went hard left, across the southbound lane, and into the desert. All the doors opened, and several people got out, running north into the desert. Oh well, I thought, this is going to be a long night.

I pulled up my Tahoe behind the car and got out, carefully clearing the vehicle to make sure no one was left to bushwhack me. I could see that they had left behind all or most of the supplies they brought with them: backpacks (real ones, not dope) with canned food, jugs of water, all kinds of stuff. There were half a dozen backpacks in the car, and as I checked for sign exiting the car, I counted about six or seven sets of prints running off.

It was a long way to Ajo. They wouldn't be halfway there by the time the sun came up, and then it would get very, very hot. I called them on the PA system, which usually was broken, but today functioned perfectly. "*Donde van? Sus agua y comida estan aqui!* (Where are you going? Your water and food are here!)"

Repeating that again, I followed up by inviting the group back to take a ride with me. My basic academy Spanish was successful; in a few minutes, they returned. One guy had kept running, the driver. The rest saw sense; they decided that it was better to give up now and try again later than to walk their asses off all night and into tomorrow, then end up giving up anyway or dying out there. If the driver was local, he probably had someone he could call.

Dirtbag

You never know who you're arresting out there. There are a ton of people crossing illegally, and most of them are probably okay, but it only takes one to ruin your day. Luckily for the Border Patrol, this happens rarely. But it happens.

One night at the end of our shift, my partner SPA Gordon and I were heading back in from our assignment near Tecate. Gordon was a soft-spoken Senior Patrol Agent, a suave kind of dude who jumped from detail to detail and from station to station whenever he sensed an interesting opportunity. He and his wife home-schooled their kids, and he took them wherever he went, using frequent moves as educational opportunities for them.

During our shift, an agent had inadvertently driven into Mexico while trying to V/R (Voluntary Return) an elderly female. The *Aduaneros* at the Mexican POE immediately arrested him on suspicion of "Invading Mexico," as they usually did when an agent was caught south of the line. Gordon had gone over to "No Man's Land" and talked the agent back out of the hands of the Mexican Government through calm rational conversation. I was busy watching his back in case something crazy went on, and didn't hear the conversation, but it seemed very smooth. Gordon got the job done and freed the agent. Got his gun and radio back, too, if I remember correctly. It was outstanding work for which he never was recognized, except by his fellow agents, as far as I know.

So, Gordon and I were headed back north after a job well done, chatting about his last detail to Headquarters in DC. As we passed an area called "The Hiltons," so named because of the sheer number of aliens who had been arrested laying up in the brush by the highway, I noticed movement by one of the ubiquitous call boxes on the side of Highway 94.

"Hold up, there are bodies by the callbox."

The 373 Callbox was a popular place for the aliens to go and try to use the phone to call for a pick-up. There isn't anything around for miles except the two-lane Highway 94, a few rural houses mostly hidden away in the foliage and canyons, and the

373. Sadly, for them, it wasn't a phone, but a direct line to the California Highway Patrol. We pulled in and there were three of them, kind of standing there not sure what to do.

"*Bienvenidos! Somos La Migra!*" I said smiling, hoping to appear jovial and nonthreatening. Then I grabbed the nearest male and sat him down. The others sat on their own, admitting to being lost illegal aliens, and Gordon and I began field-processing them.

Out of the corner of my eye, I noticed a dark figure at the end of the light cone thrown by our alley light. A guy in a black jacket stood there with his hands in his jacket pockets, shifting his weight from foot to foot, looking scared. He was right at the end of the pullout where, with one or two steps, he could run down into the canyon below. I knew from previous visits that this was full of poison oak. I dropped what I was doing and ran over to him, yelling "*MIGRA-te veo-no te mueva!* (Immigration-I see you-Don't move!)" in my best Border Patrol Spanish.

He wanted to bolt. I could see his eyes darting around, but for some reason, he did not. I grabbed him by an arm and a handful of jacket, then dragged him into the light, keeping him off-balance. Once in the light, I got better control of his hands and began a quick pat-down, or "Terry Frisk," for weapons. In his right front jacket pocket, where his right hand had been, was a small handgun. The other pocket had a bunch of .22 rounds in it.

"Gun," I stated, and immediately handcuffed the guy. Gordon turned his attention on our new suspect who gave us a bullshit name, Sanchez, and said he was from Mexico. We loaded him up with the rest and went back south to Tecate to roll his prints. He asserted his right to remain silent as to his criminal possession of the gun and ammunition. His prints came back negative for any criminal or immigration record. Sanchez, however, had several prison-style tattoos, including a swastika, and the scars and marks on his neck and back were indicative to me of an "active" lifestyle. Speaking with the others in the group, it was determined to our satisfaction that he was the foot guide, and most likely intended to rob this group.

Their story was that they were with a larger group and "got separated" from them. When they came out of the hills and crossed the highway, Sanchez told them to wait by the callbox while he "went to find food." When he left, he was not in possession of the jacket. When he returned, he was wearing the jacket and had food for the group. There was a young couple in the group who, between them, had several hundred dollars in US currency. Gordon and I believed that they had been the intended target of a robbery.

The AUSA office declined to prosecute Sanchez under 18 USC 922 for his criminal possession of the firearm. It was a 6.35mm (.25 caliber) "Bronco" pistol, a Mexican copy of the Baby Browning pocket semi-automatic handgun, a design originating from a hundred years ago. The 79 rounds of .22 ammunition he possessed would not have reliably worked in the gun, which was not loaded. Had he pulled it on me, I would not have taken the time to ask. At any rate, lacking anything else to charge him with, we decided to deport him officially since he was an obvious dirtbag.

A few weeks later, I was on detail in Ajo, Arizona. I got an email from a San Diego Sector Intel Agent thanking SPA Gordon and me for our work. Sanchez was wanted in the Mexican State of Oaxaca for the attempted murder of a police officer. He was turned over to Mexican authorities at the Tecate Port of Entry, for what I can only imagine was an unpleasant experience unless he had powerful friends.

Two Burglars on the Highway

Shortly after 9/11, the Border Patrol in the San Diego Sector changed the way it worked a little bit. Before that time, agents in San Diego Sector were all but forbidden to conduct any kind of traffic stops or smuggling cases unless there was a direct correlation to the border. The words they (management) used were always the same: "I'm not telling you to not do your job, but..."

The message was clear, and it was made even more clear when agents who defied the restrictions were harassed and retaliated against. One young agent conducted a traffic stop on a load vehicle north of Tecate, which allegedly had tried to run him over. He fired at the driver of the vehicle as he jumped out of the way, and the vehicle subsequently crashed in a canyon. I can't remember if there was ever a prosecution, but the agent was kept on the "rubber gun" squad for about two years afterward, as a punishment, in his opinion at the time.

Another agent, F., who was pretty adept at spotting loads, pulled one over at the end of our shift. The supervisors told the other shift agents to go home, leaving him to process the case alone. Then, for some unknown reason, the charges were not pursued. That particular agent became the subject of a retaliation campaign by some of the supervisors for not being in his assigned area. He ended up recording a conversation with a supervisor who was later caught in a lie. The union would not defend the agent, so he defended himself and secured a written apology memo from a supervisor that was posted in the muster room.

My intent is not to expose a lot of dirty laundry, but to illustrate the climate change that happened after 9/11. Nothing much changed operationally, from the agent's perspective. We were now able to pursue smuggling cases, and generally be less shy about investigating possible illegal activity or conducting traffic stops, as long as there were sufficient articulable facts with which to justify their actions. The only other obvious change was that an agent had to park in front of the station for "security."

In this environment, I was riding with my partner Tom. We

got sketchy information over the service radio about a possible load of Middle Eastern males heading to San Diego. Obviously, this was just basic intel and not a license to pull over any vehicle on a search for ethnic minorities, but just a lookout to keep in mind if and when a load vehicle was encountered. This was in the context of the largest terrorist attack on the United States history that had just occurred, and at least one of the perpetrators had had links to San Diego.

As El Cajon is on the way to San Diego from points east, it made sense to put agents on Interstate 8. The I-8 checkpoint may or may not have been up, but our job was to look for this vehicle and any other smuggling traffic in the I-8/Highway 79/Pine Valley area. At one point, I remember we were trying to respond to a call driving uphill on Interstate 8 in an old 90s Ford Bronco with the small-block V-8. We had our lights and siren on and I had the pedal floored, but we could only manage about 60 MPH. It was funny and a little embarrassing, with California drivers passing us right and left, middle fingers in the air.

Of course, another unit ended up responding to the call and beat us there; it turned out to be 10-19, no violation. We ended up checking various spots along I-8 where aliens typically either loaded up or crossed, such as the Pine Valley Bridge, "Shit Creek" behind the Alpine CVS, and certain mile markers we were familiar with from past apprehensions. While we were checking the dirt in the I-8 median for sign, a passing motorist pulled over and informed us that there were two guys walking westbound in the median, to our east. He had no further information, but this was not typical behavior and we thought it was either aliens or a motorist in distress, so we moved out to check.

It wasn't long before we came upon two guys ditty-bopping along the median near the eastbound lanes. We swooped in and got out before they knew who we were. The sun was going down behind us and the BP Broncos did not have the roof racks with red-and-blue emergency lights. They just had lights in the windows and on the front grille, so from the front, we could have been any normal vehicle for all they knew.

We announced ourselves and got them to sit down. They were two young males from Mexico. They had the usual alien stuff: a couple of backpacks, water jugs, etc. As Tom was interviewing them regarding their immigration status, I went through their stuff and found a bunch of coins, jewelry, and two handguns. One was a loaded Smith & Wesson .357 Magnum revolver, and the other an almost identical looking revolver, but chambered for .177 pellets. There was also plenty of ammo for both.

We had not yet secured their hands, so when I called out "gun," we took them all the way to the ground and hard-cuffed them, then thoroughly patted them down. In Southern California, both at the time and presently, carrying a concealed weapon is *verboten* unless you are law enforcement or one of the (very rare) holders of a concealed carry permit. Illegal aliens in possession of firearms are in even more potential trouble under 18 USC 922(g)(5)(A), a federal felony. We had a couple of "quality apps," as the saying goes, and took them in to the El Cajon Station for processing.

At this point, I had gotten a few aliens with guns before, so it wasn't surprising to me when the Prosecutions Agents again declined a gun case on behalf of the AUSA. A San Diego County Sheriff's Deputy was requested to respond to the station. He told us that there had been a home burglary in the area east of where we had picked these two up. Looking at the inventory of items the two IAs were carrying, he quickly determined that they were the burglars. Apparently, they had broken into the home of a local seasonal firefighter who was up in Northern California for fire season. The coins had some value as collectibles; I cannot remember if the jewelry was worth anything. The .357 was worth at least $600 at the time. The Deputy charged them for the burglary under California law.

This would be the only time I would go to court on an arrest for the next twenty years. They were convicted, in spite of their smart-ass defense attorney trying to get me to say on the stand that we never read them their Miranda rights. This was not the case, I told him; the processing room camera clearly would have shown Tom with his card in hand, reading them their rights in the language of their home country. I suggested that he should subpoena the tape. Clearly, he never did and lost the case.

We were lucky. While that processing area camera usually worked, I found out later that the tape in the very old VHS recorder was not regularly changed (tapes in old VCRs were to be changed at least every 24 hours and retained for a period of time for just this reason). Tom had read the guys their rights as required, but if the tape hadn't been properly changed we would have looked pretty bad.

Excitement in Tecate

I was working an overtime shift on a beautiful day in February of 2002. Although the Border Patrol is concerned with illegal entries in between the designated Ports of Entry (POE), we usually had two one-man units assigned to cover the small POE in our area. As the POE West agent, I decided to eat my lunch in the parking lot of a small market (TC Worthy's) adjacent to the southbound lane in full view of the scouts on the Mexican side. This was for deterrence and so that I could see if anyone ran north in the southbound lane near the store. Although it was a Wednesday, I remember there being a lot of pedestrian traffic, both northbound and southbound. In Mexico, the vehicles were stacked up in the northbound lane, waiting to enter the United States from Tecate, Baja California.

A huge chicken salad from the Bravo Cafe sat in my lap as I chowed down, observing the activity around me. Somehow I was managing not to get any on my uniform. Looking over my right shoulder, I made eye contact with a scout in "no man's land" standing on the borderline across the street to my south. He casually spoke into his cell phone, most likely to a foot guide waiting to send some bodies across and into one of the many vehicles parked nearby, where they would hide until a "shopper" made his purchases and got in to drive them away.

As I watched this guy, I noticed a blue Ford pickup moving behind him, threading its way through the stopped traffic by driving up on the sidewalk and finally turning northbound in the southbound lane, still in Mexico. I thought "Hmmm... that's strange."

Then I noticed a Chevrolet Corsica close behind him, and a low-riding Ford Thunderbird also following. There was just enough time for me to swallow some lettuce and croak into the radio.

"Agents near the POE, we got a drive-through!"

As I called it out, the vehicles came north into the US, driving up a curb and scattering some pedestrians. I pulled forward onto the sidewalk as the pickup passed me, I observed a terrified-looking man in a cowboy hat driving it. Then he passed.

My Tahoe blocked the next vehicle, not intentionally, but because there was nowhere else to go. Time seemed to slow down as I got out, a phenomenon known as tachypsychia. I forgot what I had been told at the academy - that drive-throughs equal dope, and dope equals guns - and I left the 870 shotgun in its rack as I exited the Tahoe. I ran around the front of my ride to grab the driver of the Corsica. There were people all over the place, and I hoped the Customs guys were taking notice and coming to help out. Then I saw the rifle.

Next to the driver of the Corsica, leaning against the dash, was an M-16 rifle loaded with a 20-round magazine. The driver, a middle-aged Hispanic male, was holding his left hand up and saying something I could not hear.

"HANDS! HANDS! Border Patrol! Get out of the car!" I yelled. Afflicted by tunnel vision and auditory exclusion, all I could see was this guy, the rifle, and the fact that his right hand was not visible. Suddenly, I was looking at him over the front sight of my pistol, opening his door and "helping" him get out of the car and onto the ground, yelling at him to give me his hands.

He was wearing a black nylon fanny pack, the kind that might as well have had big block letters on it spelling 'G-U-N.' He was reaching into it with his right hand as I pulled him out of his car by the scruff of his neck. I began the trigger press, and remembered to say it in Spanish, *"Deme las manos,"* my pistol inches from the back of his head. If he pulled a gun out of the fanny pack he was a dead man. I thought, "Holy shit, I am really going to have to kill this guy." Luckily for both of us, the double-action Berettas have a very long trigger pull before the hammer drops and the gun fires. He suddenly stopped reaching into the bag and gave me his hands.

"OK, OK, " he said as I placed him face-down on the ground and was assisted by a Customs guy in handcuffing him.

My vision opened up as the stress response abated, normal sound returned, and I looked up to see a circular firing squad of Customs Inspectors covering us, and each other, with their pistols out and bystanders everywhere. A guy walking up the southbound truck lane with a badge out (the driver of the third vehicle, the Thunderbird), was taken down by Customs and my partner on the east side. The Ford truck had been successfully spiked by Customs, and was resting nearby, blocking Highway 188 in both directions. Not a shot had been fired, and that was just as well, because I suspect that if one person fired, others would have, with disastrous consequences.

After everything got sorted out, there were two different stories. The driver of the pickup truck was a US Citizen, and a resident of Tecate, California. He claimed the two men following him wanted to kill him because he didn't give them money. He had no criminal record that we could find.

The other two in the passenger cars were Citizens and Nationals of Mexico, credentialed members of the Baja California State Judicial Police. They were each armed with a 9mm Browning High-Power pistol which they carried in their black nylon fanny packs along with their badges, law enforcement credentials, and one rock each of crystal methamphetamine. The guy I took down had a semi-automatic Colt Sporter 5.56mm rifle, and his partner had a Colt 9mm full-auto submachine gun. Each Mexican cop claimed that the USC was wanted for molesting a young girl in Mexico.

After much sound and fury (signifying nothing), the two Mexican cops were released into the custody of their *Commandante*, who came north to get them. We seized their vehicles; both cars were registered to separate parties out of the Los Angeles area. I never learned the disposition of the weapons, none of which had a paper trail in the United States.

The coverage by the San Diego Union-Tribune failed to disclose the origin of the 'police' vehicles or the methamphetamine possessed by each Mexican officer.

Was the dope a pick-me-up to get them through a long shift? Or throw-down meth to plant on innocent would-be extortion victims? Neither Mexican Officer had anything to say about the dope, in my presence at least. I gladly handed my guy over to Customs and retired to our little POE trailer to write my report. In the years since, I have tried to avoid any Mexican Agency whenever possible. Encounters on the line were infrequent and usually cordial, after a fashion. How there can ever be any level of serious cooperation with a thoroughly corrupt narco-democracy, which is financially and politically dependent on violating our law and sovereignty, is beyond me. The good guys down south, understandably, have to keep a low profile, and I never knew anyone able to tell them from the bad guys.

Shortly after this incident, I went to work for another federal agency. The Border Patrol had been good to me; I was not leaving angry. It was apparent to me, however, that there was no wartime urgency to anything we did on the border. There were no military units on or near the border, in spite of the threat that everyone agreed was posed. Some of us figured that the DEA and CIA had snitches in all the big cartels and would let enough dope in to pay them off. After the 9/11 attacks (in part occurring due to weak immigration enforcement regarding visa issuance and maintenance of status), there was an opportunity to largely solve the immigration problem. However, the smuggling picked up again like nothing ever happened. Some cynical agents supposed that perhaps there were powerful interests at work high above the Border Patrol who might be benefitting from all the bodies and the dope coming across. It made me think a little... too good a problem to solve?

Ramming Incident

It was sometime in 2003, and I had a trainee riding with me. I was freshly back from the other federal agency and happy to be "down south" again. My trainee was a young female who seemed pretty interested in the job. As we headed eastbound on Highway 94 from "824 Bravo," our unofficial designation of the last 7-11 before getting out to the field, I had my trainee, my Pop-Tarts, and Mountain Dew, and all was right with the world.

My buddy Tom, now an FTO, had a bunch of his trainees working a group east of Tecate. They had followed the IAs from the border fence past Crutches Pond, up to a place called the "Race Track" near Thing Road. A cluster of houses on Thing Road had a circular dirt track behind them, which local kids used to race their mini-bikes and so forth. It was also a popular place for groups of IAs to load out.

We followed Tom's progress on this group as updates were called out on the radio and made our way east. "Looks like they loaded up," Tom called out and put out the description of a possible load vehicle, an old Chevy Suburban. The kind with the "barn doors" on the back.

F., another El Cajon agent, answered up. He was always down to make traffic stops, much to the chagrin of pre-9/11 Supervisors. "I'm behind it. It looks good." Agent F. was heading eastbound on 94, way ahead of us. Another agent called out that he was going to back F.'s stop.

I explained to my trainee that we would support them but had to hang back in case there was a pursuit. Border Patrol Policy dictated no more than two units following a Failure-To-Yield vehicle. Though the suspect had not FTY'd yet, he most assuredly would do so because of Border Patrol policy limiting pursuits. The load drivers all knew that we would only pursue until they did something crazy. We followed at a distance as Agent F. called out various landmarks to dispatch; he was on Old 80.

"Chippies are at the I-8 entrance; I'm going to light him up," said F., calling out the presence of a California Highway Patrol unit, and announcing his intent to activate emergency equipment.

We were almost there. As we came around a bend, I could see the red-and-blues up ahead.

"FTY, FTY, he rammed 'em!" someone yelled. I spotted the Suburban as it flipped a U-turn in the median, hit a BP vehicle, and headed straight at us. This time I did not forget the shotgun; I grabbed it and stepped out, racked a round into the chamber, and aimed in at the driver of the smuggling vehicle, activating the weapon-mounted light. The bright "Surefire" light reflected back and washed out my view, however, so with no target, I stepped aside. The 'Burb went past me and crashed into a big tree behind my Tahoe. The agents and Highway Patrolmen on the scene converged on the vehicle, trying to break open the windows and get the doors open. One of the chippies looked at me disapprovingly.

"You better clear that thing," he said haughtily, as if I was about to mow everyone down or something. At that point, the doors of the vehicle were opened.

As they pulled everyone out of the loader, I made a safe weapon and returned it to the rack in the Tahoe. I can't remember how many bodies were pulled from the 'Burb, but it was quite a few, over twenty at least. They were stacked in there good. We found out later from the aliens that the load driver spotted the CHP vehicle, rammed it, U-turned and rammed a Border Patrol vehicle, then saw me with the shotgun. He then made himself small under the dash rather than control his vehicle. If I had fired, there would have been no driver, only an empty seat and 20 or more bodies crowded in the back; what a 12-gauge slug would have done to them made my blood run cold.

I am reminded of the firearms training maxim, "Be sure of your target and what is beyond."

Soon the FBI responded. It was the Civil Rights Squad, not the Assault on a Federal Agent Squad. They were very interested to know why the Border Patrol was picking on poor illegal aliens again, and why an agent would consider deploying a shotgun when all they did was ram multiple vehicles. One of my supervisors, whose name I sadly can't remember, told them to pound sand. He wisely had me write, but hold on to, a memorandum detailing my reasoning for the shotgun deployment. Nobody ever asked for it. I think the load driver ended up getting prosecuted for this one due to assaulting Federal Agents. I believe he was also prosecuted by the State of California since he had also assaulted their officers.

Tom's trainees ended up doing the smuggling case, but even then those cases were few and far between, compared to today. I can't remember what happened with that case. In any event, it was a good night for my trainee as she got to see all kinds of craziness, and no one got hurt. Not even the aliens.

Quality App?

Tecate, California, around 6:00 PM. I was working around the POE with some other guys and we were spread out both east and west of the small town with its two-lane Customs facility. My classmate Tom was up on a hill we called Customs Overlook, or something like that, and he had his binoculars. I was on the west side, lurking in the truck lots for the small groups that would jump the fence and run into the stores, or jump into waiting cars to blend with traffic. Sometimes, legitimately documented border crossers would cross legally, park a car in the truck lots, and leave the keys in it. They would then just walk back south, leaving the car for a group to jump into later.

We had hurried out right after muster to beat the shift-change rush. Our shift "flexed" from 4 PM-2 AM during winter, to 5 PM-3 AM for the summer. For a couple of days after the change, we would get a lot of apprehensions around the port of entry until the smugglers got the message and adjusted their operations.

Tom called out a group; they crossed on the east side where the other guys were. They were running across behind the POE and heading straight for the Amerimex convenience store just north of the Highway 188/Thing Road intersection. I can't remember how many there were, but it was a small group. They ran into the store as we came out from our hiding places on the west side to get them.

One of my partners went inside the store and talked a couple of aliens out, but the last one would not emerge. Nobody wanted a big scene, so as they took the two IAs across the street to our little processing trailer. I waited near the door for the last one. Eventually, he came out. He was in "transition." A tall dude with what appeared to be a convincing boob job, very feminine looking with short brown hair and jewelry, but the prominent Adam's apple was kind of a dead giveaway. Tom, through his binoculars, could not see this level of detail from his hilltop vantage, about a quarter of a mile away. He thought he was looking at a tall female.

101

"That's a Quality App," he laughed on the radio.

The guy spoke pretty good English; he told me they were supposed to wait in the store for their ride to San Diego. Also, he said that he was scheduled to have the transition "completed" very soon. I asked him where he got the money for all the surgery and hormone treatments, and he replied that there were many well-off people downtown who spent a lot of money on him for "services rendered."

The Tecate Processing Center was a single-wide trailer with three cells, a couple of offices, and a bathroom. It was a place where you brought your apprehensions for entry into the biometric identification systems and processed them for removal proceedings or V/R, whatever was called for. More serious cases were taken to the station. The Detention Bus would show up periodically and take all the bodies off to El Centro or San Ysidro for removal.

So, I got this guy and was writing him up, and one of the senior agents asked aloud where we thought he should be held. Male or female cells?

"He's pre-op, should be male," I said. This is 2001-2002 before all of today's gender categories and subcategories.

"Well, are you sure?" He asked. I wasn't. The cells were small and nothing bad would happen because we were right there, a few feet from the plexiglass; any funny business would be dealt with quickly. But nobody wanted to commit.

While we were thinking about this, a few newer agents showed up, including a young female agent whom I didn't know.

"Ma'am," the senior agent said, indicating the transexual, "this person might have dope on her; we need a female to do a good search."

It didn't take long before we heard the telltale "Aah!" and the red-faced female agent came out, alien in tow. Even the alien was chuckling.

"You assholes," she said. She was going to be all right.

Delta Tango

Sometimes PAs use jargon or codes when the regular words are fine. A "Delta Tango" is the phonetic alphabet for D-T, or Drive-Through, when a suspect vehicle drives right through the border between legitimate Ports of Entry, usually smuggling bodies or dope. In my opinion, saying "Delta Tango" doesn't save you any effort over saying "Drive-Through."

It was my first day riding solo at the Sonoita Station, July of 2004. Frank, one of the more outstanding agents at the station, had given some of us newcomers a quick tour of the major roads the day before, and we were expected to learn the rest by doing. I wished that I could ride with their latest group of trainees for a bit first, but this has never been allowed in any station I ever worked. Maybe they are afraid that surly journeyman agents might pollute the impressionable minds of the trainees.

Deciding to get right down to the immediate border area, I took the most direct route to go south. Sonoita Station agents called this "going down the middle." There is a place south and maybe a little east of Sonoita called Canelo Pass, which bisects the Canelo Hills and accesses the San Rafael Valley which opens up as one continues south. Proceeding through the pass, I followed some unfolding events over the radio, consulting a hand-drawn map a trainee had made of the area, complete with PA-specific designations of various landmarks. These types of maps are ubiquitous in the Patrol, at every station I ever went, and the best ones always seemed to live forever.

As I followed the progress of a supposed drive-through that had been called out from "The Big House" by the Arizona Fish and Game Ranger that lived there, I figured out that I might be in a good spot.

By the time I got down into the valley, I couldn't see anything. It seemed a good idea to go as far south as possible in case the loader tried to TBS. After a while, I decided to pull over and climb up a small hill for a look. No sooner did I get up high than I saw the dust trail. A rooster tail of dust headed northward by

Shelley's Bus Stop, followed by the buzzing of a "Foxtrot" air unit. A Border Patrol OH-58 helicopter flew low over the valley and got right down on that vehicle, an old Ford or Dodge pickup truck. The truck then turned around and started heading south, towards where I was.

I ran down the hill and was in the middle of one of the Forest Service Roads when the pickup came barreling around the bend, starting to lose traction. I could clearly see the wide-eyed driver and front-seat passenger gaping at me as the driver corrected himself and kept coming. They couldn't stop if they wanted to. One of them held an object out the window. I thought *"gun!"* and brought up my shotgun, but then chose instead to get my ass out of the road.

They blew past me; I jumped in my little Jeep Rubicon and hauled ass right after them, going cross-country now. Of course, I couldn't keep up; load drivers were generally very good, and they were utterly unconcerned with property damage or the safety of others. I, on the other hand, was just OK, and had a lot to lose. Also, the steering wheel's tilt mechanism came unlocked repeatedly as I bounced across the valley after them. At one point, I could see the OH-58 almost land on the roof of the load vehicle, and again on the hood. The pilot was quite a cowboy. Later, I learned it was Pilot K, the heroic pilot who would later come to the aid of Agents Brinkhoff and Villa when they got shot up by smugglers.

Between us (mostly the helicopter), we chased the pickup south. It crashed through a gate at one of the ranches, then through the barbed wire fence that marked the International Boundary and made a getaway.

I went back to the spot where I had chosen not to get run over by the truck. In the grass, just past the curve in the road, was a small handheld radio. It was of the type commonly used by the scouts. A small handgun with a loaded magazine inserted was right next to it. Hah, I thought, it really was a gun!

We seized the weapon (a cheap semi-auto pocket pistol, no paper trail in the United States) and the radio (useful for some of the native Spanish speakers to listen in on the scouts) and called it a day. Later, my supervisor, Nikita, asked me why I didn't shoot the guy.

"Because I didn't have to," I said. "And it was more important to get out of the way."

"Next time, you shoot." He said, seriously.

Trash Mountain

On one of my first shifts at the Sonoita Station in July or August, I had the east side. It was a beautiful drive down State Route 83, past Parker Canyon Lake, and into the valley. Some guys say the drive gets old, but no matter the area, I always enjoyed the drive south. Southern Arizona is a sight to behold, especially in this particular area. Many people spend their vacations here, camping, hunting, catching bugs, and birdwatching. Deserts, mountains, grasslands, and animals; there is plenty to look at. On this particular day, I remember going all the way down near Lone Mountain on Forest Service Road 61, turning east, and beginning my "cut" for signs of illegal traffic.

Even in the summer, here in the San Rafael Valley, it was about 10 degrees cooler than up in Tucson. I rolled down the windows and got set up to lean out the window at 5 mph for the next few hours, looking at the edges of the road and the dirt patches beyond, as well as the grass or weeds, in case they were pushed down. It was late in the morning, so the sun wasn't going to help me.

FSR 61 wasn't the best cut as it was an improved road; not so much dirt as gravel, or something in between. Also, I wasn't familiar with the area yet. Other better cuts were not yet known to me. This is what I knew how to do, and it would be a start, so I went for it.

It didn't take long to find a group. The freshly pushed-down trail in the tall grass off the road jumped out at first, and then as I continued, I could see them clearly in the dirt next to the road. I called it in and let the station know I was getting out on a group, the approximate number, and the dominant sign. I pulled all the way off of the road and grabbed my stuff: gloves, Camelback, shotgun, and a green boonie hat.

There was no art to it as this was a group of about 30. Even though they did not always walk in the dirt, no matter where they went, it looked like a herd of buffalo went through. I walked for a while, looking around frequently for flashes of color in the brush.

The ground was rising as we closed in on the Huachuca Mountains. The group stayed northbound. At one point, I lost the sign on the side of a ridge. Working my way up to the crest of the ridge, I paused for a moment before topping out, to listen for a bit and catch my breath. Being a big slow guy, I had no problem taking my time; if someone was laying in for me, I wanted to be ready for them. Then I heard them talking.

Someone was speaking in a low voice. Pressing further upward along a brush line, when I came to a break in it, I took a look. There were several aliens taking a break along a creek bed. I wasn't totally sure this was my group, but there were definitely more than a few bodies down there. I could only see about a dozen Hispanic males. They all had small backpacks indicating that they were typical illegal immigrants as opposed to dope mules. In Border Patrol vernacular, they would be called "10-45," radio code for an alien smuggling case, or "Title 8" which is the part of US code that covers immigration. Dope was known as "10-46," or "Title 21."

Though the brush concealed them, I could hear more along the creek bed. Having only two sets of handcuffs and a small bundle of flex-ties, busting them all now would be stupid, I thought. Sometimes, I would just wade in and get what I could; usually just a few. In this case, I figured I'd shadow these guys a bit from a distance and try to call in help later on.

For the first couple of hours, it was easy. When they went over a ridge or behind some brush, I would beeline towards it along the easiest ground. A few times they got away from me, but again, the signs of their passage were pretty obvious. They were spitting, blowing snot, and throwing their trash on the ground constantly. Though shoe booties were a thing now, nobody bothered in the mountains, so occasionally I would check the ground to confirm their sign. It was all there, the major patterns: Converse, Nike swooshes, running W, cheese graters, fine lines, and the Mexican Vibram. There was more underneath these, but these guys were the ones bringing up the rear. I would catch a flash of red or blue through the brush as a brightly colored shirt or bandanna passed by.

Whenever I thought I could speak without being heard, I would update the station on my location. Unfortunately, the terrible Arizona radio comms were not helping. As a former San Diego Sector agent, I had no idea what bad comms were until I came to Arizona. I would put out GPS numbers and group size periodically, but never could hear anyone talking back to me. There were not many agents down south, but if anyone heard me, I did not know it. This went on for several hours.

The last time I saw them, I was coming over a small ridge as they were creeping around a dry waterfall, and I just caught sight of the last ten or so guys in line. By now, I was out of water and getting concerned about how to get back. Not exactly lost, just concerned. I knew which way was north and roughly where I was on a map, but the roads and landmarks were still largely unknown to me. The lesson here is don't go on a hike alone when you don't know the area, especially trailing a group.

I ended up climbing uphill to a spot where I thought the handheld radio would get out. Working my way up to what I thought was a peak, the foliage became thicker. Soon it opened up under all these trees. The place had been hollowed out by years of groups coming through and laying up here, out of sight of aircraft, and leaving their trash. Then the animals got to it and spread it around some more. I topped out and saw all down the other side of the hill, as far as the eye could see, a layer of garbage carpeting the ground. Old clothes, backpacks, opened cans, pouches, and empty jars and plastic bottles of all kinds. Wrappers, cigarette butts, dead lighters, and plastic bags fashioned into raincoats and groundsheets were all over the ground and hanging from trees like Christmas ornaments. It was nasty, and I could only imagine what the more inaccessible areas looked like. It wasn't the first or last disgusting lay-up I ever saw, but the biggest one in my career. I later heard that an effort was made to clear out the trash, but who knew how high up they got. At least the dopers usually cleaned up after themselves to evade detection.

I called out group numbers again, along with their approximate direction of travel and requested a pick-up. It sucked to let the group go on, but you should never wait until you're in distress to exercise discretion and ask for help, no matter how much it burns you. One of the original Sonoita guys answered up to me, and between us, we figured out where I should go to meet him. It ended up being one of the Forest Service Roads out by Sunnyside, I think. It was a long day, and my head was throbbing with dehydration by the time I got into his vehicle.

Later, the duty supervisor (who will be a Chief someday, and probably a good one) let me know that they heard all of my updates and had been tracking the progress of the group all day. He was pretty nice about it, considering how stupid I had been going off on my own after a big group in the mountains. This was a transitional period when the Border Patrol was starting to realize that the old way of doing things was not necessarily the best way. One agent on his own in the Huachuca Mountains with a group of 20 was just as likely to get his ass kicked as come back with a group. Also, my water discipline was lacking. As it was, he advised me to get with someone else next time and left it at that.

The group was never caught as far as I ever knew, but it wasn't the only big group out there at that time.

I am a slow learner. It took another time humping up to the Crest Trail through one of those canyons on the southwest face of the Huachucas and running out of water before I got smart. At least on that occasion, I had an original Sonoita guy with me; my comrade, Terrible Terry. That day taught me that I had about two or three hours, after running out of water, to walk before heat exhaustion really set in. It's different for everyone, but that was my red line. From that time forward, whenever my Camelback ran dry, I either got more water, turned around, or called for a pick-up, no exceptions.

Animal Encounters

In the course of twenty or so years of walking around the mountains and deserts, one is bound to have interesting encounters with animals. After being chased by dogs a few times, I figured out that they only chase you if you run; once you make up your mind to fight them, they almost always back off. If not, well, that's why you have a gun and a baton; posture with confidence!

PJ vs. Pit Bull

Border Patrol Agent PJ was near some campers in the canyons west of the Huachuca Mountains looking for some traffic, when somebody's pit bull had a go at him. He stood his ground, but the dog was not impressed. Before the pit could bite him, he drew his pistol and fired. While missing the dog, he deterred the attack and was swiftly cleared by the FBI (All Border Patrol shootings, whether they hit anyone or not, are investigated by the Border Patrol Critical Incident Team, the FBI, and local Sheriff's Departments).

Big Cats by the Burning Bush

One early evening, in the El Cajon Station AOR near Tecate, CA, a sensor went off in a creek bed north of the "Burning Bush." This is a place on the Border Road that had been set on fire years prior by some aliens. I was out on foot concentrating on the patches of dirt in between the rocks and looking for sign when something made me look up. About ten yards away, as I shined my light, a set of glimmering eyes stared back at me. Not knowing what it was, I slowly reached for my pistol and raised my Maglite. A big mountain lion turned broadside and casually walked away. It had been checking me out from a rock above, and well within pouncing range. It was a hot summer evening, but I shivered a little.

Months later, while manning a FLIR scope truck on Scott's Hill just a little east of the previous encounter, I panned over to the Burning Bush after a sensor was called out. Zooming in, I could just barely see the top of the bush where it stuck up from behind a slight rise. The Border Road came straight towards it from the east then broke hard north, following the creek bed for a bit before a hairpin 180 turn back south. Directly past the bush, the border road went back west. I watched for a while before I noticed a cat-like silhouette walking along the Border Fence from east to west. Then, another one further north paralleling the first.

It was like they had done this before: The southern cat would move for a bit then sit, at which time the northern cat would move. Then the southern, and so on. Kind of a cat version of bounding overwatch; these cats were stalking something. After a minute, I saw them: two heads poked up just north of the Burning Bush, bobbing up and down as they walked northbound in the creek bed, bent forward under the weight of their backpacks. They were blithely unaware that two mountain lions had them in their sights.

"I got a pair heading north from Burning Bush," I called out. "Anyone available for two, west of Scott's?"

An agent answered up. He came in "quiet," lights-out in a Bronco, from the base of my hill, nice and easy. The sun was setting, so he had to be careful.

"Be advised, there are two kitty-cats stalking them."

The patrol vehicle sped up and blazed in with its lights on, scattering the cats and sending the aliens back south.

"Two TBS - good work."

The newer MSC trucks have a recording and play-back feature. I really wish I could have gotten this on tape or on a cellphone camera. It was very cool to see the mountain lions acting in tandem like that.

Stalked by Big Cats

A similar story was relayed to me by a BORSTAR Agent, Brian. He was following some foot sign one day in the El Cajon Station's area up north somewhere, walking in a canyon solo. The canyon had steep sides and as Brian walked, it got narrower. Something made him stop; was it the group? They could easily bush up in one of the nooks and crannies, but the sign kept going, so that wasn't it. Deciding he was hearing things, he kept on following the group. Eventually, the canyon made a sharp turn. Here an echo definitely got Brian's attention; someone was behind him. Another group? He made the turn, climbed up the side of the canyon, and hid behind some rocks and brush, waiting.

After a while, they came around the corner. A medium-sized mountain lion and her cub, also following the sign, freshly trod upon by our agent Brian. He shifted his weight to make a noise, alerting Mom to his presence before she got too close. The cats took note and turned around.

I always wondered if, or how many, aliens out there ended up *hors de combat,* at the tooth and claw of wild animals. We definitely ran into several who had been bitten by snakes and spiders, but never by the bobcats, bears, or mountain lions. Maybe the cats liked to stalk us for practice, like the mother cat teaching her cub, or were they just naturally curious?

Cougar Stalks Chris

Once while operating a scope truck east of Sonoita near a hill we called The Biscuit, I put a K9 Team in on a sensor that was in a wash beneath Highway 82. As the agent, Chris, and his dog went under the bridge to check for sign or scent, right behind them, a big mountain lion slunk along. How could they not know? It was too far away to honk the horn. I called repeatedly on the radio, to no avail. I called for another agent to get in there and make some noise, but nobody was close. As I prepared to lower the boom and get over there in the scope vehicle, I heard Chris calling. He said there was no sign, the activation was probably animal, and they were heading back to their truck.

You bet it was.

I met up with him later and told him what was up. He was not happy.

" Why didn't you say something?!

"I did, but either you couldn't hear me or I wasn't getting out."

Chris explained that the wind direction was coming from in front of them, so the dog never smelled the giant cat behind them. It must have been pretty silent because it was *close*. Chilling.

Bears

When you got into mountains like the Huachucas on the east side of the San Rafael Valley, Arizona, that was bear country. Again, it is amazing how quiet they are for their size. Although these bears are not big by North American bear standards, they look pretty big in the wild when they are looking at you. When I was told to escort some Army guys from Fort Huachuca to check out some sensors of theirs, I brought along an 870 shotgun and loaded it with 1-oz. slugs. The soldiers, who were in the National Guard deployed to the fort, were unarmed.

We turned off of Forest Service Road 61 and headed up one of the roads leading into a canyon. All of the canyons went up towards the north and east, into the mountains. It was a very popular place for dope and aliens. There are a lot of trees and other foliage under which groups could conceal themselves from aircraft. We got on some sign and followed it up, getting on a pretty well-used trail. As we broke into a grassy clearing in the trees, we saw the trash first. It was a well-used lay-up, littered with trash, as they all were. There were several backpacks about twenty yards away, all torn apart, and a young bear was chomping on a can of "tuni," Mexican tuna fish. We watched him for a few minutes as he worked on the can with his teeth while holding it with both front paws. It was pretty fascinating to me, watching him work. I'm not a huge animal enthusiast, but to see them in real life doing interesting things always commands my attention. Eventually, the bear got the can open, and wet tuna got all over the place, at which time he cleaned it all up.

"I'm glad you have the shotgun," said one of the Army guys. The bear heard him, and looked at us, but didn't pay much more mind to the puny humans as he went about his business. We went about ours, and when we came back through going the other way, he was gone. It occurred to me that placing a tracker on a bear would quickly map all of the most popular trails and lay-ups the aliens used to further their illegal entry.

Not long after that, there were several of us agents working a large group in this same area, again heading up one of the canyons into the woods. I found a promising creek bed and decided to cut it, stepping away from the other agents as they continued uphill. It was getting dark. With my head down, Maglite out, I was concentrating on the rocks and dirt when I looked up to see a bear cub about ten yards away. He ran off to the west, towards the trail the other agents had followed up. The hair on my neck stood up as it dawned on me: here was this cub, where was mommy?

She was right there, on the other side of the creek bed. She made a chuffing noise, from way too close, and it was almost too much to take. I couldn't immediately find her in the dark, but when I did, I could see that she was big, and the cub had already circled around and rejoined her. Thus reunited, they turned and walked up the hill to the east, into the trees. I had never heard a thing until the mom called her cub. The shotgun was in my hand, but I doubt it would have been possible to use it in time, had she decided I was a threat.

The creek bed was no longer interesting, and I rejoined my partners immediately.

Later, another agent, Mani, had a similar bear encounter in the same area. After he busted a large group on one of the trails, he left the "10-15s" (the aliens they initially apprehended) with a partner and went off up one of the hills to chase down the runners. After dispersing, groups of runners will usually circle back to the same place they had run from after the agents leave and softly call or whistle for their buddies. Mani figured he might catch them resting, so he moved lights out.

The bear must have been upwind and paying attention to the aliens nearby because Mani took him by surprise. This is rare; in my experience, agents are not very stealthy when tromping around the mountains. What is not surprising is that he didn't see the bear until it turned around on him and stood upright with a grunt. Mani quickly drew his pistol and fired a round over the bear's head; the bear took off.

When he told me this story later, we both agreed that he was pretty lucky, because his little .40 caliber hollow points would not have made much of an impression on the bear, had it decided to press home an attack.

10-99

In June of 2005, a bunch of us were in processing at the Sonoita Station, when we heard a call on the radio:

"Shots fired. 10-99, 10-99..."

Everybody froze. 10-99 is the code for "Officer down." The BP has recently gotten away from using 10-codes most of the time. Usually, plain English is more easily understood and, to put it honestly, the smugglers know our ten codes too. They are still useful for brevity though, and this one makes your hair stand up.

The general details of the gunfight near the Line Shack in the Nogales Station area of responsibility are widely available on the internet. Years later, CBP produced a short documentary for showing at musters, using the real guys and re-enactments, kind of like those crime shows on the Investigation Discovery Channel. The basics are that two Border Patrol Agents, Brinkhoff and Villa, cut some sign across a fence line and were following it towards the International Boundary Fence when they were ambushed by unknown assailants and pinned down from the high ground with accurate rifle fire. Both agents were shot and unable to move, so they had to return fire in place while calling for help. A heroic BP helicopter pilot, Pilot K, flew his little bird right down into the line of fire to draw off the bad guys and buy time for the responding agents on the ground to get in there. The shooters fled back into Mexico where, as far as I know, they have never been apprehended for this attempted murder.

At Sonoita, while some agents were turning up the radio and asking each other what the hell they just heard, a few quietly exited processing and went straight to the armory. In a moment of clarity, I followed them, got my M4, and an 870 shotgun too. It was my practice to always bring all of my gear to work no matter what the assignment was so that I could be ready for sudden changes (think the Blackhawk Down scene when the Rangers were told they didn't need night vision or heavy armor). I always had a few extra M-4 magazines loaded, so I grabbed those and looped 12-gauge rounds in my tricky bag with water, gloves, lights, flex-ties, etc. In this case, I was one of a few. I got outside in time to see Terry, a giant red-headed Viking-type guy who I thoroughly enjoyed working with, had jumped in a truck. I hopped in with him and we hauled ass on State Route 82 towards Patagonia and Duquesne Road, where we could turn west and get close to the Line Shack. No plan, just go. We figured someone smart would have come up with a plan by the time we got there.

Turning roughly south on the Harshaw at Patagonia, we hit the dirt and had to stop for an agent who had a flat. It was one of the supervisors, who I will call Iceman; he was also a member of the Tucson Sector Special Response Team (SRT). He said that he had to get going and ordered a very disappointed Terry to get out and take over the immobilized vehicle. With that, SBPA Iceman and I re-commenced speeding down to the area of the Line Shack.

It took a while on the dirt roads; this being summer, there were other people on them, too. When we got closer, we could see it was obviously way too late. We dusted out a well-known (and not well-liked) TV news personality from Tucson, blew by a bunch of senior management officials, and rolled up on some PAs who were obviously wanting to get after it. I felt fortunate. SBPA Iceman, as the senior SRT agent, assumed command of the scene and began deploying the agents present. Some of the SRT guys had shown up; they had apparently been doing something else, and some didn't have long arms or ammo, or even complete uniforms. That was weird. They would be deployed for the "tactical tracking" op, so I gave one of them the 870 I had brought along with the 12-gauge shells I had in my bag.

"You guys go up that hill there to the east and cover the trackers," Iceman told me and a couple of others. To this day, I cannot remember their names but I felt comfortable with them in the event of any incidents. On days like this, people show you who they are. Speaking of quality people, Terry had changed the flat and still made it out to the scene a little later than we did. He was like that. Another few agents were sent up a hill to the west; this meant that between our two teams, we could cover the agents tracking on the low ground from two sides.

I remember a valley, bordered east and west by ridge lines that went south towards the border, which was also elevated, so the SRT "tac-track" guys would be moving southward at the bottom into a perfect trap, the base of which was closest to Mexico, where the bad guys had gone. We went up the east side and the other guys went up the west side, and the SRT team performed their tracking op down low, very slowly. Some only had gym clothes under their heavy plate armor, and it was HOT. One of those poor guys was vomiting from heat exhaustion in short order.

In the end, we came up empty. The bad guys probably beat feet as soon as Foxtrot flew in; the actual border wasn't far away. Tucson has a great Trauma Center and the two stricken agents got first-class medical treatment. Brinkhoff and Villa conducted themselves like the outstanding agents they reportedly were. I remember hearing later that both of those guys had M4s, which were left in their vehicles "to just check this sign out really quick."

Lesson learned: if you have a rifle, take it with you!

I also learned from SBPA Iceman that it was He Who Knows What To Do who should be in charge, regardless of rank. In this instance, apparently, nobody questioned him, and he did a fantastic job with what he had.

It was not the first time, nor the last, that I would find out in the moment who the guys were that could be counted on. I wish I could remember all of their names. Brinkhoff and Villa recovered and returned to duty. They helped the Border Patrol by putting together some very good two-man tactical training devised specifically for Border Patrol Agents, who usually work alone or in pairs. They called it TATP, or Tactical Awareness Training Program. I attended the training and it was excellent. Initially meant to go BP-wide, it was soon discarded. Discarding much-needed training in favor of getting more agents on the line is all too common, in my opinion.

Ideally, TATP would be integrated with firearms and defensive tactics qualifications; the latter two are quarterly events, but there is enough other training that a four- or five-day training cycle every six months could be instituted, which could take care of all of it. This would require bargaining and planning, but I am sure it could be done.

Rollover

It was a chilly evening in Sonoita as a few other agents and I returned from the Nogales Station. It escapes me whether we were coming back from the range (we conducted much of our firearms training in Nogales), or if we had been processing at the station itself. At this time in the early 2000s, there was an awful lot of traffic coming into the United States, and the entire manpower of the Sonoita Station was detailed to processing bodies in Nogales, according to someone's Operational Plan. One agent was left "at the crossroads," at the intersection of State Routes 82 and 83, with another agent and a supervisor at the Sonoita station manning the phones. The entire border area that Sonoita agents were supposed to cover was left open.

As we headed eastbound on Arizona 82, we heard on the radio that a sensor had gone off near the winery in Elgin, Arizona. This particular sensor was located on a dirt turn-out next to the paved road where illegal aliens would come out of the brush and load up in vehicles to further their entry into the United States. The agent on the radio stated that the sensor was "good," meaning that a vehicle had just picked up a load. Sign for numerous pairs of footprints, blown out by tire tracks, would indicate this. The agent, whom I'll call Bob, was fairly squared away and as we entered Sonoita, we picked up speed in our giant lifted Ford Excursion to make it to an interception spot on SR82 before the loader got there.

"There's tail lights ahead," called out Bob on the radio. "Dust cloud; I gotta stop," he continued. We all knew that there was a tight curve north of where the suspect vehicle had loaded up. A sudden dust cloud indicated that the loader had left the road.

"It's a rollover, multiple injured. Roll medics." Bob's voice was mechanical. He was a recently trained Emergency Medical Technician about to earn his pay. We called out our response and arrived to see a big Ford dually, upside down, with many bodies lying around, some of them groaning. Agents were posted north and south of the scene to divert traffic away. Others assisted Bob as he attempted first aid on the many injured. While many of the aliens were miraculously unhurt, some of them were beyond help.

Bob told us later that as soon as he saw tail lights, they disappeared in the dust cloud. When he could not see, he halted and got out, and discovered the load vehicle with the aliens strewn all over and around the road. Some of us got down to business separating the uninjured and securing them off to the side. Bob and a few other agents rendered first aid. Luckily, ambulances began arriving very soon, and Life Flight birds were in the air.

There were many injured, and about eight or nine dead out of the 20 to 30 illegals that had been in the truck. There were children. I think all the young kids made it, but I'm not sure. I saw one adult with his spine exposed, and internal organs falling out of his back, but he was conscious for the moment. Others were also pretty grievously injured. Some, inexplicably, were just fine.

I saw one man whom I will never forget just sitting on the road. In the dark, it appeared as if he was scratching his head; upon closer inspection, he was digging his fingers into a heinous wound atop the skull, much of which was missing, where crushed bone and gray matter were apparent. He would pick out some goo, look at it, and flick it onto the road nearby. By this time, I was assisting a Fire/EMS medic with triage tags. Green meant good; yellow, serious; red, critical; black, dead.

"That guy's a black tag," she told me, "He's already dead."

One nearby agent kind of freaked out and stepped away. On the other side of the spectrum, a senior agent happened to be walking by when I taped a black tag around the wrist of the alien.

"Anyone got any chips?" he asked offhandedly. Both agents' reactions are normal in the face of trauma; one of sudden illness and revulsion, and one of inappropriate black humor. In both cases, the agents continued taking care of business in spite of their initial reactions.

It took a while to clear out all the bodies. There were several Life Flight helos landing and taking off on the road, and ambulances, and then the real police showed up. There were Santa Cruz County Sheriff's Deputies, Border Patrol Agents in and out of uniform (BP Critical Incident Team), and Arizona DPS State

Troopers.

When everything cleared out and it was just agents, DPS, Sheriff's Department, and CIT. Somebody noticed there was a peculiar, but somewhat familiar, smell. We looked at each other and shrugged.

"Anyone burning meat?" asked an agent.

We looked around and eventually zeroed in on Bob's vehicle. It was still parked in the middle of the lanes where he had gotten out in the dust cloud because he couldn't see. It was what we called a "Barbie" Jeep, that is, not the Rubicon model with the off-road package, but the cute little low one that high school girls might have preferred.

Bob's Jeep had come to rest atop the body of one of the aliens, and the heat shield of the still-running vehicle had been cooking the flesh of the dead man this whole time. With all of the other smells - smoke, dust, and helicopters landing and taking off - no one had noticed. It was kind of ghastly.

One of the CIT agents who had been on the scene told me later that the Santa Cruz County Attorney, or one of his employees, threatened that "if you prosecute the load driver with murder, I'm going on your agent for the same thing." This was of course, outrageous if true, and nothing of the sort ever came from this incident. The Border Patrol doesn't prosecute anyone anyway; we set up cases or "prosecution packets" that the Assistant US Attorney reviews and either does or does not approve for prosecution.

ATVs

ATVs are not as fast as motorcycles but are much more safely operated in the dark. Care must be taken, but it is very doable. The motorcycles are great for darting up trails at speed, while the ATVs, at least those operated in the Tucson Sector, are more suited for bulling through the sandy washes, heavy brush, and carrying out loads of narcotics.

At some stations, these were "checked out" like shotguns or Milcams, as an item to be used by the shift agents. In recent times, however, this has changed. With a large number of injuries and accidents, the training and requirements to be on these off-road units have become more standardized. The use of the "off-highway vehicles" (OHV, in government-speak) has been limited to members of their specific units that have been trained and are supervised by qualified instructors and supervisors.

The death of Border Patrol Agent Manuel Alvarez in September of 2016 is indicative of the hazards of working alien traffic on motorcycles or ATVs. While responding to nearby activity, BPA Alvarez and another Motorcycle Unit agent had a terrible accident resulting in Alvarez's death. The effect of Alvarez's death on the agents of the Casa Grande Station was immense. He was a popular and very effective agent. This event led to changes in the Tucson Sector Off-Highway Vehicle policy to increase safety; while policy changes might have some positive results, it is still a dangerous job. It is one thing to go out to the dunes or to a track and go nuts; it is entirely another to pursue people who do not want to be caught across open desert, washes, canyons, and fence lines.

I was selected for ATVs first at the Sonoita Station, then at the Tucson Station as a supervisor. Before 2007, we were distinguishable from line agents by the green one-piece flight suits we wore, the ones worn in the US military by armored vehicle and flight crews. There were plenty of accidents, and some serious injuries as well, so the flight suits were half-jokingly referred to as "bone bags." After the mid-2000s, they were no longer authorized. They were great, but replaced by the new rough duty uniform.

It seemed that the most dangerous part of the day was at the end of it when we were trying to get back to our trailer and head back to the station. Getting the ATVs, or "scoots" as they are sometimes called, back onto the trailer is another source of injury. I suspect that this is due more to impatience and being tired.

From 2005 to 2007, the Sonoita ATVs were rotating through details to the Ajo Station, which was getting hit pretty hard back then. Usually, when we returned from a detail in Ajo, the ATVs were broken, and took some time to get ready for the next detail. But we made do. Riding a mix of Kodiaks and the big 4x4 Polaris, all of which had been broken and repaired many times, including the welding of broken frames, we caught a lot of bodies and dope. Mixed in with the Ajo guys, we had a great time working their area from the bombing ranges up north, all the way to Gu Vo and Pisinemo to the south.

On one outing, we got on some sign near the Border Road and were following it north near Red Hill in the Mesquite Mountains. Working in relays, a couple of agents would stay on the sign on foot until the mounted agents, cutting the washes to the north, found the sign and called it out, dismounting. Then the former foot agents would get back to their scoots and bypass the other team, to begin the leap-frogging process over again.

Working this way for a few hours, we ended up at a small village called Santa Cruz, in the Pisinemo District of the Tohono O'odham Indian Reservation. The foot sign had been tracked non-stop from the border to the doorway of a specific house, near the church in Santa Cruz. We surrounded the house and waited. Border Patrol Agents are generally discouraged by training and policy from making entry into private dwellings in the course of their duties. In this case, it would have been perfectly legal to do so, since there had been constant contact with foot sign directly linking this house with an illegal border crossing. Time was on our side, however, and nobody wanted to get in any trouble. The senior Ajo agent, who had a satellite phone (cellular signal was nonexistent here at the time), called a supervisor at the Ajo Station, who in turn called for a TOPD officer to do a "knock and talk."

It took hours to get a TOPD officer out there. He asked us if we had knocked on the door. Of course, we hadn't. None of us were supervisors or in public affairs, which was why we had called him. Needless to say, the Border Patrol and the TOPD had and have their differences, especially when it comes to relevant authorities and operational techniques.

While agents covered the alternate exits, the officer knocked on the front door. It was only superficially attached; as he knocked, it fell off the dilapidated hinges, revealing a dark and disgusting interior with trash bags (full of trash) up to the ceiling that had been broken open by the rats, spilling foul-smelling garbage all over the place. The smell was impressive. All kinds of clothing and personal articles littered the floor as well, and one (non-tribal) illegal alien watched cartoons on a TV that was connected to a satellite dish placed in a window. He surrendered peacefully. As we entered to arrest the alien, I turned a corner and saw a large number of marijuana bales stacked up high. The marijuana smell had been obliterated by the trash and rat turds. Grabbing the alien and cuffing him, I noticed that he was pretty solidly muscled, clearly a well-fed backpacker and not just some guy watching the house.

Over the next year and a half, we would get a lot more dope out of Santa Cruz and the vicinity.

While on detail to the Ajo Station, the ATV agents and the Horse Patrol Agents (HPU) had an informal competition to see who could get the most apprehensions. It wasn't much of a contest; though the ATVs got close sometimes, HPU ended up with more. Horses can see in the dark; they know what they are looking for and will see or smell aliens and move to them. An HPU guy would post himself on the mine tailings south of the town of Ajo and scope the area with a Mil-Cam until he found a group. Then they would ride out and get them.

ATVs tried it on one of the bombing ranges one night. A guy climbed up to a high point with the Mil-Cam while the rest of us rode to a place where he had a view of us, and where he thought the aliens would come from. We dropped the scoots just inside the gate and rode in slowly, lights out, with NVGs. I had a hard time with this, nosing into a wash and hitting my NVGs (and them hitting my face) on the speedometer. But we managed without doing too much damage and staged up in a wash near the foot of a hill where the Ajo guys thought the aliens were headed.

Before long we had contact. The Mil-Cam operator called out a group coming towards us. I can't remember how many, but it was a good-sized bunch, and they came pretty close to us. A few of us walked up with NVGs and integrated ourselves into the group. When the agents up ahead "busted" the group (announced themselves), we went lights on and put them down fast before too many of them could run. It was a good night out for us, but I think the Horse Patrol got more apprehensions that night anyway. Not such a great night for the aliens, who had walked about 60 miles to that point since crossing into the US. Only the "blue flag" water stations set up by immigrants' rights organizations, and the caches placed by the smuggling organizations, could keep them alive long enough to make it that far.

There was one cut we did every morning. Federal Route 28 is a long wide dirt road, between the villages of Gu Vo and Pisinemo, called Crossover. We would drop scoots at the west end and ride eastbound until we found a group big enough to be worth tracking. Yes, worth tracking. With so many groups crossing at all hours of the day, it was a matter of screening for the groups that you had the best chance of apprehending before running out of water, gas, or both. In those days, a group of 20 was about the minimum we would go after unless there was a reason to suspect it was backpackers. We were pretty fixated on dope at that time; it was considered to be the more dangerous type of group with the highest likelihood of criminal aliens (CARPS).

One fine morning, I was riding with a partner, Mikey. Mikey was a fun guy to ride with, he had a good sense of humor, and was a Marine too, so we had that in common. He had been way more of a Marine than me though, having been in the Military Police in Quantico while I was picking up cigarette butts in Camp Lejeune.

We rode slowly eastbound, noting sign from various groups

over the tire tracks of the regular east-west road traffic. I really wanted to go after a group of bicyclists, otherwise known as TOBs, or Tonks On Bikes. They were known to travel in large groups of 20-30, and bicycle sign is really easy to track and catch up to.

There were stories of agents on foot who would lay in with cargo straps when they saw a group of bicycles coming. In the desert at night, far from any human habitation, it would be easy to hear the squeaking of the chains as they pedaled furiously to beat the dawn's break. They allegedly would fasten two or more straps together and pull them taut across the aliens' direction of travel when the group got close. In the ensuing chaos of crashing bicycles, it was easy to get the majority of the group. Needless to say, this was not sanctioned by management. I never saw this happen, but it was one of those stories that everyone believed.

With ATVs though, none of this was necessary. We would ride hard on the bike sign, and when we got close they would always ditch their bikes and hide in the washes, hoping we would only get some of the group. It would have been pretty stupid to try to out-ride ATVs on a bicycle.

After a bit, Mikey and I found a group of 20-plus and went after it. Other ATV guys were cutting State Route 86 up north of us, and soon they had the sign across 86 near San Simon. We hauled ass up to that point. By the early afternoon, there were three teams of ATVs after three separate groups of 20-30 aliens. As the day wore on, it became a little more difficult to cut for them; the soil dried and there was less color from the foot sign. There had been so many groups over this area for so long, it was easy to get off on the wrong traffic if you weren't careful. In the morning, a big group would leave sign in the desert you could cut from space.

Mikey and I made good enough time. We got our group before hitting the next paved road. The other guys got theirs too. By mid-afternoon, three ATV teams had over 60 bodies in custody. Later, one of our guys was interviewing an alien who told him that in the morning, the foot guide woke him up at the sound of our motors, saying: "Listen! They're coming. We have to go now."

No dope, but a good haul of aliens. We waited for several hours while the two available vans assigned transport ferried our apprehensions back to the Ajo Station.

ATV Pursuit

From an interview with an agent of over 20 years in the field, many of those patrols on ATVs:

"It was September, so it was warm but it cooled off at night. Another agent and I were cutting sign in an area known as "The Parking Lot." This is a couple of miles west of [paved road], near Williams Ranch, on a [large Indian Reservation]. We rode Yamaha Warriors, no 4x4. They were fast but sucked in sand or mud. We did our sign cutting with the headlights since we didn't have cut lights back then."

Cut lights are small LED lights, with magnets to attach to the metal on patrol vehicles; some are welded to the frames of Border Patrol ATVs. The lower you fasten the cut light, the easier it is to find the sign, due to the cast of the shadow on the sign. Mount it too low, and it will be ripped off by rocks or brush.

"Three vehicles had gone through; we caught two of them on ATVs. They were laid up against the mountain. I think there were about 18 [bodies]; they were all asleep, laying around the vehicle. We tracked out the second one further north, in between the pass out there and the 'beef stew tank,' where all those cows died."

Beef stew tank got its name thusly: A herd of cattle, dying of thirst, had followed their usual trail to a tank to find water. There had been water there recently due to monsoon storms, but it had all been absorbed into the mud. The cattle walked into the dirt tank where they became stuck and all died. That area of the Sonoran Desert is so remote, and during monsoon is so inaccessible, that it was a long time before anyone reported it; by that time, the cattle had become badly decomposed.

"We caught the bodies again, sleeping around their [load vehicle]. After that, we chased the [third] one all the way to [the paved road], mile marker 12. They were laid up in the wash, but they weren't sleeping yet. They saw us coming on the ATVs [got in their vehicle], and took off. They were going down that [dirt] road, and at that mile marker 12, they just hit it."

Mile marker 12 is where the load vehicle hit pavement; when it straightens out, high speeds are possible. The load vehicle was trying to TBS and get back to Mexico.

"We were actually able to chase it down on our ATVs. I remember it was a white Chevrolet pickup truck with a blue line all the way around it. I remember the adrenaline as we were chasing, I could feel the bugs hitting my neck and how much it hurt because of the speeds we were traveling. We weren't really able to keep up with it much because we were on ATVs, but we actually pushed that vehicle all the way back through the gate [on the International Boundary Fence], so we were 3 for 3. It was funny because I would see the lights go far away, and then when we would start catching up, they would pull away, and so forth. Cat and mouse."

Needless to say, it is not encouraged to pursue load vehicles on ATVs. Pickup trucks can hurt you on an ATV. Also, in this area, there are horses, cattle, and donkeys crossing the road all the time who are not looking both ways! Even a deer or a coyote can ruin your day if you're going 60-70 mph on a quad. But at that time, in that area, things were a little crazy, and PAs adapted.

"There were a couple of transport vans following us. They were full but followed just to make sure nothing happened. We were able to manage and get that group south.

It was fun chasing these people around. You know, a lot of guys would see a vehicle [and say] "aah, it's gone!" But you never knew unless you tracked it. Most of them, we found out, crossed in the early morning and hid up against the mountains in various little ravines, and they would all get out of their vehicles and sleep under bushes.

Once we learned that information, my partner and I were killing it out there. We would catch two to three [loads] of 20, 30, 40 bodies at a time... but yeah, we got in a pursuit with a truck."

The mission of the Border Patrol is to arrest those crossing the International Boundary between the Ports of Entry. Is it dangerous? Yes. Can it feel pointless, like trying to hold the ocean in your hands? Sure. Can it still be "fun?" Absolutely. Again, the purpose of this book is to share a few accounts of what your working Border Patrol Agents are doing out there. The larger strategic/operational approach is beyond their sphere of control or influence (except as voters) and is dictated by politicians and their appointed servants.

If it seems, by this point, that the effort and expense of Border Patrol Operations are senseless and random, then you are getting somewhere. Is progress measured by the number of apprehensions and pounds of narcotics? Is more actually good? Yes and no.

If you catch a lot of bodies and dope, great, you are successful. But you are also a failure, because why do they keep coming? Failure of deterrence.

If you catch very few bodies and not a lot of dope, you are successful. But you might also be a failure, because how could they get away? If there are a few gotaways and you aren't catching much, then you are a success! Your resources will be taken and sent elsewhere.

It's kind of a "Catch-22."

This is why government numbers can be misleading. There are numbers for all kinds of things, but how do you count what you never saw? Are the numbers verifiable, or conjured up in a bureaucratic plot to conserve resources? Ask yourself what wages are for illegal aliens. If it's peanuts, then immigration enforcement is a failure. Ask yourself, how expensive is it to OD on opioids? If it's cheaper than ever, then drug enforcement is a failure. This is where we are.

Riding with Serge

One of the real characters on the Ajo crew's ATV unit was Serge. He got a K9 later on and I'm sure he was very productive with his dog. I only rode with him a couple of times, but it was always interesting; there was a lot of traffic, and we always got into something. Also, he was a big fan of movies and we had a few favorites in common.

One of them was a 1994 Luc Besson title, *Leon: The Professional*. It stars Jean Reno as a hitman "Leon," Gary Oldman as "Stan," a dirty law enforcement agent, and a very young Natalie Portman as "Mathilda." There is one scene near the end where Stan, upon learning the location of his enemy, Leon, calls it in to his team: "Bring me everyone," he says.

"Everyone?" asks the voice on the other end.

"EV-RY-ONE!" shouts Stan.

Serge once told me, "I always wanted to say that into the radio: 'Bring me everyone!'"

Hopefully, he never had to!

Serge and I were cutting the Crossover, west of the village of Pisinemo on the TON. He rode a Grizzly ATV, while I had either a Kodiak or a huge (and very worn-out) Polaris. There were groups here and there, but we finally settled on one of the bigger ones; the sign was pretty fresh in the dirt of the well-trafficked road. The Crossover is very wide and very straight for a dirt road, and it was always worth cutting. A large number of big groups crossed it every day, many packing dope, coming out of the Mesquite Mountains and heading north to San Simon and State Route 86, as well as points north.

The group was at least 20-30, as I recall, and it was pretty easy to follow at speed. There is a way of "zooming out" your concentration and looking way ahead for the faint trail of color left by the group; this allows a daytime rider to make time on the group. At night it's much slower. On ATVs, you also have to temper your enthusiasm a little, so as not to crash. If you go too fast or get too focused on the sign, you might miss a barrel cactus or a critter

135

warren. A barrel cactus will stop your ATV cold, but you the rider will keep going. Ask me how I know.

So, we're following this big group, calling for air support, and zigzagging back and forth. When we came to the San Simon Wash, we had to slow down and really look at the dirt for where we thought they were headed, and then find a way across. With our crude handheld GPS units, we would typically mark the spot, dismount, and follow the sign on foot through the wash and the thickets around it until breaking out into the open desert again. I would usually then make a long dark line in the dirt with my foot to mark the egress; some guys would just go by the GPS waypoint. Then it was back to my scoot and ride along the wash until there was a good spot to cross safely.

There were two of us, so one of us did the dismounted thing while the other guy hauled ass to get back on the sign quickly. It was probably Serge since I was there on a detail, and he cut sign way better than me. When we met up later, we stayed on it as the sign broke east towards Federal Route 21, a paved north-south road that connects Pisinemo with the rest of the world.

Pushing hard, we made good time to FR21, around milepost 20 or 22. There was, and still is, an elaborate monument to the deceased victims of a car crash at that spot, a *"cruz de memoria."* The Tohono O'odham Indian reservation has hundreds of these monuments, each representing one or more traffic fatalities, and tended to by family and friends. They usually have some kind of cross or plaque, with flowers candles, mementos, etc. The Border Patrol has its own memorial crosses for agents; these are marked with the United States flag and a small marker.

The long, straight roads invite tired drivers to sleep. There is a serious problem on the reservation, and in Arizona as a whole, with drug and alcohol abuse and impaired driving. There is the poor fencing of the roads as well. Donkeys, wild horses, cattle, and even locals in dark clothing are often struck with fatal consequences, especially at night. Even if you are alert and looking for it, a herd of horses can cross right in front of you before you can do anything about it.

In this case, as in others, the uniqueness of the monument served as a landmark for a group of illegal aliens to meet up with their load vehicle, or vehicles. The foot sign made a beeline for the monument, milled around, then went for the road. Right next to the road, tire tracks had blown it out as the vehicle took off. I checked the opposite side of the road, and the dirt was clear of sign.

Serge was already calling it in.

"873, this group loaded up at mile post 22 by the monument. About 20-30 golf." "Golf" is Border Patrol speak for "gotaway." We used it often; though most of the stories in this book end in apprehensions, most signcutting operations do not.

Military Encounters

The US-Mexico border is the most militarized border in North America. The US just hasn't shown up. The Mexican Army, known as SEDENA, is not shy about aggressively patrolling their side of the border and sometimes coming over to ours. To be fair, until recently there have been large areas where the International Boundary is not clearly delineated, and US Border Patrol personnel have been known to go a little too far south at times. At best nobody notices. At worst any US Officer caught south of the border is arrested for invading Mexico and faces a very uncomfortable stay while his or her release is negotiated.

Mexican soldiers caught north of the border used to be pointed south and told to go back. After 9/11, they are now apprehended like anyone else, if there are enough agents to convince them to give up. Sometimes, like in Texas several years ago, they so outgun the US authorities that they are allowed to take their dope and go south on their own. Once or twice they have tried to apprehend our agents in the United States, but to my knowledge have not succeeded.

It is not my purpose to impugn the Mexican Army; of course not every unit is dirty and involved in smuggling. Some are. Plenty of Mexican soldiers and police defect to the cartels for better pay and benefits and take their uniforms and weapons with them. Others contract out. Personally, I have encountered many who appeared to be just doing their job and patrolling their side of the border. Once, I helped to jump-start a SEDENA HMMWV that was stuck on the other side of the fence. Other agents have had plenty of positive interactions with them. Many BP Agents are veterans and have empathy for enlisted troops of most armies. It's just that because so many of the cartels field such well-equipped units, it is difficult to tell the difference between legitimate soldiers and cartel shooters, and often unwise to get close enough to make a determination.

Federales Near Campo

On one occasion, I observed numerous men in gray uniforms with black nylon tactical gear carrying FN-FAL battle rifles southeast of Campo, California. One of the agents at the station later told me they were Federales. I don't know for sure and definitely did not ask them at the time. They were in an area where a large group was staging to cross the line.

Strange Soldiers at BM 103

Sometime around 2005-2006, I was west of the Huachuca Mountains near Border Monument 103. I was slowly driving the Border Road westbound at a leisurely pace looking for brush outs or any other sign. Something I saw on the south side looked good. I pulled north of the road, over a small hill, and walked back to take a look... and totally forgot what I was looking for when I spotted a squad-sized element of what appeared to be Mexican soldiers walking up a draw about 50-100 meters south from the line. I got down near a tree and watched them for a bit.

There were about a half-dozen guys in full military battle-rattle with HK G-3 battle rifles, tac gear, and helmets. Then there were about four or five guys in dark gray with giant black backpacks the size of military seabags or hockey bags. The hair on the back of my neck stood straight up, something which I have learned to never ignore.

In Arizona, most of the dope that is carried on foot across the border is wrapped in cellophane and tied up in a homemade burlap backpack. In San Diego, most of the backpack dope was in actual nylon backpacks or duffel bags. On the northern border, a lot of it is carried in hockey bags. So, this was weird to me but still looked like a dope load.

I tried to get out on the handheld radio, without success. I looked around at all the high points on the south side, wondering if someone was looking back at me, knowing that they were. Was it actual army soldiers or cartel guys? Was it army soldiers working for the cartels? Who knew, and who cared? I watched as the group dropped out of sight over a small rise and into another gully further west, then I ran back to my ride and got on the radio. Nothing.

Since there wasn't anyone else working nearby, no comms, and no realistic way to succeed, I bugged out - loudly, with no attempt to conceal who or where I was. Hopefully, this would deter them for a little bit. There was no way to get out of the area without them seeing or hearing me, and I am sure there were scouts calling me out the whole time. Dope at that time, in that area, was never moved without heavy scouting. I called it in as soon as I had comms and later came back with a partner to cut for the group. The bad guys were either very good or chose to cross somewhere else because we never cut sign for them.

BP Helicopter Lands in Mexico

There was a drive-through at the border in the San Rafael Valley, that is to say, the Sonoita Border Patrol Station's AOR (Area of Responsibility). Agents responded and chased it back south where it then crashed. These were crazy times; around the same time frame, a load vehicle drove through the border and got cornered by agents, one of whom foolishly approached on his ATV. The loader backed into him and the agent fired several shots through the back window of the pickup, intending to hit the driver, but missed. Nobody was hurt that time.

This time, the loader had crashed south of the line and, as luck would have it, a Border Patrol Foxtrot (air) unit was flying around nearby. He came on the air saying something like, "There are injuries; I'm going in."

The guys on the ground tried to tell him not to, but he was on detail and didn't understand where the border was. He thought they were being callous, or something like that, because he insisted on landing and deploying a BORSTAR Agent on board who could help the wounded. Unfortunately, the BORSTAR agent was also on detail, and unfamiliar with where the border was.

"No, Fox, don't do it! See where the ground agents are?" Sonoita agents at the actual International Boundary Fence were waving emphatically.

"I have BORSTAR, they need help."

"FOX! You really shouldn't land!"

Nobody wanted to get them in trouble, but that was the gist of the radio traffic. The helicopter landed, and the BORSTAR agent got out with his med bag to help.

Sadly, the Mexican Army was also nearby. HMMWVs with soldiers showed up. For some reason, they were almost always close when the DTs happened. They arrested the BORSTAR guy at rifle point. While they were doing this, the pilot spooled up and took off, leaving his partner behind to the tender mercies of the Mexican Army. At the time I thought that was a dick move, but I guess he figured he had to protect the bird. Who knows, no one ever heard from him again.

My buddy, Joe, was there, and he drove right up to the fence and hit the lights and siren, trying to get SEDENA's attention. The incident was happening about 1/4 mile south of the line.

Joe waved over one of the soldiers and explained to him that the BORSTAR guy was a Border Patrol medic, and that we thought there had been casualties; that he was not trying to arrest anyone, just trying to render aid. Both Joe and the Mexican *soldado* joined in cursing the pilot for leaving a ground guy in the lurch; apparently, this soldier had had a similar occurrence in his career. After a few more pleasantries, the Mexicans in their HMMWV gave our BORSTAR guy a ride back to the border, and freedom.

Campini Drive Through

The next time I bumped into the Mexican Army was also kind of strange. There had been a drive-through at the Campini Mesa. Another agent, Dave, had spooked this load vehicle back south in a cloud of dust. I raced over to the Mesa from wherever I was and met up with Dave. We went south on the D.T. Road and noted the type of tire sign that had been left behind so we could pass it on to the next shift. Surely they would try again.

We stood there shooting the breeze when a dust cloud coming from the south side heralded the approach of a vehicle. There were two of us; I had an M4, and they could surely see and ID us as BP, so we waited for them. It turned out to be an HMMWV with SEDENA markings. An old guy clambered out, followed by three other soldiers with their G-3 rifles. The old guy had two stars on the front of his ball cap. A General. The General's companions all looked like they were 16 or 17, and their uniforms did not fit them well but had legit-looking patches and insignia. They were all smiles, and we shook hands and exchanged greetings.

Dave informed the General that we had just had a drive-through that got TBSed and had he seen it? *El General* replied in the negative; he asked us if we had seen people on red ATVs doing doughnuts on the Mexican side. He pointed out to us some tire sign on the Mexican side of the cattle guard that indicated this. I happened to notice that the tire tracks of Dave's TBS load vehicle were on top of the ATV doughnut sign.

We said no, but that we would be in the area all night and would be on the lookout. He laughed and told his lads, *"Vamanos muchachos!"* We parted friendly, but not friends.

Dave and I agreed that *El General* was probably curious as to why his load never made it through. In my very short three years as a United States Marine, I never saw a General rolling around with teenage enlisted men or without a bunch of Captains and Colonels in tow, taking notes and telling him how great he was. This guy, real General or not, was up to no good, and I learned we could count on any dope loads having military support.

144

Encounter at Lochiel

Craig's voice came in low over the radio. He had a vehicle in sight trying to drive through near the cemetery at Lochiel. "It's a load." He was a soft-spoken, witty kind of guy, and one of about three or four agents covering the entire border area for the Sonoita Station. Of course, it was a load, trying to drive around the end of the border fence late at night without inspection.

Lochiel is a somewhat occupied semi-ghost town right on the border near Washington Gulch, about 25 miles east of Nogales, Arizona. Its days as a mining town and a working Port of Entry were over by the mid-80s. By this time, in the early 2000s, there was only one occupied house in the whole town, and the old Customs House was boarded up. Craig was on the hill between the town and a narrow draw that went roughly northwest towards Washington Camp. The bottom of this draw from where it climbed up to the west was where the west end of a chain-link border fence was which continued eastward across Lochiel.

A Chevy pickup truck had tried to skirt around the end of the fence, and got stuck at the moment of truth, with the passenger's side of the vehicle hung up on the fencepost right where the cab met the bed. Craig called all of this out while sitting in his ride on the hill west of the town, backed up to the cemetery, watching through NVGs. Josh and another guy were partnered up in the Canelo-Campini area and were en route. At the station, I figured I was no more out of pocket than Josh and his partner, so I grabbed a ride and took off.

It took a while to get there, and I arrived at about the same time as Josh. Our plan was for Craig and me to sneak down to the truck and ID the plates and VIN and try to get it unstuck to seize it. Craig had observed the occupants unload several bundles from the back of the pickup. Another vehicle came up and they loaded the bundles in it and it took off south. We were pretty sure there was no one left around but posted Josh and his partner on the hill to cover us. It was, after all, right on the border in a notorious area for dope smuggling. We also called for air support.

We snuck down with M4s and NVGs out. If there were scouts, hopefully they would have seen us and stayed clear. That was fine with me. When we got down near the stuck pickup, we waited a minute, listening. When Josh reported no activity around us, we went lights on and commenced getting numbers off the vehicle. I remember it was registered in the US, and as we ran the plate through dispatch, Josh called out vehicles heading our way from the south.

There were three of them, lights on, coming up fast. Craig and I decided it would be best to take off, and we ran to the north. We could hear guys getting out of the vehicles on the Mexican side. They yelled at us in Spanish, and I immediately fell right into a hole.

Dazed, I crawled up to the edge of the hole, facing south, and raised the M4 up to peer through the ACOG, a kind of military low-powered scope. It was only 2x, but at the 50-70 yards I was looking, I could clearly see that there were three military-style HMMWV trucks and about ten to twelve soldiers in combat gear milling all around their vehicles and the load vehicle. Some of them were north of the line. All had the ubiquitous G-3 rifles issued to regular Mexican Army units. They were slowly moving north.

Oh, shit, I thought. If I'm fucked, so is one of those guys. I aimed in on one who seemed to be giving directions, backlit by the HMMWV headlights. If they came into the US and found me, I was going to open up and then disappear in the confusion. No way would they be taking me south, not from here. I didn't know where Craig was, but he had definitely been ahead of me, going north, when I fell down.

"Somos La Migra," I called out. "Somos Patrulleros!"

I tried to call out to dispatch the armed incursion, in probably too loud a voice. Of course, it didn't get out on my handheld.

Everything was drowned out by the sudden appearance of a Foxtrot helicopter. The chopper flew an orbit around the north of us and lit up the area with the night sun. OK, I thought, there's a witness. In my peripheral vision, I could see Josh and his partner sauntering very casually down the border road towards the Mexican soldiers. I tried to call them on the radio to get them back out of sight but wasn't getting out to them.

Oh well, so be it. At least the bird was here. I got up and waved.

"What's up, guys?" Josh said amiably.

He met up with one of the soldiers and they conversed animatedly. I joined them, and so did Craig, appearing silently from the darkness.

Josh wasn't a native speaker, but had grown up on a farm in Dateland, AZ, and might as well have been. He was another great agent. He translated for us that the soldiers had been tracking the loader from their side and were there to seize it. They were from a unit that had just been transferred into the area from a conflict zone in the southern state of Chiapas, Mexico, where they had fought the Zapatistas under *Subcommandante* Marcos (AKA, Delegate Zero). They definitely looked more squared away than the General's men from the Campini drive-through, that was for sure.

We called off Foxtrot since everything was cool.

Now that we were all friends, Craig and I tried to move the truck, without success. The leader of the Mexican soldiers said that he could get it out with a winch on his HMMWV but then he would get to seize it. I shrugged. If he could get it out, then he could have it. The pickup was still mostly in Mexico, and the dope was gone, so it no longer mattered to us.

If these guys were involved in trafficking, it didn't seem like it to us. They didn't have the aura of dirtiness exhibited by the General and his teenage squad from Campini. Or the mystery men earlier from BM103 with their big black duffel bags. Since we didn't have any way to move the pickup, and the Mexicans did, there wasn't much we could do about it. We called in the loader TBS, in custody of the "mike-mikes (Mex Military)," and two individuals TBS, also. Another successful deterrence.

Woman in the Well

It was near the end of shift, around 2:00 PM, a stifling mid-summer day in the Sonoran Desert. Border Patrol Agent and K9 handler Tulley was turning eastbound onto Federal Route 20, passing a triangular-shaped hill known amongst Border Patrol Agents as "Little Egypt" on the Tonoho O'odham Nation. A seasoned agent, he scanned the desert brush back and forth on the roadsides. He slowly drove along the two-lane paved road, dodging frequent potholes and slowing for some horses that grazed next to the road.

As a K9 agent, he drove an unmarked F150 pickup truck. The back half of the crew cab was fitted with a kennel for his partner, Tessa, a Belgian Malinois. She paced and panted, needing a "break." Although the shift was almost over, there was a little time, and Tulley wanted to take his dog for a walk. The Mals were notoriously high maintenance; they were good at their job but very high-strung.

He turned off onto a road known as Gravel Pit, and headed south on it, towards the foothills of the Artesa Mountains to the south and east. These "mountains" are not really that high, but very rocky and rugged, grown over with cactus, mesquite, and other desert scrub. The temperature in the shade hovered around 105; he would have to monitor Tessa carefully, as the Mals did not know when to quit, and would keep going until they became heat casualties.

The second wash south of FR20, Tulley turned eastbound into it and drove along the wash in 4x4 low. The bed of the wash had been rocky, but the rocks gave way to soft sand, and it narrowed to the point where the sides almost scraped the side view mirrors. He had been just four-wheeling but was concerned about vehicle damage now.

As the wash opened up a little, the south side towards the mountains dropped off and was now more gradual.

"I'm not sure what happened first," Tulley says, "Tessa whining, or me seeing the little girl waving me down." At the top of the bank, a young girl, about six to eight years old in dirty jeans and a t-shirt, stood frantically waving and crying. Her long dark hair was tied back in a ponytail. Tears streamed down her cheeks as she called to him.

"She came down the side of the wash, sliding her way into it. My Spanish isn't great, but I could hear her saying that her mom was in trouble and needed help." He pulled up onto more solid ground and got out, trying to calm her. "It's okay honey, we'll help your mom."

As the girl sniffled and sobbed, Tulley got Tessa out of the back and hooked up her leash. The Mal was great with kids and gave the girl a sniff. It was stifling in the wash; the normal heat was magnified here as there was no airflow. The dog led them as Tulley picked up the girl and carried her up the side of the wash. He set her down on level ground and said, "*Busquemos a tu mama.*" Let's go find your mom.

The kid had left clear foot sign in the dirt, and Tessa had her scent; they set out with the girl holding her hand on the dog's back, and Tulley following them.

They walked for a bit when Tessa alerted. A K9 alert can be many things, and an alert handler can tell. Some dogs might sit and some just tense up. It depends on the dog. Tessa started pulling hard towards a low, circular stone wall about three feet high. There was a rope crudely attached to a nearby tree stump, thrown over the wall and down into the well. Tessa circled around, looking at Tulley as if to say, "Right here, dad!"

He looked into the well and saw a white oval in the pitch black: a face. The young woman had planned to draw water out of the well with the bucket, but it had either fallen in or was missing. She decided to use the rope to climb down into the well and find the bucket but slipped and fell into the water. Already suffering from heat exhaustion, she had panicked when falling into the icy cold water 30 feet down, treading furiously before finding the rocky walls and drawing herself upward far enough to breathe.

In his broken academy Spanish, Tulley tried to coach her into tying the rope around herself so he could haul her out; it didn't work. She was too tired to hold on while he pulled up on the rope and kept slipping out of it. The dog was whining and the little girl was crying. Tulley was getting frustrated. He got on the radio and was able to contact a nearby Border Patrol air unit, "Foxtrot." He guided Foxtrot in, talking him southward from Sells. Foxtrot relayed for additional help for "a woman stuck in a well," and the Tohono O'odham Fire Department was requested.

When the bird had spotted him and was overhead, some BORSTAR agents (Border Patrol EMTs with search-and-rescue training) overheard, and Foxtrot directed them in. It took a while; Tulley was worried about the woman in the well who had started out as a heat casualty but was now shivering and probably hypothermic due to being soaked in cool water 30 feet underground. Shock was a concern. He reassured the woman and the girl that help was on the way, and that she would be out soon.

"BORSTAR responded, with TO Fire," says Tulley, "they set up a pulley on a ground mount, like a sawhorse, and lowered a harness down to her." The woman was hooked up and on her way up in no time. "Once everyone showed up, I was relegated to the sidelines." He made sure to reward Tessa, throwing her toy and praising her in a high-pitched voice, one the dogs can understand.

"I stuck around long enough to see that the girl and her mother were reunited, then I had to get out of there. Tessa had been out in the heat for too long."

The Malinois, highly specialized and well-bred K9s, were known to succumb to heat stroke if not very closely monitored. Tessa needed to get back into the air-conditioned truck as soon as possible. As the BORSTAR agents and the firefighters tended the apparatus, and the girl hugged her mom, Tulley and his dog went back to the truck, and then home for the evening.

"If I hadn't needed to kill some time at the end of the shift," he said, "that would've been the end of them both."

The Real Deal

Bob transferred to the Tucson Station from San Diego Sector in mid-2005. He was already an experienced Border Patrol Agent, as were many in the great Voluntary Relocation Program instituted by the Patrol in the early 2000s. Many agents at the time were getting restless; there was no way to transfer from one station to another unless you took a promotion. In years prior, a journeyman agent, GS-9, could theoretically put in for a promotion to Senior Patrol Agent, pick up a raise to GS-11, and a transfer. With an agency-wide grade increase from GS-9 to GS-11, there were effectively no more Senior Patrol Agents; journeyman agents were left with no option to move around unless they became a supervisor. Not everyone wanted that.

The Border Patrol, to its credit, recognized and responded to the change in traffic patterns away from the cities of San Diego, El Paso, and others. Narcotics and alien smugglers were moving their operations to the outlying areas due to the increase in Border Patrol manpower, fencing, and infrastructure (Operation Hold the Line, Operation Gatekeeper, etc) that radiated outward from the cities, but was still largely absent from the rural desert and mountain areas in between. The Voluntary Relocation Program was instituted, an opportunity for qualified agents to request a lateral transfer to a number of stations that were seeing traffic increases. It provided agents with a lump sum of money for relocation expenses in exchange for the agent's commitment to work at the new station for a minimum of one year. There was a huge response.

As Bob tells it:

"I transferred to the Tucson Station in 2005. The Tucson Sector was having an increase in traffic and needed boots on the ground. Agents transferred to Tucson from all over the country. One, in particular, DG, stood out. He and I became fast friends and still are to this day. DG and I had the same work ethic; we came to Tucson to work and not just for a change of scenery. DG came from Texas, and I from California."

The influx of agents was not always welcomed by the

receiving stations. Many of them were "young" stations, meaning the agents already present did not have much seniority, on average. Suddenly, a large number of senior agents moved in and pushed these guys way down on the list for details and special units; this caused some hard feelings. An agent at the top of the list for an assignment to Sector Public Information Office, or Horse Patrol, with five years' service, might suddenly be at the bottom of the list if enough transferees with more time displaced him/her.

Bob continues: "You have to understand that the Tucson Station at that time was a very junior station, with the average time in service [for field agents] of about four to five years; most of the agents transferring in had ten or more years' service. Needless to say, we weren't welcomed with open arms.

"It was late 2005 or 2006. DG and I were assigned to the Tres Bellotas Ranch, which is literally on the border." TB Ranch, as it is known, is also one of the two most remote and desolate assignments for Tucson agents. "Once we got to our assigned area, we began to cut the road for any sign... we didn't find any...

"After about two hours, we received a call on our service radio asking us to give our supervisor a 10-21 (phone call). We went to a high area where we could get a cell signal. the Duty Supervisor advised us that a Ranger had seen a large group crossing the Tres Bellotas Road north of our area and asked if we could look into it. DG and I didn't even give our sup time to finish!"

The TB Ranch Road goes north to south before turning left and follows the International Boundary roughly eastward for a few miles before petering out. Bob and DG turned around, cutting back over their own tracks, and "sure enough, the sign was there. We figured the group waited for us to get south of them before they crossed.

"I always thought I was a better-than-average sign cutter, but DG was exceptional! I learned much from him during our time working together over the years. We geared up and began following the sign. When I would lose the sign, DG would pick it up again, we did this on and off for a couple of hours."

They finally lost it. This is where the most important characteristic of a successful Border Patrol Agent kicks in: persistence. If you never lose the sign, it's about endurance and your supply of water; if you lose it, persistence is the difference between a good agent and a great agent.

"This is where DG and his excellent skills kicked in. He kept telling me, 'They gotta be somewhere because they can't be nowhere.' We searched and searched, even backtracked, but nothing. After about an hour, DG found a single partial heel print. He exclaimed, 'I found these fuckers!'

"The group had gone into a canyon that was rocky and hard to cut. We continued our sign cutting and came to a finger in the canyon." The agents could smell them; they were close. "Groups walking for days and days without showering or basic hygiene emanate an unmistakable odor."

They came up with a plan. They would walk into the finger quietly, Bob in front, and spread out. The bodies were all bushed up, spread out on both sides of the finger, playing the "I don't see you/you don't see me" game. DG stayed back and Bob walked all the way up to the head of the group before a single body rose up and took off running.

Bob: "To my surprise, no one ran until I got to the front of the group. I figured he was probably the guide. He wasn't worth chasing; I didn't want DG to have to deal with the group [by himself] in case they got 'froggy.'

"We identified ourselves as Border Patrol Agents," and issued commands "to comply with our orders. To our surprise, they did."

Officer presence accounts for a lot in these situations; as has been said before, you win every fight you do not have when making an arrest. The two agents, with their command presence and spoken orders, established dominance quickly, and "once we walked the group out and did a head count, DG and I had managed to apprehend 65 undocumented aliens... if I'm not mistaken, that was one of the largest apprehensions by two agents at the Tucson

Station."

It paid off. "Remember when I said that when we transferred in, we weren't well received? Well, we managed to impress the Tucson agents that we were the 'real deal.' Not long after, junior agents were asking to work with us. Good times!"

Short Walk in a Hot Desert

It was summer, somewhere between 2008 and 2010. Tulley, a K9 Handler, with his partner "Tessa," was working a noon shift, driving southbound on Federal Route 19 on the TO Nation. It was about 2:00 PM, so the sun was still high and the temperatures were about 100-110 in the shade. The landscape is desert rocks and scrub, interrupted with lines of spiky thickets and washes that are dry most months out of the year. As he passed through the Artesa Mountains, there was an "S" curve, and then the terrain opened up as the road continued southbound towards Baboquivari High School and the village of Topawa.

In the long straightaway north of the high school, there was a long line of vehicles along the east side of the road, facing southward. There were cars, trucks, ATVs both marked TOPD, and all kinds of unmarked law enforcement vehicles. As he came upon them, Tulley slowed, looking for someone who seemed in charge. Nothing had been mentioned at muster about ongoing incidents near Topawa.

One of the vehicles, an unmarked law enforcement pickup truck, had a plainclothes cop standing near it; one of the "Shadow Wolves," a tribal unit of the US Customs once known for their tracking skills.

"What's going on?" asked Tulley, "Need any help?"

"A lost kid, we don't need any help," was the reply.

Tulley went south, made his cuts, and came back north the same way at the end of his shift. The vehicles were still there and searchers still out. Usually, the Tohono O'odham Nation let the stations know when such things happened, and we were often asked to assist with search and rescue on the TON. After all, that's pretty much all we did with the aliens anyway. No one wanted any help, so Tulley went back to the station, and then home for the night.

The next day, coming south the same way, he saw the same scene. A long line of vehicles on the east side of the road, people out searching, and still no request for help. On his own initiative, he continued on to the high school, which was south of the scene on the west side of FR19 in a fenced-off area. Tulley turned into the high school and saw a janitor, still at work after school hours; he asked the guy what the story was.

"Two kids got in a fight," said the janitor, "and one of them decided to walk home to Little Tucson instead of taking the bus." Little Tucson is a small community about 5 miles northeast of the school, as the crow flies. Kind of a long walk for a kid in the brutal Arizona summer heat, and it had now been over 24 hours since the incident. Tulley thanked the man and set out across 19, past the Topawa cemetery, and onto a dirt road that paralleled 19 to the east. If the kid had walked off on the most direct route, he would have crossed this road and left foot sign.

Tulley noticed right away that the road had not been heavily trafficked. As he drove north of all the vehicles parked on FR19, there it was, sign for one in the dirt as it broke out of the brush from the west. The tracks turned north for a bit, and then there was a TOPD black and white Ford Expedition, with three officers standing around it. While Tulley's Ford pickup was unmarked, it was still a law enforcement vehicle, with antennae and subdued red and blue lights installed fore and aft. He briefly flashed them to ID himself on approach.

There was a Field Training Officer with two trainees. They were posted there for who knows what but must have driven in directly from FR 19.

"I got sign here," Tulley advised them, "you want one of your trainees to come with me?" The senior TOPD Officer agreed and sent one of the female trainees with the Border Patrol Agent. Tulley pulled off the road and got Tessa out.

The Belgian Malinois was excited to be out, but she was a good dog and panted patiently while Tulley hooked up her leash. As soon as the fastener clinked, she was off, looking for her toy. The tracking canines don't look for people or drugs, they look for their toy, which (through hard training) they have learned to associate with certain odors. When they detect the odors that have been associated with the toy, they alert, and wait for their reward. BP dogs are trained to detect the odor of people and drugs, among other things. They are very, very good at it.

The sun was just right, and there was still some shine to the foot sign for one individual walking up the road. Tulley didn't need the dog at all, it was easy. He chatted with the young policewoman as they walked up the road, advising her to stay behind the dog. Then the sign started weaving.

"This isn't good," he told her. "He's not far."

The sign went into a bush, milled around, and came out. Then it continued, zigzagging up the road. As they continued, the sign went off the road into a thicket. A single tennis shoe lay there. Tulley tried to prepare the trainee for it.

"It's been over a day, in the summer. We're about a mile and a half from the school. This kid is going to be in bad shape; he's disrobing, which is common with heat casualties."

The agent, his dog, and the policewoman turned into the thicket, and then, right in front of them, the dead teenager lay under a bush. His shirt and the other shoe were nearby. The young lady called it in on her handheld radio. When help arrived, Tulley cleared out in disgust.

"They spent two days looking way north on the roads when they could've accepted my help and found him right away," said Tulley. "Was it an interagency thing? Why not ask for a hand? I had the dog right here."

Relations between the Border Patrol and the Tohono O'odham Police have improved dramatically in the last ten years. It was too bad for the young boy that no assistance was requested; he would have been found very quickly by agents cutting the parallel road on the day of his disappearance. Why the local authorities did not do this, they never said.

Runner from the Point

It was July, about two in the morning, and still hot. The bugs buzzed and swirled around the bright checkpoint lights as bats and small little birds swooped in, eating them. Periodically one would get zapped in the blue electric bug-zapper with a loud sizzling and sharp smell. The two local coyotes (the actual animals, not smugglers) warily circled the outer limit of the light thrown out into the desert. They fed on bugs, rabbits, and trash that got away from the cans at the point; sometimes PAs, bored at the checkpoint, would feed them. The less-wily coyotes got run over pretty regularly whilst trying to scoop up dead things on the road. Buzzards eat pretty well in the desert.

There were several light generators that were hooked into the electrical wiring and thus not running. The Connex box that served as the checkpoint trailer sat along the east side of the two lanes that make up the 40-plus north-south miles of Federal Route 15. Over everything, a giant aluminum canopy with lights wired into the underside of it, and cameras attached covering all angles, arched. At this hour, the agents had retreated into their air-conditioned vehicles, which faced southward so they could see oncoming traffic.

A pair of headlights about a mile south and coming northbound was the signal for the agents to get out and do their duty. At least two agents would clamber out of their patrol vehicles, one going to the primary position between the north and southbound lanes at a break in the orange barricade separating them, and the second agent going across to the secondary position opposite the primary agent on the side of the road.

The primary agent was responsible for making contact with the driver; identifying himself as a Border Patrol Agent and announcing that this was an immigration inspection, then questioning each occupant of the vehicle as to their citizenship and/or immigration status. The secondary agent would peer into the vehicle, looking for hidden persons or contraband in plain view, and inspecting the outside of the vehicle for any hint of smuggling-related modifications, or a cracked open trunk. If there was a K9 team, the agent and his or her dog would sniff the air around the outside of the vehicle for an odor the dog had been trained to detect, such as that of people or narcotics not in plain view. An alert from the dog would prompt a non-verbal signal from the K9 handler to the primary agent to refer the vehicle to secondary inspection. If it was clear, the K9 agents would usually just say "clear."

This night, there was no dog. As the approaching vehicle became visible to the agents, they got out their flashlights and got ready for the inspection. Another set of headlights appeared behind the first.

It was a Chevy Traverse sport-utility vehicle, gray in color, with several occupants visible. The primary agent introduced himself and began the spiel; the driver stated that he was a United States Citizen. As the agent proceeded to question the others, they avoided eye contact and mumbled unintelligibly in answer. This is usually a clear indicator of illegal alienage. Before they could be referred to the secondary inspection lane, the driver of the Traverse floored it and took off.

There was no time to throw the spikes. The next vehicle to approach was a marked Border Patrol F150 pickup truck driven by BPA Rotceh. He was an experienced and alert agent. He saw the whole thing, immediately recognized it for what it was, and did not hesitate to engage his overhead lights and siren, calling out via department radio that he had a runner from the checkpoint, the make, model, and color of the suspect vehicle.

The load vehicle went north on FR15 until it got to FR422, known to agents as the "Dam Road." They turned westbound and as the Traverse slowed and squirmed to avoid the numerous potholes, Rotceh announced, over his Public Address (PA) system, for the driver to stop. The suspect vehicle kept going westbound until it hit FR42 when it turned north and punched it again, reaching extremely high speeds for a loaded SUV.

The Watch Commander was following progress at the CAG Station. He terminated the pursuit and ordered Rotceh to stop following the vehicle and turn off his overhead lights and siren.

Simultaneously, the Duty Supervisor at the station was on the phone contacting units of the Pinal County Sheriff's Office and the Arizona Department of Public Safety with the type and location of the suspect vehicle. They took over the pursuit and followed the vehicle for some time onto Interstate 8, and then Interstate 10, where they also terminated due to the erratic and unsafe driving of the suspect.

Load drivers know that if they drive recklessly enough and fast enough, pursuing law enforcement will back off. If there is no air support to follow these vehicles, they either crash or get away. Often, they crash with serious consequences for their passengers and/or the driving public.

Vehicle Stop near the Checkpoint

As has been mentioned before, working even a small, two-lane checkpoint requires agents to pay attention. They must focus on vehicles coming from one direction to be inspected while always looking over their shoulder at what is coming from behind them. Even when inspecting the occupants of a vehicle, attention must be paid both to them, as well as the surroundings, which can change at any time.

It was summertime in Southern Arizona and typically, sweltering around 100-110 in the shade. The two-lane Border Patrol immigration checkpoint near an Indian village on a large reservation was staffed with four agents. The senior man was K9 handler Tulley. After doing his time as "primary" agent stopping northbound traffic and briefly speaking with the passengers of the vehicles, Tulley was relieved and went to his truck to cool off. With four agents working the point, there is usually one in primary, one or two in secondary, and one or two in the truck cooling off. The next guy up, Border Patrol Agent P, took Tulley's place on the road in the heat. It was so hot that his Vibram-soled boots made sticky noises on the asphalt. Vehicles were coming north pretty regularly, as is normal for the 12:00-8:00 PM shift, so the primary agent had to stand there. The rest of the agents were near Secondary in front of a huge fan.

A large aluminum canopy had recently been installed that shaded the entire checkpoint to include both lanes, and there was a large air-conditioned Connex box we used for storage and for lunch breaks. The canopy made a big difference, but the heat was still oppressive. The agents in their dark green uniforms, equipment on their belts, and some with body armor were eager to be out of it.

Tulley relaxed for a minute in his vehicle, an unmarked F150 crew cab pickup. The back of the cab was fitted with a large dog kennel for his partner, "Cammy," a spirited Belgian Malinois. She whined a greeting. He guzzled some water.

All of a sudden, a white pickup truck blew southbound

through the checkpoint at high speed. Agents were focused on looking southward at oncoming traffic and didn't hear the vehicle coming until it blasted over the rumble strips placed at intervals in the lanes. In primary position, standing on the double yellow line between the lanes, Agent P jumped out of the way.

"I'm going to pull that over," P said angrily and ran over to his marked patrol vehicle. As he took off, the other two agents, who had been standing over by a large fan, came out to assume primary duties.

"I'll go with him," Tulley said to them and pulled out.

About half a mile down the road to the south, there is an old mine entrance on the east side. That is where P caught up to the white pickup. As he was running the plate with dispatch, Tulley approached them. They were still going fast, and the driver of the white pickup was not stopping. If there was a failure to yield and the white pickup tried to lose them, P would break off and Tulley would be able to follow at a distance in his unmarked unit. If there was a bailout, he could use Cammy to track the driver out. It's always good to have a K9 team nearby on a vehicle stop.

The plate return came back as they approached the village on the reservation, one of the larger ones in the area. The suspect vehicle was registered out of a small town in the county to the north. Maybe the driver was up to no good, or maybe just hurrying down to the Port of Entry to go into Mexico. Blowing through the checkpoint like that at 60mph in a 15mph zone, endangering the life of an agent, gave them enough to stop him for a chat.

The village sprawled, dustily, to the east of FR 15, and had two entrances off the highway. All the roads were dirt; the main group of run-down houses, some abandoned, surrounded a central church. By the time the three vehicles passed the first entrance, P. lit up his red and blues and chirped the siren to initiate a stop.

The suspect vehicle turned left at the southern entrance to the village, coming to a halt just inside the cattle guard; there was just enough room on the dirt for the two agents' vehicles that followed. This part of the dirt road was raised up on a berm. The surrounding brush, which was normally unruly thick mesquite and other desert scrub, had recently been cleared. The three vehicles came to a halt within a few yards of FR15 in a column with the white pickup, P's marked BP vehicle, and Tulley in his unmarked K9 unit.

As Tulley was getting out of his ride, he could see that P had approached the driver's side of the suspect pickup. P made it as far as the driver's door, then quickly turned about and ran back, eyes wide.

"He's got a gun!"

Tulley could see the silhouette of the driver through the back window of the cab.

"What I saw was... he fired three shots. One straight up through his roof, one through his windshield, and one straight out through the passenger side window." Pistols out, the two agents moved quickly to the rear of Tulley's truck.

"10-10, shots fired, shots fired," Tulley called out over the radio. Luckily, the transmission got out. Comms are notoriously bad around that checkpoint in Arizona. The agents at the point heard and responded immediately.

"There was no room anywhere. No cover, no concealment anywhere," he said later. It should be emphasized that, in spite of what is shown on TV and in movies, a vehicle is not cover. Cover stops bullets. Something that hides you but does not stop bullets is concealment. The only things on a passenger vehicle that will stop a bullet are the engine block, and possibly the wheels. A common pistol bullet can go through a typical car or truck; in one side and out the other.

The driver of the suspect vehicle opened his door. Tulley watched as one foot and then the other stepped out. The suspect was a heavyset white guy, middle-aged, wearing a T-shirt and shorts. In his right hand was a medium-sized pistol, possibly a 9mm. With no cover to their left or right, and the suspect advancing after having fired shots, the agents would have been absolutely justified to shoot him on the spot.

Before using deadly force, Border Patrol Agents must be able to articulate that the adversary has the means, intent, and opportunity to cause death or serious bodily harm to the agent, or another person. Only then can the agent use deadly force, as a last resort, to stop the threat. In this case, the agents could clearly articulate these things based on the behavior of the suspect driver. He brandished a weapon, he fired the weapon, and he advanced on the agents.

The agents decided to retreat; they moved back west, keeping Tulley's K9 ride between them and the suspect. They quickly crossed both lanes of FR15.

"I don't have my vest," P said.

"Get behind me," Tulley told him, as they hit the dirt on the opposite side of the lanes from the vehicles. Tulley was in the habit of always wearing his body armor in an external carrier over his uniform. They got down low just about thirty feet from the tailgate of Tulley's K9 ride. As they took their position, the suspect stood casually right where they had just been. His gun was out at about a 45-degree angle. While not pointed exactly at them, it was definitely pointed in their general direction.

Responding to the calls of their partners on the radio, the remaining checkpoint agents had quickly moved out to assist, leaving the checkpoint unmanned. An emergency is an emergency, they probably just kicked over the stop sign and turned off the red light on their way out. Acting Supervisor Ron, and his partner, Randy, had jumped into a marked 4x4 pickup and approached the scene at high speed.

The suspect seemed unfazed when the other two agents arrived. Lights and sirens on, they skidded to a halt between him and the agents on the ground. In the southbound lane, blocking it, they clambered out.

Ron had an M4 carbine and leveled it across the hood of the Tahoe. Randy had his pistol out like the others.

"Don't do it!" The agents called across the road.

"I *will* kill you if you point that thing at me!" yelled Ron.

Tulley was thinking about his dog. Cammy was still in the back of the K9 unit. A gun battle would endanger her. The whole incident happened in way less time than it takes to read this; he hadn't had the time to let her out before seeking cover.

"Hey," Tulley told Ron, "I'd rather not get in a gunfight. My dog is still in the truck, but if he fires, we do what we have to!"

The suspect just stood there. "He didn't seem agitated," says Tulley. "Didn't seem like he wanted to shoot us." Without pointing his gun at the agents, the suspect raised it to his own head, then dropped it down pointing at the ground. Whatever he had been thinking before, the intent was no longer demonstrated.

"There's only gonna be one more round fired here," he called out.

At that point, Tulley thought, "I knew what would happen next."

The agents called over to him to relax, and he did, for a moment. They told him it wasn't worth it, that whatever the problem was, there was help out there. They told him they would call for help. All the things you would want to say, in that situation, they tried.

"I don't want to hurt anybody," said the guy. Then, smoothly but quickly, he raised the pistol under his chin and pulled the trigger.

"It wasn't like you see in the movies; no spray of gore and all that," says Tulley today. "He just dropped. I could tell right away that he was dead. There was a little blood spatter on my tailgate and a small pool under his head where he fell. Right under my tailpipe." The blood was quickly soaked up by the dirt.

Tulley helped clear the white pickup while the other guys called in the "subject down." There were no other passengers, but there was a baby seat in the back of the extended cab, luckily empty.

A passing motorist, a local tribal member, stopped by as the agents awaited medical and the local police.

"Is he an Indian?" he asked.

"No," the agents replied. Without a word, the man drove off.

Tulley: "We found out that the registered owner and the dead driver came back to two different addresses," Tulley continues. "We requested Sheriff's Office to respond to both addresses to make notifications."

Then the local agency, the Tribal Police, arrived and began taping off the scene. Tulley: "We had to leave everything the way it was. Vehicles running and the dead guy's head right under my tailpipe while the scene was processed." For hours. In the summer heat. It was not a pretty picture.

"The only other big thing was the senselessness of it all," Tulley related later. "That's the biggest thing I took away from it."

A couple of weeks later, Tulley was standing in line, waiting to pay for a snack at a Petro gas station after muster broke, before heading down south to the checkpoint for duty. An older couple, obviously from somewhere else, saw his uniform, stopped, and addressed him: "Thank you for your service," they said. "Is it like that TV show?"

They meant "Border Wars," a National Geographic reality show focused on Border Patrol, CBP, and Coast Guard patrolling America's borders.

"No," Tulley replied, "it's 90% boredom and 10% adrenaline. I did have a guy commit suicide right in front of me though." That would *not* be something you would see on Border Wars.

Then Tulley was next. The cashier looked up. "That was her uncle," she said pointing over to another employee, a young woman stocking the shelves nearby. Tulley knew her; he paid for his items and walked over.

He wanted to say something to reassure her. "I was there when your uncle died... I just wanted to say that I am sorry for your loss." He explained that they had tried to talk him down, to prevent what happened, but to no avail. The young woman told him that the baby seat in the back of the truck was for her daughter. She took it well and asked if he would be willing to talk with her aunt, the man's widow.

"Sure, I have to talk to my boss first, but I will let you know."

They set up a date and time and met at the same Petro Station a short time later. There were some tears as he explained what had happened. The lady was nice and said that her husband had been drinking and that they'd fought before he took off in the truck. She gave Tulley a hug and thanked him.

This kind of closure is pretty rare, and probably helped Tulley as well as the widow. Another perspective, from P's point of view, follows:

"That's mostly how I remember it went down, with some small tweaks. I'll tell you what happened from my perspective... what was going through my head from beginning to end, and finally the aftermath.

"It was my Friday, nearing the end of the shift. My mind was on where I was going to grab some drinks that night. When the white truck flew by me, it pissed me off. My roommate from the academy and good friend Mike G. was killed by a drunk driver [on the reservation] about 5 years earlier, and that was too close for comfort. When I ran the plate and it came back [to the small Arizona town], it made me wonder why it wasn't [tribal]. I was still pretty mad at this point. I remember thinking that I should quickly throw on my vest, but before I could, he pulled over.

"I got out and started to approach the driver's window, but the hairs on the back of my neck stood up; it just didn't seem right (the whole situation). It seemed like he wanted us to pull him over for that stunt, but why would he want that? I was mad, but something told me not to rush up to the driver's side window. I stopped about halfway down the truck bed and I could see his window was cracked. I noticed a child seat in the back as well, and I didn't know if a kid was in there or not. I yelled out, 'do you know why I pulled you over?'"

Agents are trained to always obey their instincts in these

types of situations. If it doesn't feel right, it probably isn't. You don't have to wait to identify what's wrong, before taking corrective action of some kind.

"He replied with no hesitation, 'I have a gun and it's loaded!'

"Almost simultaneously, he squeezed off a round through the roof. This is when I jumped back for better cover, and then Tulley stepped out of his vehicle. Tulley was a good 10-20 seconds behind me. [The suspect] then fired a shot through the window and passenger side as I backed off.

"I called on the handheld radio (probably hysterically) '10-10 shots fired.'

"Later on, Ron said I yelled 'Bang-bang-shots fired,' which I may have.

"Mostly what was going through my head was my body armor sitting in the passenger seat. I can't remember exactly what I yelled at Tulley, but it was something like 'he's shooting' or 'he's got a gun,' and then I said, 'My damn vest wasn't on.'

"Tulley did say 'Get behind me,' in full New England accent, which was ballsy and makes me laugh in hindsight. I was definitely glad he was there. The guy with the gun had the high ground, we were in a bad spot. We both had our guns pulled and aimed toward him. We just couldn't find good cover, but he never fired directly at us, and he waited awhile until getting out of the truck. When we backed off on the other side of the road, Randy and Ron [agents coming from the checkpoint] pulled up and we got behind their Kilo truck."

A "Kilo truck" is Border Patrol-speak for a fully marked, four-wheel drive, 1/2 or 3/4-ton pickup truck used as a patrol vehicle.

"I can't remember exactly when he stepped out of the white truck, but he did point his gun either under his chin or at the ground when he exited. When all 4 of us were behind the Kilo truck all aimed in, that's the first time I felt comfortable. At this point, he was above us on the berm about 30 feet away. We told him it wasn't worth it, etc. I remember I said, 'Tomorrow is another day.' Looking back, it seems poetic now, because the sun was just starting to set as he held the gun under his chin. I remember him saying he didn't want to hurt anyone... And I'm pretty sure his last words were, 'There's only going to be one more bullet (or round).'

"He braced himself and shot. When he shot himself, he crumpled immediately and seemed to almost melt. There wasn't that much blood, as Tulley said.

"Ron ran up and kicked the gun away. I yelled 'The truck wasn't clear,' and kept my gun aimed at the 99%-sure dead guy on the ground while they cleared the truck; thankfully, with no child inside. There were just a few crumpled-up beer cans on the passenger side floor.

"This incident is something I will remember forever. I've never been in combat, and this was the first person I've seen die in front of me. I do often think of what might have happened if a few things went differently, and [whether or not] I acted correctly. What if I had run up to the window demanding an explanation, considering how mad I was?

"He said he didn't want to hurt anyone, later, but he obviously wasn't in his right mind. I'm glad I never gave him an easy target. If my vest was on, would I have been more emboldened to run up to the window? What if one of us was in the southbound lane, not paying attention when he barreled through at 60+ mph? Could I have said or done something to keep him from killing himself? Should I feel guilty about having felt some relief when he did finally kill himself because he didn't make me do it? How's that kid doing these days that sat in that child seat? He obviously wanted suicide by agent but ended up doing it himself, looking at the setting sun over the Sonoran Desert with an audience of 4 agents. He must've known these were his last moments when he barreled through the 15 checkpoint.

"The whole-body armor debacle certainly doesn't make me look like John Wick, but maybe other agents and LEOs can learn from it."

There is plenty to learn from this incident. On duty, try to focus on what's happening around you; this is admittedly difficult after standing in the heat all day when it's 100-plus in the shade. At the checkpoint, someone should always be looking the other way. Always wear your body armor. Drink plenty and take more breaks when you can. There's more there, but not necessarily suitable for this book. Once again, the stereotype of the ass-kicking jackbooted gunmen of the US Border Patrol is shown to be false. Thoughtful, even under stress, about using force, is something they rarely get credit for.

Drunk Driver at the Checkpoint

On a nice night in May 2020, agents at the Immigration Checkpoint were alerted to the impending arrival of a vehicle that had been spotted driving erratically that was headed their way. The suspect vehicle was northbound on Federal Route 15, south of the village of North Komelik. The checkpoint is just north of the village. This is on the Tohono O'odham Indian Reservation; while Border Patrol does not enforce drunk driving laws, we are a major law enforcement presence on the Reservation and also (at night) the majority of the driving public on the roads. BP frequently encounters drunk drivers and alerts local law enforcement, in this case, the TOPD.

At the point, there were four agents present - an Acting Supervisory Border Patrol Agent, two BPAs, and a K9 team. A plainclothes agent in an unmarked vehicle had followed this suspicious vehicle for a time and witnessed it bounce between the fog line and the double yellow line on the two-lane highway, which usually indicates a distracted or impaired driver. Since BP Agents are not technically empowered to perform traffic stops on suspicion of DUI, it is usually preferred in such situations to follow the suspect into the checkpoint where everyone must stop and detain for a "reasonable" amount of time to allow local law enforcement to respond.

Mark was the agent on primary. He readied the Controlled Tire Deflation Device, or CTDD, usually referred to by agents as spikes or a spike strip. It was a three-foot-long long plastic sheath with three sides that, whichever way it landed, had a row of hollowed-out sharp spikes pointed upwards and was designed to puncture and rapidly deflate the tires of a vehicle when deployed.

There are many rules regarding CTDD deployment, and agents are trained, minimally, once a year on their use. In this case, if the incoming vehicle did not stop at the stop sign in the primary inspection area, it would be "spiked." Every vehicle must stop in primary at a Border Patrol Immigration Checkpoint.

Karl, a northbound agent, who had not been paying

attention to the radio traffic, stopped in the primary inspection lane and leaned out of his truck. He started to tell the agents about how the possible drunk driver that was coming up whom he had seen earlier. The checkpoint agents could see the vehicle approaching, and Mark shouted, "Go! Go! Go! He's going to hit you!"

Karl pulled off of the road immediately before the suspect vehicle, a white Chevy Cavalier, sped through without even slowing down. It was a close call. Mark stepped aside like a bullfighter and nonchalantly threw the spikes down, over his shoulder, as the Cavalier passed. The other agents scrambled to get out of the way. The front driver's side tire was spiked successfully as the Cavalier kept on going. Had the first agent not gotten out of the way, there absolutely would have been a collision resulting in injuries or death.

Mark recovered the spikes and threw them out of the way as agents jumped in their vehicles to pursue. The unmarked vehicle with the plainclothes agents sped through first, followed by the other guys in marked vehicles. They caught up to the Cavalier about a mile down the road and agents took the driver, Norbert, into custody on suspicion of High-Speed Flight from an Immigration Checkpoint.

Norbert was a tribal member, and obviously under the influence of something. Border Patrol Agents do not like to take custody of persons under the influence of alcohol or drugs, so the local tribal authorities, the Tohono O'odham Police Department, responded. An officer arrived quickly and administered a field sobriety test. Norbert failed this test, but the TOPD Officer advised the agents that because he did not personally witness Norbert behind the wheel of the Cavalier, he could not arrest him for DUI.

Since the TOPD would not take him in, the agents decided to pursue charges under 8 USC 758: High-Speed Flight From an Immigration Checkpoint, a felony. He was transported to the Casa Grande Border Patrol Station for processing under the felony High-Speed Flight charge. This charge is usually a slam-dunk when smuggling is involved since there are arrays of cameras around and in the various Border Patrol checkpoints; identification of drivers is a non-issue.

Agents prepared a prosecution case for Norbert, for High-Speed Flight From an Immigration Checkpoint. As far as any of the concerned agents know, these charges were not prosecuted.

From the Cover: A wash north of Sells, AZ with sign for 60-plus aliens walking north towards Interstate-8.

Winter in the Patagonia Mountains, south of Patagonia, AZ

BPA Eberle near Harshaw, AZ

Village near State Route 86, Southern Arizona

Hills northwest of Quijotoa, AZ

Illegal Aliens, spotted on a train from the air, taken into custody by Border Patrol

Border Patrol ATV Agent speaks with a Union Pacific conductor regarding illegal aliens on the train, 2006

Aliens attempt to conceal themselves from Border Patrol helicopter while riding on a train

Abandoned building, known as 'The Love Shack' for reasons long-forgotten, on State Route 86 near San Simon, AZ. Such landmarks are used by smugglers for picking up loads of narcotics and/or illegal aliens

Bootie sign. Can you see it?

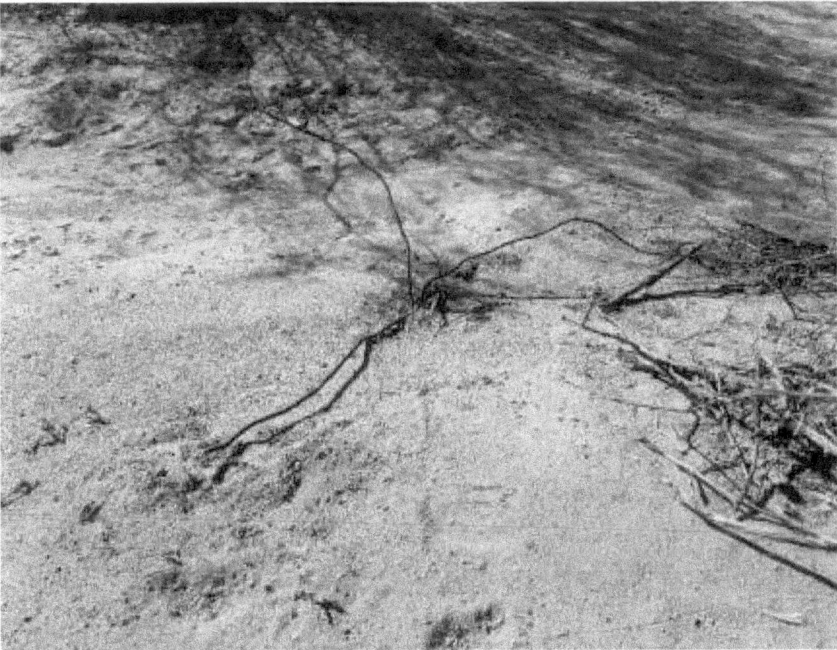

Bootie sign for 2-3 bodies crossing a wash

Good sign for 3-4 bodies

More good sign crossing a road. Cutting with a flashlight is still the only way to do it at night. Ideally, a partner will be nearby to watch your back.

Walking out a group with ATVs.

ATV Agents writing up a group, filling out 826 Forms with basic biographical and apprehension information, whilst awaiting transport.

Swing shift ATVs: from the left, Dan, Gabe, Wingo, author, Bob 'The Real Deal,' Roberto, Serge, and Norm. Photo by Norm.

Discarded shoe booties along State Route 86

"The Piss Road" near Quijotoa, watered nightly by travelers between Tucson and Why, AZ. There are very few facilities along State Route 86 on that stretch

Discarded alien clothing along State Route 86. It's everywhere in Southern Arizona. The camo works pretty well, especially at night.

Walking out a group. Transport will meet them at the next road.

This group has no backpacks. It could be a group of 'packers' who discarded their dope load in the desert before apprehension, or the dope packs have been loaded on the ATVs.

Bob supervises securing marijuana-laden ATVs for transport back to the station. The towing vehicle was already full of dope.

In this view one of the burlap backpacks is still intact.

Another group being walked out by ATVs.

Eberle earning his pay southwest of Three Points, AZ in 2010. Tucson Station ATVs got their share of dope and aliens in this area at the time, in this case working with Horse Patrol units as well.

Desert Donkeys. They are damn near invisible at night, and often hit by vehicles.

Large group from a traffic stop on Interstate 8. Note that the trailer they were stuffed into is already half full of some kind of cargo. There were about 60 aliens in this load. This is inhuman, and hopefully, smuggler was prosecuted vigorously.

BPA Rotceh interviews a group of smugglers, without packs, arrested after a foot chase. Their dope was found later with a Border Patrol K9 team.

Typical Sonoran Desert terrain

Traffic check

Looking South at FR15 Checkpoint

Looking North at FR15 Checkpoint

Front cover: BPA Cory was tracking a group of 15 when he came into a wash with sign from several groups, totaling more than 60.

Agents and aliens get a fire going while awaiting transport. The relaxed posture indicate they have been searched, and there are enough agents to go after any runners. Also, everyone is most likely hungry, cold, and tired.

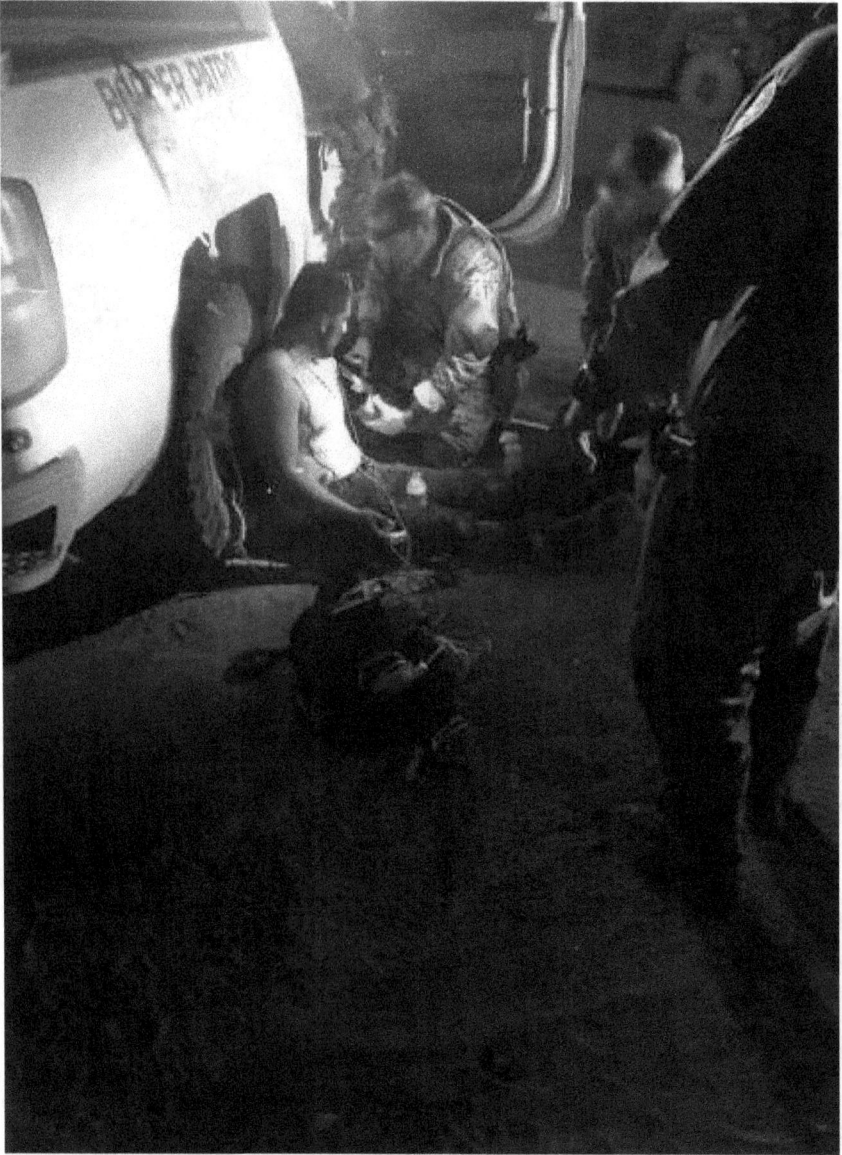

Lucky alien being treated by Border Patrol for heat injury shortly after apprehension

Typical desert loader, packed with marijuana in cellophane-wrapped bundles

A memorial stone for Manny at the site of his death near Vamori, AZ

My friend PJ after a successful walk

PA takes a break after scaling a mountain

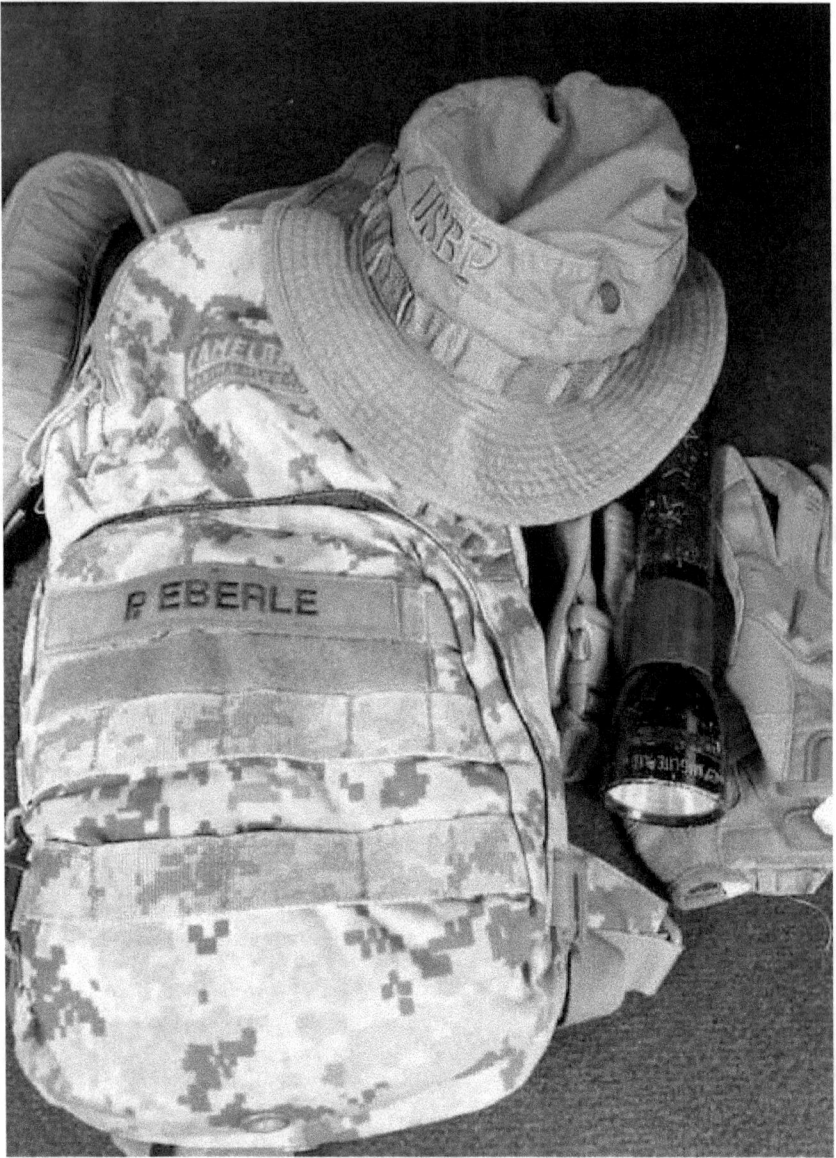

Some of the items used the most by working agents: Camelback hydration pack with 100-oz. bladder for water (small first aid kit, liquid IV packets, batteries, and flex-ties in the pouch; bush hat; 3-cell Mag-Light; gloves.

IV. Supervisor

New Sup

It is often said in the Border Patrol that the first-line supervisors have the toughest job. They are beholden to two masters: management types with their organizational goals and operational plans; and the troops, the line agents who get out in the weeds and make things happen. It can be a difficult job in the best of times, though being on a good patrol group makes it easier. For my part, it was nice to have a small measure of control over immediate working conditions, and the opportunity to positively influence the working lives of those agents around me.

Luckily, there are many excellent agents who take care of business and police themselves. In exchange, it is good to treat people like adults and try to minimize the worst of the hassles coming from management, or at least deliver it in the gentlest possible ways. As one instructor said in a supervisory communications class:

"They do not work for you; YOU work for THEM!"

His name is Jim Glennon, a retired police lieutenant from Illinois. His book, *Arresting Communication* is a must-read for law enforcement officers and new supervisors.

What follows are a few stories relating to first-line supervisors, as well as some of the reports received from agents in the field.

Shortly after arriving at the Tucson Station, as a newly-minted Supervisory Border Patrol Agent, I was out in the field with another Tucson Sup who had been at the station for a while. It was towards the end of shift, so we staged up at a crossroads where off-going agents in our area would have to pass on their way back in from the field. This at the time was how I learned to get the details of what happened on shift from the guys, as radio comms are spotty at best, and you can't always know what all of your guys are working at any given time.

One truck came up and we waved him down to get his "intel." The front bumper was held together with baling wire and burlap string from a dope bundle, and there was all manner of brush hanging off from the undercarriage.

"What the hell? Run over any aliens on your way north dude?!" I asked, grinning, in what I thought was a joking manner. I had forgotten that I was 1. A new supervisor; and 2. At a new station where no one knew or trusted me.

The agent in question got extremely defensive and loudly protested that he had done nothing wrong, the bumper had fallen off while working a group, etc., and that he wanted a union rep. Thankfully, the other sup with me had a good rapport with his agents and got the guy calmed down. This was the first time, but sadly not the last, that I learned my lesson to remember who I was talking to before I began running my mouth.

New Sup in Douglas

Mark had just recently made Supervisory Border Patrol Agent (SBPA) at the Douglas, Arizona Station. He was unfamiliar with the area, but quickly identified the agents who were interested in working traffic. Then, as a good supervisor, he would link up with them in the field to learn the area, and the Douglas way of doing things.

For those considering a career in the Border Patrol, or agents considering promotion to Supervisor, I cannot overstate this point: The best way to gain a good reputation as an agent is to find out who the productive agents are and follow them. Unless it's some sort of "Training Day" rogue cop situation, then you should do what the good agents are doing. Volunteer for transport. Do not run away from processing. Get in the dirt with the real agents, and you will be successful. This is also the best way for a new supervisor to gain rapport with field agents and learn the area when at an unfamiliar station.

Being a good agent, my friend Mark already knew this. He made arrangements with some of the guys to meet up out in the field, near an area that had a stretch of railroad tracks on the US side that came real close to the border. A rip crew operated there, preying on the hapless groups of IAs and ripping off dope loads. They were known to be armed. The agents' plan was to leave the vehicles about a mile away, and hump it in on foot, lights out. They would lay in at the tracks and try to get some bandits.

As it happened, Mark was held up at the station with "sup stuff," various and sundry menial administrative tasks that any BP supervisor or military noncommissioned officer might have. He got out to the field late and found where the agents' vehicles were stashed. He then walked in solo towards the line where they were supposed to meet up before laying in for the bad guys.

It was dark, being a moonless night, but still possible to navigate. Stars still count for illumination, and your night vision gets better the longer you're out in the dark. He moved slowly and carefully. Mark wasn't all geared up. As he says today: "I was a

DGL (Douglas Station) sup and I never carried gear at night except for a boom stick (the Wilson Combat Scatter Gun Technologies BP shotgun)." Preferring to travel light at night is understandable; nothing extra hanging off him to get caught on brush. At night in the desert, sound travels pretty far.

After a while, Mark made it to the track formation, the elevated earthworks upon which the rocks (called "ballast") and railroad tracks are laid. He waited in the dark, looking each way along the tracks, trying to find some clue of where the agents were, and listening up for company. As a Border Patrol Agent, whenever you reach a blind spot like this or get close to the top of a hill that may or may not have someone already there waiting for you, it is a good idea to pause and catch your breath and listen. He didn't want to get on the radio, again for noise discipline, it was too close to the border.

After waiting and listening for a bit, he decided to get up on the ballast and peek over the tracks to see if there were any agents or aliens nearby on the other side before proceeding. It didn't sound like there was anything or anyone there. Shotgun in hand, he climbed up and had a good scan.

"... I did stop at the bottom to listen before creeping over the top," Mark told me later, "same as the bandit I am sure. Rocks are surprisingly loud at night when hunting bandits. Then I slipped up to the top of the rail bed (that's what I would call it) and was startled just a bit when I saw an 'agent' with a rifle go over the top at the exact same moment. We nodded and I continued south and he went north."

Mark kept going, hitting the International Border Fence, then turned west to where the other agents were.

They met up on the line, devising their op plan. "I bumped into your guy laying in over there on the tracks."

One of the agents looked at him, "We don't have anyone over there."

Says Mark today:

"I wonder how the bandit tells the story, and if it would have been a one-on-one shotgun v. rifle fight if the moon had been up. But that's how the game is played."

One might wonder how agents in the field keep track of who is who, and where. The answer is good communication and knowledge of the terrain. The landmarks, your partners, and the aliens all come into play. Sometimes you can tell just by looking, smelling, or hearing who it is coming up on you in the dark. The mountain lions often come to mind. They are stalking, poised, and moving slowly and deliberately. The aliens are hesitant, hunched over, and bunched up. On a black and white screen in a scope truck, every person is a black (hot) humanoid blob with a white (cold) backpack on. The agents and aliens are pretty easy to tell apart by their demeanor and behavior.

Mark bumping into the bandit in the dark is both alarming and understandable; to an extent, they were both hunting.

Having a plan amongst yourselves, before going in to apprehend a group, is very helpful. Especially at night, it is useful to work with the same guys as much as possible; the more you work together, the more you just "know" who they are. Even in the green haze of the NVGs, you can tell who it is by the way they walk if you work together enough. Of course, this is not always the case, especially if you're the new guy.

At least one Border Patrol Agent has been killed, that we know of, in a friendly fire incident. A sensor activated. One agent came from one direction to check it out, while two others came from another direction. Shots were exchanged, and one was killed, another wounded, and the third was unharmed. Out of respect for the agents involved, that is all I will say about it. There are some articles out there. Bottom line: This is serious, and you have to keep your head.

The Border Patrol has attempted to improve agent ID in the field by issuing everyone a smartphone with "blue force tracking." While not useless, it only works where you have signal. Agents have to have it on their person, and turned on, at all times when on duty. Also, the Department loaded the phone up with multitudes of apps, some more useful than others, and the battery drains pretty quickly. It will surely improve over time and is usually a good tool when used as directed.

Use of Force

On one warm summer evening, I was fortunate enough to be nearby as agents from my shift apprehended a group of several aliens near a place called "Solar Panel" in the Casa Grande Station's AOR. One agent, who I will call Rick, ended up in fisticuffs with a combative Guatemalan who did not wish to be arrested. My supervisor's notes, used in part to document the use of intermediate force for a memo later on, will be quoted along with what I can recall of the event.

"On June 27, 2014, at approximately 12:15 AM, I was informed via radio that a Border Patrol Agent (BPA) may have been assaulted. Several agents had spread out along a series of washes, attempting to apprehend a group of about 13-14 illegal aliens. Due to the ongoing operation, and general communications problems, the agent did not speak to me until about an hour later."

There were a few agents involved over an area of about a half a mile of typical Sonoran Desert terrain... rocky hills, cholla, Saguaro, and barrel cactus; scrub-covered flats, and many crisscrossing washes filled with critters and thorny brush. Falcon-1, a contracted fixed-wing aircraft with sophisticated night-vision equipment, had responded to the area where some agents were checking a wash for sign. Falcon-1 was well-known to agents throughout Tucson Sector; the sensor operator had a very calm, southern-accented voice and was very keen to help agents get the dope or the bodies.

According to my notes, the alien, later identified as Sanchez (not his real name) had already been apprehended and was being escorted through some brush by BPA Rick when he attempted to escape. Rick chased after him and caught up, directing Sanchez to the ground. In spite of Rick's commands to stop moving, Sanchez continued to struggle with him on the ground, including striking Rick with elbows and feet. There were other aliens at large in the area, and no agents near enough to help, so Rick delivered strikes to the torso area of Sanchez to gain compliance and prevent escape. There were no further witnesses to this incident, save for the crew of air asset Falcon-1.

Typically, when working a group, the appearance of an aircraft causes the group to either dig into the brush and hide, or to run in several different directions so that some of them get away. The aircraft can only track a few and following agents generally will only go after the ones "on screen" first, picking up some sign later on for the rest. This is what happened.

The aircraft was overhead, and the group busted before agents got into position to box them in. Rick was put in on a single runner who he pursued and apprehended. The alien was initially compliant before attempting to take off. When Rick caught up to him the second time, the fight was on.

Though agents were around, they were all seeking other aliens, and if Rick called them on the radio, they did not hear. Only the aircraft, who spotted the fight, was able to "get out" on the radio and alert us. By the time anyone got to Rick, he had Sanchez handcuffed.

"I spoke with Sanchez. He had scratches on his face from struggling in thick brush but was otherwise in good health. He gave me a false name, date of birth, and birth certificate, and claimed Mexican citizenship. He did not indicate a wish to make a complaint at the time. After he was loaded up and transported (separately from the rest of the group) to the Station for identification and processing, I called the Duty Supervisor from the field and reported the incident."

This was a happy ending, and if there was a complaint generated, we never heard another word about it. Rick continued to be a happy warrior, and an aggressive field agent, who eventually got a K9 partner and is still working.

As far as anyone who was there knows, prosecution was not pursued for the assault.

Assault/Use of Force

The threat of agents being disciplined or prosecuted for doing their job is ever-present, but rare if the agent in question is aware of his or her authority to act, and what is an appropriate action in a given situation. Sometimes, however, irresponsible Use of Force instructors, Sector Attorneys (like the one who suggested that only a bear hug while falling to the ground is an appropriate non-reportable use of nonlethal force), and journeyman agents' war stories can influence the junior agents to question their own judgment and common sense.

BPA Rollo was laid in with another agent on a trail in the remote Baboquivari Mountains south of Kitt Peak. These mountains are absolutely crawling with illegal aliens, backpackers, rip crews, and at times USC militia LARPers (Live-Action Role-Players) playing Border Patrol. It was late at night, and the pair had good reason to believe that packers were going to be coming down the trail. Both were excellent junior agents; well aware of the local traffic patterns and sensor activity, and it was a busy time of year.

The agents waited; each was wearing his green RDU uniform with clearly displayed patches and badging. They were carrying all of their assigned duty gear to include pistol, flashlights, pepper spray and/or collapsible steel baton, radio, handcuffs, gloves, and Camelback hydration packs. In spite of all this gear, the dark, green-colored uniforms are almost invisible in the dark. A well-disciplined agent remaining motionless can often have a group of aliens walk right up to him.

About half a dozen packers eventually came down the trail, swishing and grunting their way through the grass lining the trail, bent forward under the weight of their 50-lb. homemade burlap packs of compressed marijuana wrapped in plastic. One of them probably carried the food pack and the leader, if there was one, probably had the radio or even a pistol. Dressed head to toe in camouflage, they blended in perfectly with the mountains at night.

When the group got very close, the agents unholstered their pistols. At the academy, the instructors were clear: dope means guns. The two PAs hit their flashlights and went loud, shouting in Spanish, "Stop, we're Federal Agents, get on the ground!"

Some dropped their packs and ran back the way they had come, a couple more complied, dropping to the ground, and one or two hesitated to do anything, stunned. One agent went after the indecisive ones, "helping" them to the ground and patting them down real quick.

The lead alien in the group dropped his pack and, head down, charged right at Rollo. Before he knew it, Rollo had been wrapped up by the alien and was falling backward with the packer on top of him. Gun in one hand and light in the other, he began hammering the alien on the top of the head with his plastic-framed HK P2000, opening up a nice gash and breaking off a piece of the handgrip of the gun.

Eventually, Rollo and his partner got control of a few of the aliens who were secured and then walked out of the mountains back to the vehicles, and to camp. The assault was reported, dope seized, and a case was prepared for the assault and for the narcotics trafficking charges. Rollo was not hurt, and the alien got a few stitches; I never learned whether or not he was prosecuted for going after the agent.

The next time I saw Rollo I asked him, "Why didn't you shoot?"

BPA Rollo replied matter-of-factly, "I didn't want to get in trouble."

Another Use of Force

It was a cool December evening near Cowlic, Arizona, when one of the MSC trucks spotted a group running through the desert between the upside-down car and Middle Gate. The upside-down car had been gone for years but was still a known landmark west of Cowlic. Middle Gate was a little north of the village which was on the Tohono O'odham Indian Reservation. The whole reservation is a known thoroughfare for both narcotics and alien smuggling, and there are plenty of Tribal members who are actively involved in the criminal enterprise, though most are not.

I was on duty, but not near enough to respond, so my heart was warmed to hear the ATV guys answer up. From the normal "drop spots," places where they unloaded the ATVs from the trailer, they could get there very quickly on their Yamaha Grizzly quads. Still, nothing else was happening so I began to move over their way.

About half an hour later, the call came out for a Supervisor over by Middle Gate to take a Use of Force report. These days, with the enhanced scrutiny of law enforcement, any incident generating the possibility of a complaint must be thoroughly reported through the chain of command so that no manager is surprised by it if there is blowback.

When I arrived near a three-foot wash surrounded by thick brush, I saw the group of about twelve illegal aliens all sitting in a line while the agents field-processed them. Everyone was calm. One of the ATV Agents, J., stood off to the side.

He reported to me that when they got into the area where the MSC truck had lost visual, they quickly found the group hiding in the wash. The subjects were commanded not to move as the agents approached.

These types of washes crisscross the desert and are strewn with rocks, roots, animal warrens, cactus, and garbage left by generations of illegal alien groups traversing the terrain. Erosion makes their structures unstable; both agents and aliens are frequently injured just by walking through or near them. When aliens resist arrest in a wash, this is a dangerous situation and, if allowed to escalate, can have potentially serious consequences for all involved. Agents are almost always outnumbered by the aliens and while the aliens are usually just trying to get away, any fight can be unpredictable. It is critical for agents to gain control as soon as possible when dealing with a superior number of aliens whose identities, criminal histories, and motivations are as yet unknown. These issues are even more pronounced in hours of darkness.

As it happened, the aliens ignored commands and began running in every direction up and down the wash, as well as trying to scramble out of it. Agents jumped in to try to stop them from fleeing and to effect arrests. In the scrum, J. grabbed one of them and they both went down hard into the wash, with the alien on top of the agent, scuffling and striking out. J. yelled commands to stop, delivering a few strikes of his own, and eventually gaining compliance with an arm bar. When it was over, the three ATV agents ended up with twelve aliens "10-15."

I took reports from all of the PAs, and then briefly interviewed the alien, Wilfredo. He admitted to being in the United States illegally, and to trying to get away from the Border Patrol. He did not wish to file a complaint. Still, I took all of his information, photos of J. and Wilfredo (separately, to document injuries, and the agent's clearly badged uniform) and called everything into the station. Often, an alien will change his or her mind by the time they are being processed for deportation and decide to make a complaint. In this case, it was a pretty straightforward use of nonlethal force. At worst, in six or so months the Office of Professional Responsibility (OPR-basically Internal Affairs for CBP) would issue J. with a Notice to Appear at their office in Tucson, where they would interview him, any witnesses, and go over the facts of the case before proceeding with charges, administrative discipline, or choosing not to pursue the matter any further. It is almost always the case that agents act appropriately in these situations; poorly written reports often open the door to OPR investigations. In this case, nothing came of it.

Assault on an Agent

It was a cool December evening when supervisors heard a call on the radio about some agents who had a group in custody, and that one of the apprehended aliens was assaultive. This was pretty serious, as has been covered. The terrain in this area is extremely rugged and rocky; the peaks rise up to 4000 feet. Walking through at night is treacherous in the extreme, between the different types of cacti, loose rocks, mine shafts, vent holes, thickets, washes, and brush lines throughout the area. The fact that each agent is carrying about thirty pounds of gear doesn't help; the aliens, while traveling more lightly, have been walking for days by this point and sleeping in the desert. The agents have a bone-jarring ride on disintegrating roads to get to where the group is supposed to be, and by the time they get there, they have to pick up the sign and follow it on foot. After the agents make contact with the group, there is the issue of identification (agents identify themselves in Spanish and English, however, some aliens do not always hear or comprehend what is being said due to exhaustion and/or trauma i.e., recent victimization by bandits). Agent exhaustion and faulty radio communications are also challenges to overcome.

In this case, the group of aliens had been spotted by a Mobile Surveillance Capability (MSC) truck, using both radar and the night scope. The mountainous terrain where they were is extremely remote and getting to the area necessitated an hour-long drive over very poor dirt tracks and old mining roads before the agents could get to the area of the sighting. Then it was a hike along the side of a mountain through the thorny foliage to get to the spot.

Luckily, the aliens were still visible to the MSC, and its operator talked the agents into the group of nine suspected illegal aliens. As the agents approached, the aliens bushed up. The MSC operator got them closer, then several of the aliens broke and ran in different directions. By now, backing agents were close by and heading that way to assist with transport. BPA M. called out, via handheld radio, that an alien had fought with him and was now refusing to walk.

A suspect refusing commands is a leading indicator of resistant or assaultive behavior. In this case, the assault had already allegedly happened, and there were several more aliens still running around out there. The two agents on foot, M. and his partner, BPA R., had a total of five in custody with four more still running. Other agents were getting closer, traversing the mining roads to get there, but were still pretty far out.

An Office of Air and Marine (OAM) helicopter had been on station, orbiting high above the agents. He kept them in sight and lit up the vicinity with his night sun while giving the responding agents a visual of where the group was. Eventually, running low on fuel, he had to leave, but there were no further incidents. Backing agents, including a supervisor, arrived on the scene, and M. reported that the alien, Zeno, had become assaultive while resisting arrest, including kicking the agent and grabbing and twisting M's finger before running away. When M. would close in on him, he would feign giving up, then try to fight with the agent again and run off. While this was happening, his partner R. was away rounding up the others and securing them.

Zeno was sullen and covered in dirt, handcuffed behind his back. He did not want to walk further. He was assisted to one of the patrol vehicles and placed inside, separated from the others in the group, for transport north. Later, at the station, agents prepared a case for Assault on a Federal Agent.

Here is M's perspective, edited for clarity:

"At approximately 4:45 PM, I was working with my partner, BPA R., when the... Mobile Surveillance Capable scope truck spotted a group of nine people on the west side of the Mountain. This area is an extremely remote portion of the Sonoran Desert... with no serviced dirt roads. BPA R. and I were on mile marker 101... on the highway, with our service All-Terrain Vehicles (ATVs), when we responded to work the group via service radio.

"It took us approximately 30-40 minutes to drive into the area of the group. Upon our arrival, the MSC was directing an Office of Air and Marine (OAM) helicopter to the last area he had [visual] of the group. I immediately drove to the helicopter's positioning, [and] spotted two people in camouflage hiding underneath a palo verde tree. Once I was five or six feet away, the two subjects looked up at me and I identified myself as law enforcement... and instructed them not to move. The subjects decided to ignore my commands and run. BPA R. was quick to pursue them with me. I drove my ATV behind one of the subjects before dismounting to chase on foot. After a brief chase, the subject was apprehended. BPA R. was able to apprehend the other subject. The two subjects were handcuffed together and I started to walk them back towards BPA R., who was attempting to locate more people from the group. I noticed that while walking, one of them looked back at me and attempted to toss a cell phone into some brush. I retrieved the cell phone, and the same subject then indicated that he wanted it back. One of the subjects then complained that his handcuffs were too tight. I checked the handcuffs by placing two fingers between the handcuff and his wrist [this is what is taught at the Border Patrol Academy]. I was able to fit my fingertips at the top and bottom of the cuffs but still loosened them by one or two teeth. They continued to complain, but I told them that I was not loosening the handcuffs anymore (I was concerned that they were trying to find an opportunity to break out of the cuffs). The two subjects then refused to continue to walk and sat down. I waited with them for a few minutes until they decided to walk again... to meet back with BPA R. (the total distance traveled was about 150 yards)."

M. met back up with R., who had apprehended another alien in the meantime. They secured the four together and sat them down. R. remained with the group while M. went out, picking up another, making four apps. Then he went out again to search for more.

"Once the fourth subject was secure, I set out on foot north to search for more subjects. When I was about 100 yards from BPA R., and out of his view, I noticed three camouflage backpacks in a small wash. I was about to inspect the backpacks when I noticed a person wearing camouflage, hiding underneath a palo verde in the wash about 20 feet away. The sun had already set at this time, but there was enough light to not have need for a flashlight.

"I quickly closed the distance and another subject (one I had not noticed before) stood up and immediately ran away. I announced myself as a Border Patrol Agent, and the subject who was hiding looked at me and started to get up from his hiding spot. I instructed the subject in Spanish to stay down and noticed that he was still attempting to stand up. While attempting to grab the subject to place him in handcuffs, he extended his arms out... to keep me away. I... tried to break through his active attempt to keep me from arresting him. In doing so, the subject started to put his hands onto my body armor rig (containing my handcuffs, pistol magazines, a knife, and a handheld radio), and also in my face."

This is serious; the illegal alien, having crossed the border and making it about 15-20 miles into the United States, is actively resisting arrest (extending his arms to keep the agent from going hands-on), and assaultive (sticking his hand in the agent's face; any kinetic force directed into an arresting agent is considered assaultive). According to the Use of Force Continuum, at this point, M. would have been within policy to use pepper spray, a Taser, or his collapsible steel baton to protect himself and effect the arrest. He continues:

"While we were scuffling with our hands, the subject gained his footing and stood up. I broke physical contact with [him] and took a step back. I again instructed the subject [in Spanish] to get on the ground... [he] said "OK, OK," but was still standing. The subject indicated that he wanted me to approach him standing to make the arrest. I did not and instructed him to get down. Moments later the subject attempted to run past me. I grabbed him and he was only able to take a few steps before falling down on his butt and back. I fell forward, with the subject, and noticed that he had hold of my hand. I pulled my hand away, however, he was able to retain a deliberate grasp of my left index finger. I remember thinking his intentions were to break my finger. I quickly swung my left arm up, and then down, to break his grip on my finger. I then thought about hitting the subject with closed fist strikes but refrained because I did not want to give him another opportunity to control my hands/arms.

"After I was successful at breaking his grasp, he made a deliberate, forceful kick to my leg with connection. Knowing that this subject was willing to deliberately inflict pain on me, I drew my service weapon and pointed it at him. I did not want the subject to get up and keep attempting to harm me. I continued to give verbal commands and the subject continued to ignore them. I quickly realized that my firearm was not going to be needed at that time nor would I be able to put handcuffs on him, so I holstered."

It is not being stated here, but in the moment, even a very fit person would be getting tired. It is not just the exertion of the struggle (in body armor, while yelling commands), but the uncertainty of the outcome that also drains one's reserves of energy. Border Patrol Agents are not supposed to get in fights, they are supposed to make the arrest consistent with the law and department policy. The encounter was not going M's way, and although help was coming, it wasn't there yet. BPA R. was out of sight and could not leave handcuffed aliens unattended. Notice how M. is adapting his response according to the subject's actions, an indicator of an experienced agent. He ramps up and throttles down his use of force according to the subject's actions.

"By this time, most of the light was gone. After [I re-holstered the pistol], the subject stood up again. I commanded him in Spanish to get back down. The subject indicated as he did before, that he was going to give up again. However, the subject was standing, ignoring my commands to get down, and he seemed to want me to place him in handcuffs on his terms. After the subject realized I was not going to approach him standing, he tried running again. He was only able to take about three strides before tripping over a bush. He fell face first and I was quick to put my body weight on top of him. The subject then immediately pushed up, and I could feel him lifting me up with him. As he was getting to his knees, he started to turn and face me. Thinking that he was going to try and grapple with me or hit me, I immediately broke physical contact again and pulled out my OC spray. I separated from the subject and stayed about six feet away. The subject got back to his feet.

He was facing me and I again instructed the subject to get down. He did not comply and again tried to bait me to come to him. I did not, so he ran. I holstered my OC spray and lost sight of the subject briefly. I then radioed [the] MSC that I had a subject that fought with me and to look for the last person they saw running from me."

In a moment, the helicopter arrived; the MSC operator spotted the guy hiding and directed the bird to him with GPS coordinates. M. ran over, following the sweep of the aircraft's spotlight, the "night sun." He continues:

"He saw me as I approached, stood up, and started to run. I pursued and after about 50 yards, I quickly extended my arms to grab the subject. When my hands contacted the subject's back, [he] fell forward. I placed my knee in the small of the subject's back and commanded him to put his hands behind his back. He complied and I placed him into handcuffs."

It took agents an additional hour to get there with 4x4 vehicles to transport the prisoners out, and another three hours for M. and R. to get them back up to the station for processing. In this case, Zeno, an illegal alien from Central America, was presented for prosecution for Assault on a Federal Officer. The case was dropped by the AUSA the next day.

One can read reports like this over and over ad nauseam, as I have, but what does not always come through is that uncertainty in the moment. In this case, with two agents on five aliens, the odds were pretty good in favor of the agents. If the aliens are not armed and only one or two fight, then the agents have an excellent chance of success. Though possibly tired and encumbered with their gear, agents had not been walking for a week up and down hills and in and out of washes. They have on them, at least, a collapsible steel baton and a handgun, and probably more than one less-than-lethal device like pepper spray or a taser. However, once the agents become separated, anything can happen. Once a suspect knows he is about to be handcuffed, anything can happen. Your partner might also be in a fight, and you might not be able to hear each other. Your radio might have bumped a branch and changed channels. A couple more aliens could have circled back around to attack you, as has happened in the past.

That is just the uncertainty on the part of the agents. The aliens' own situation cannot be ignored. As has been said, they may be exhausted, or have been recently victimized by bandits or their own foot guides. They may be on the verge of heatstroke or hypothermia, and not thinking straight. They may not hear or understand (they may not even speak Spanish) agents' commands or comprehend that it is the Border Patrol as opposed to a rip crew. They may be wanted for serious crimes, and willing to do anything to escape apprehension.

Most apprehensions are pretty straightforward, involving nothing more than a foot chase and a takedown, at the most. But there is always the possibility that it gets deadly, fast. After all, the agent brought a gun.

The murder of Border Patrol Robert Rosas on July 23, 2009 is illustrative of this uncertainty. There are different versions of the story. In the CBP version, Rosas was investigating "suspicious activity" near the Shockey Truck Trail in the Campo Border Patrol Station's AOR, when he was shot from ambush by illegal alien Christian Daniel Castro-Alvarez and two other illegal aliens. In another version, from the Officer Down Memorial Page, it is also stated that Rosas was shot several times as he exited his patrol vehicle on the Shockey Truck Trail.

(From CBP.gov and odmp.org)

The San Diego Union-Tribune had a more detailed story by Kristina Davis dated March 20, 2014, after the last living murderer was sentenced. According to the article, the five were smugglers who decided to cross the border specifically to lure an agent and rob him of his equipment. Night Vision Goggles are valuable commodities to smugglers and scouts, and according to the article, a set had been stolen from the smugglers recently. They "brushed out" over the Shockey Truck Trail in a way that was sure to be noticed, and when the BPA Rosas began tracking the sign, three of the smugglers jumped him and shot him nine times. They took his gear bag, pistol, handcuffs, and NVGs as they escaped back across the border.

This murder prompted the Border Patrol to "flood the zone" around the Campo and El Cajon Station AOR with agents detailed in from all over the country. It resulted in the shutting down of smuggling activity through that particular *plaza*. Different cartels run different *plazas*, so they cannot necessarily just shift traffic to another area, which may be run by the competition. It is supposed among agents that to loosen up the law enforcement coverage and get the drugs and money flowing again, an arrest needed to be made. Castro may have been strenuously urged, by persons unknown, to give himself up.

Maybe someone more highly placed than I knows the real reason Castro gave himself up. His story was that he was forced by the others to participate; many convicted felons have similar stories. Some of them might be true. Emilio Gonzales-Arezanas also claims he was forced into the murder, in which he also fired bullets into the wounded Border Patrol Agent.

Castro-Alvarez and Gonzales-Arenazas were convicted and got 40 years in prison. Marcos Rodriguez-Perez, who also fired shots, got 56 years. Jose Luis Ramirez-Dorantes, who remained just south of the International Boundary as a scout, received 55 years. Another scout, and the alleged ringleader of this conspiracy, is still at large and supposedly dead: Juan Chacon-Morales.

Another incident was relayed to me early in my career at the El Cajon Station. An agent was assaulted at the Tecate Port of Entry by three assailants. According to the story, they had run up just west of the POE. This is behind the T.C. Worthy's store, immediately north of "no man's land." They were confronted by an agent as soon as they got into the parking lot. A fight ensued in which the aliens overpowered the agent, one of the bad guys even attempting to strangle him with his own radio mic cord. Another alien tried to get the agent's pistol. As the pistol was removed from the agent's holster, he kept fighting and discharged a round into the ground, causing the aliens to give up the assault and flee back south into Mexico. While I have not been able to corroborate this story, it was a point of instruction among our Field Training Officers and is entirely believable. This incident was never far from my mind when I confronted groups alone.

Three Agents Get Eleven Scouts

Every once in a while, agents are able to score a major coup against the smugglers. In one such case, three agents temporarily shut down traffic in the western AOR of the Casa Grande Station by patient and stealthy Border Patrol work. This occurred a few years ago in Las Lesnas Mountains, a heavily used terrain feature on the Tohono O'odham Indian Reservation. It is notorious for the presence of illegal alien and narcotics traffic, as well as armed rip crews, operating in some cases with the cooperation and support of local tribal members on the US side.

Three agents working the area, Chris, Darvy and Phil, were alerted to the presence of four scouts on Las Lesnas when an agent on the MSC truck miles away spotted them. The agents carefully approached on foot using dead ground that could not be observed by the four suspects on the mountain. Even with the assistance of NVGs, it is a tricky thing sneaking up on people who are looking out for you. With the night vision, your sense of depth perception is altered, although later models are better to operate with. The agents took it very, very slowly.

Once they had arrived at the approximate elevation where the initial four were spotted, they waited. For about 45 minutes, the agents remained motionless while the aliens got comfortable. They had the GPS coordinates of where the aliens were, and no one had been spotted leaving, so they were confident in their plan to slowly surround the area where the aliens had been and apprehend them there.

They moved to the last known "grids" provided by the technology operator and smelled before they saw the group. In the green light of their NVGs yawned the opening of a large cave overlooking a commonly used road through Las Lesnas. They moved in closer and could make out several people in sleeping bags, snoring away. The agents moved in from two sides and were able to take eleven out of twelve into custody. As they were quietly and calmly doing this, the MSC Operator called out a single individual running off the hilltop to the south, back to Mexico. Most likely, this was the negligent lookout for the group who failed to spot *la Migra*.

The three agents had taken the eleven aliens, as well as eleven pairs of binoculars, eleven handheld radios, twelve cellular phones, six solar panels, eleven radio chargers, many spare batteries, twelve sleeping bags, as well as a large amount of food and personal effects, all packed up and ready to be deployed. All were turned over to the Targeted Enforcement Unit for intelligence exploitation.

The entire group was taken up to the Casa Grande Station, where they were interviewed by the targeting agents. The subjects interviewed freely admitted to crossing the border to work as scouts for "*El Veinte*," a known narcotics smuggler in the CAG AOR. They intended to deploy in small teams from the border to State Route 86 in order to facilitate the movement of three to four groups of backpackers per day, spotting for law enforcement and rival gangs' rip crews.

While the dope probably got through at some point, taking eleven scouts out of operation was a serious tactical blow to the local smuggling outfit. Scouts know the terrain, know how to use it to their advantage for camouflage and concealment, and are skilled at escape and evasion. They stay on their hilltop posts for weeks at a time if necessary, being relieved or resupplied by other groups passing by. When their mission is over, they melt back south to get paid and party.

Ten of the scouts were prosecuted. The eleventh, a juvenile, was removed administratively. Juveniles, even if they are days from turning 18 and have long rap sheets, are rarely prosecuted for anything that doesn't result in death or serious bodily injury.

The prosecutions, the disruption of the smuggling operations in the CAG AOR, and the intelligence harvest all added up to a good night's work. Chris, Darvy, and Phil exhibited patience, persistence, planning, and commitment to action, and their Watch Commander wrote them up for a Commissioner's Blue Eagle Award so that they could be feted appropriately by CBP. Unfortunately, in spite of several attempts to follow up, the award got lost or tossed at Sector Headquarters, and nothing ever came of it.

Burning Dope

The Casa Grande Station Motorcycle Unit is probably the most effective unit at the station. It is staffed exclusively by the best and most aggressive agents, and they can cover a lot of ground very quickly. They work early mornings, so that the sun is low for sign cutting, and the moisture in the ground really makes the foot sign pop. The downside to the bikes is the lack of transport capability. When they go "10-15 (suspects in custody)," they pretty much have to wait for a 4x4 to come find them wherever they are, which can be pretty far out.

In March of 2014, a hard-charging pair of PAs, Pat and Rich, had worked since 0500 on a group of seven packers, whom they caught up to in the early afternoon near Pisinemo. The seven aliens had been carrying six burlap bundles of marijuana wrapped in cellophane, with the seventh guy probably humping the food pack. As they waited around for transport, the agents wrote up the aliens' biographical information on field processing forms. Before the van got there, they had all of the aliens' personal belongings in small bags in front of them, shoelaces, belts, and jackets removed, and ready to be loaded up. When they had been searched again and carted off to the station, only then could Pat and Rich ride back to their department vehicle, load up their bikes and head up to the station to process their dope case.

Most of the vans can carry thirteen or fourteen bodies and maybe their personal *"mochilas,"* or bags with their extra clothing and personal items. There would be no room for dope. So, the bike unit guys usually put one or two packs on their back, maybe one on their front if possible, and one in their spare hand while riding however many miles back to the vehicle. ATV guys had it easier, we had bungee cords and small cargo racks on our ATVs and could carry bundles more comfortably!

On this occasion, on their way back to the truck, Pat smelled something burning. He had hung one of the packs off of each handlebar, and the right side one had rubbed against the tire, hilariously, igniting. Pat stopped, threw the packs off of his handlebars, and stomped out the fire. The left side pack was okay.

They called it in, went back to the station, and completed their case along with a "CYA" memo to explain what had happened to the dope. Another day in the Border Patrol.

Packers Near Cowlic

Most times, there is no drama. You get out on a group to follow sign or respond to a sighting, and you get smoked. Sometimes you end up chasing animals who looked like people from a faraway scope truck or follow sign for hours only to find that the aliens have loaded up on a road and got away. Then again, sometimes everything goes according to plan.

It was a chilly night in February. Agents had been following a group of 20-plus near the Alvarez Mountains for some time, picking up two apprehensions from it (the slow ones). I was getting close to them, having gotten south a little late, when one of the MSC operators called out a group of four backpackers moving in single file along Federal Route (FR) 31. A couple of agents broke off from the other traffic to respond. This new group was north of the village of Cowlic, Arizona, on the TON.

At 10:00 PM, on the Indian Reservation in the wintertime, there was not much reason for any normal hikers to be out in the desert carrying large, square-shaped backpacks. In fact, I have never seen anyone on the TON legitimately hiking with large backpacks; to us, big square backpacks meant dope. This area north of Cowlic is sparsely populated; there are a few houses, widely spread out, but zero businesses, and not much of any activity at this time. As we approached in our vehicles, the MSC operator gave out the last GPS coordinates he had for the group's location. They had last been seen moving northbound towards the intersection of FR31 and FR20; at this point, the paved road basically did a 90-degree turn from north-south (31) to east-west (20).

The other two agents with me were Ric and Mike. Ric would "keep the road hot," meaning he would drive back and forth in front of the aliens' apparent line of travel to try and keep them from crossing FR20. Mike, an excellent tracker, and I would get out and try to pick up some foot sign.

Then the "getting out" ritual: gloves on, Camelbak, hat, and neck gaiter. Grab the M4 out of the rack, Maglite out of the door pocket, double-check that you have the vehicle keys, lock the doors, and get after it. Mike was already out and moving towards the numbers; I followed him at a few paces to give him room to work. It did not take long for him to find some sign.

It was a kind of vague sign; foot-sized smudges in the dirt, which indicate booties worn over the shoes of the group. Normal people do not wrap carpet fabric around their shoes when hiking in the desert. The sole purpose of the shoe booties is to make it harder for the Border Patrol to track your foot sign. These are not the shoe booties you give to the plumber or the electrician who comes into your house; they are well-made, with carpet on the soles and camouflage on the top. Some are secured with elastic to grip the wearer's ankle, others have laces or wire twist-ties. In this case, we noticed that one guy's booties were wearing out. The tread of his heels was poking through, revealing a partial print of finely-lined half circles in the heel, which made it a lot easier to follow him. Designs like you see on the soles of athletic shoes or boots are not found in nature; when they are imprinted on the ground, they really jump out at the observer.

Our disadvantage was that we had to use our flashlights to follow the sign. Any suspect looking over his shoulder would know exactly how far behind we were, as well as our relative position. It's the downside to working nights. When you are laying in, they have no idea, but when you are following them, you are the one who has no idea. At this point we were no longer in view of the MSC operator, so could not rely on any more updates for the group's position relative to ours. Then Mike's light went out. Dead batteries. Before I became a supervisor, I always carried extra D-cell batteries in a pocket of my Camelback. After one set got wet and broke open (I fell), the guts of one of the batteries leaked out all over the inside of the pocket and made a big mess, so I stopped. Too bad; we had to walk all the way back to the road to grab another light before taking up the trail again.

After a bit, the sign seemed to be getting close to the road, then turned around and headed back between two inhabited properties about 1/4 mile apart from each other. They might have been spooked by Ric driving back and forth. As we made our way between the houses, Mike concentrated on the sign while I kept my head up, looking beyond him and to the left and right, trying to keep my light off or pointed away from him. This method of covering the primary agent minimized backlighting my partner and making him a target; it also kept my light from interfering with his signcutting. Additionally, I would be able to spot any approaching threats while Mike concentrated on tracking.

We dropped into a little wash and I had to go lights on to keep from falling down or poking my eyes out with brush. Before long, Mike found a bundle: one homemade backpack of two burlap-covered bales of cellophane-wrapped marijuana tied together with twine. The sweat stains on it were still warm.

A little bit further on we found another, then the first body. Ernesto was a 26-year-old from Mexico, wearing a blue outer vest with a black sweatshirt underneath. As I secured him, Mike found another guy, Carlos. He was another young Mexican male, curled up just past two more backpacks and hiding in a bush. Both of these guys still had their carpet booties on and burlap fibers all over their sweaty, dark clothing; good evidence that they were part of the group we were pursuing.

We ended up with three double-bundles of dope, plus Ernesto and Carlos. Both of them admitted that they were illegal aliens without legal documents to enter, pass through, or remain in the United States legally. Of course, they had no idea what was in the packs and would not claim any of them as their own! As we searched our aliens and grabbed up their dope, a couple of midnight agents showed up to continue the signcutting operation. There were still two more bodies and possibly another bundle out there.

We loaded everything up and took it the 100 miles back to the CAG Station. There, they were officially read their Miranda Warnings and both invoked, or "lawyered up," in TV speak. We weighed the dope and it came to 137.8 lbs, or about $110,248.00 worth of nasty, stinking Mexican ratweed. We took the sweaters, outer vests, and ball caps of both of the men, which were covered with the same burlap fibers that constitute their homemade backpacks, and bagged them for evidence. We took their shoe booties and bagged those as well. We took and bagged their cellular phones for possible later exploitation. We also had them remove their shirts and checked for strap marks. These two were apprehended about 15 miles from the border. Packers generally travel for days on foot in Mexico before they even cross the border, so they are routinely checked for strap marks. Both Ernesto and Carlos were pretty marked up, even after sitting in our warm trucks for a couple of hours driving north. We also photographed their knees, which they had scraped up pretty good crawling away from us. The photos also became evidence.

With all of that evidence booked and stored, and the aliens identified and booked, we completed the prosecution packets for each under 21 USC 841, Narcotics Trafficking. Since they had both invoked their right to remain silent regarding their felony charges, we had no further contact with them. They were also processed for deportation just in case the dope case was dropped. I never heard back if charges were filed and was never called to testify in court. Most likely, they were tagged in the system as dope mules and charged with misdemeanor Entry Without Inspection; there are just too many dope mules and other criminal aliens to even prosecute a plurality of them to the fullest extent of the law. The next time they get caught and printed, there will be a note describing their narcotics trafficking arrest, and hopefully, they will get charged.

Motorcycle Unit Rescue

In the Sonoran Desert in the summer, almost every apprehension could be called a rescue. The temperatures get up to and sometimes over the 110s when it's hot, and only come down to the 90s. There is little water around, except for what one might find in disgusting dirt cattle tanks, rancid ponds, and the occasional well. That is when things are bad. Even during the rest of the year, the aliens cannot carry enough water and frequently fall out from their groups, dehydrated and lost. The lucky ones have cell signal and can call 911 or make it to one of the many Rescue Beacons dotting the area.

It was a very warm morning in April 2019; I was in the area of San Simon, AZ, on the Tohono O'odham Indian Reservation near the intersection of State Route 86 and Federal Route 21. The Motorcycle Unit was out, following a decent-sized group up from the San Simon Wash. They had been pushing it all morning. I noted their location and continued on an errand to the next station west in Ajo, AZ.

A few hours later, on the way back, I heard that they were pushing the group up into the Sierra Blanca Mountains. This is several more miles northeast; if the bikes didn't get them soon they were in for a rough hump into the mountains. I drove up ahead of where I thought the aliens were going and got out with all my stuff, hoofing it around one of the foothills near the Sierra Blancas. Before long, I could hear the bikes approaching and I climbed up a hill to try to see them. It was too late; the group was already way past my location and up high somewhere.

The thing with bikes is they move very quickly. The agents riding them are extremely good at sign cutting. Even at slow speed, they are moving twice as fast as the aliens on foot. They generally start early in the morning when the dirt is moist and the sun is low, so there is more shadow and color from the foot sign, and they can move faster. Combine a good eye with wheeled transport that can take you almost anywhere, and a group that is 6-8 hours or more ahead of you can be caught.

Today there was air support out. The National Guard was supporting us at the time, and the two little birds' call signs, Rogue 11 and Raven 11, were working it from the sky as the bikes made time on the ground. It took about ten hours from the time the bikes got on the sign to when they made contact with the group at the crest of a ridge high up in the Sierra Blancas. By that time, they had left the motorcycles behind and had been on foot for a few hours.

From the report recommending them for awards:

"On April 24, 2019, at approximately 9:00 AM, the Casa

Grande Station (CAG) Motorcycle Unit (MCU) picked up sign for eight to twelve suspected illegal aliens on Federal Route 28 (FR28) west of Pisinemo, Arizona. There was no timeline for the last cut on FR28, but the sign looked good, so they decided to follow it. National Guard air assets Rogue 11 and Raven 11 took turns supporting the agents as they crisscrossed the desert to the northeast, towards Arizona Route [State Route]86.

"Over the next ten hours, the temperature rose to or above 100 degrees, and the bikes covered about 15 or more miles following the sign across AZ 86 towards the Sierra Blanca Mountains. By about 2:00 PM, the agents had reached the foot of the Sierra Blancas and they were able to apprehend three illegal aliens at the bottom; by 5:00 PM, they had apprehended twelve more and were at the top. At times teetering on the brink of catastrophic falls due to the rugged terrain and the rotor wash of the various aircraft, the agents exhibited tenacity and endurance in continuing the signcut operation in spite of the conditions. The last apprehension was an unresponsive female on top of the spine of the mountains.

"Border Patrol Agent C., a certified emergency medical technician (EMT), administered first aid with what gear he had brought up the mountain. This was fortuitous for the alien in distress, for she was apparently not far from succumbing to heat stroke, according to his initial assessment. It was clear to BPA C. that additional medical care would be necessary, and this was requested. In the meantime, Office of Air and Marine (OAM) air asset, Omaha 02Y, landed at the bottom of the mountains to take on water from other agents that had staged there. This was then flown up to where it was needed.

"After a fashion, it was decided to evacuate the patient via "long-line" extraction as suggested by the OAM pilot; Arizona Ranger Rescue was brought in to lift out the patient and drop her off at the previously utilized Landing Zone at the bottom of the mountains. From there OM 02Y picked her up and flew her to the Sells Indian Hospital.

"BPAs C., M., N., M., J., E., and D. executed an outstanding example of detection, determined pursuit, and apprehension followed by a complex rescue mission that was successful in saving a human life. Their courage, discipline, and devotion to duty are an example to others [of] what it means to be a Border Patrol Agent, and cannot be underestimated..."

It ended up being a group of over 20 aliens that were taken off the mountain. After everyone was loaded up and transported away, the MCU agents came out, exhausted and covered with dirt and salt-lined sweat stains on their uniforms. The next day they were back at it.

ATVs - Expensive Dope in San Simon

On the 6:00 PM shift, near the end of the night, BPA Rotceh worked with the shift All-Terrain Vehicle unit to apprehend a group of four subjects. They had been spotted by a Mobile Surveillance Capability truck. These tools are expensive and sophisticated night-vision scopes, mounted on large military 4x4 trucks. They utilize a FLIR infrared camera with a laser pointer slaved to it, and ground sensing radar to locate and identify sightings as far as miles away. As Rotceh tells it:

"We were on 6P. Responding to the Nine Mile traffic just south of San Simon High School, for a group of 4. We went out there on ATVs and got 3 of the bodies. I took custody of the bodies while ATVs chased the foot guide. While sitting on the bodies, I noticed they didn't have backpacks."

It is common for all aliens, especially far away from roads and populated areas, to at least have regular backpacks containing food, clothing, and other personal articles. When aliens are apprehended without them, especially when their clothing has tell-tale sweat stains where the straps of a backpack might have been, it is indicative of either a dope "mule," or an unlucky alien who lost his pack. It is always worth further inquiry.

"I asked about their *maletas* (dope bags), and two of them denied possession. One of them looked south towards the direction they probably stashed them." This was a big mistake. An alert agent will notice tells such as this and other tics people get when questioned; many of them transcend culture and language and are universal signals of distress, deception, etc.

Rotceh then "asked Nine Mile [MSC] if he saw them carrying any bags he replied yes, but due to the distance, he couldn't tell if they were abnormal."

At this point, as the local supervisor, I arrived on the scene to assist with transport or to help look for the outstanding dope.

Rotceh continues, "[I] took the bodies to you guys and went to get the foot guide that the ATVs apprehended. After taking custody, he started asking me to let him go; he was desperate. The guy was scared.

"When I got to you guys, I got him off the ride and he kissed the ground, defeated. Smugglers that lose a precious load can get tortured or killed. While patting down the subjects, I pulled an orange string that I've seen on bales they wrap with. I told you that I'm pretty sure there is dope here somewhere. You said you were gonna advise K9 Agent Katy to go search afterward. She was on midnights.

"That time, she ended up with 7.5 gallons of THC oil. That was a good one."

I do remember that after the agents spent a lot of time looking for the dope stashed out in the brush, we eventually called it off. BPA Katy, a K9 handler on the following shift, was very proficient with her dog in finding the dope that eluded us! She batted clean-up for 6P shift regularly. I gave her an outline of what had transpired, along with GPS coordinates of where the group of three were arrested, as well as where ATVs had gotten the foot guide. Between those points, her dog alerted.

The THC oil was in three plastic bottles and was seized and taken to the station for processing and disposal. While they were written up for trafficking narcotics, I am not sure if the mules were ever charged. It is unlikely.

Rescue in the Sierra Blancas

Some stories in this book are rooted in my supervisor's notes for award recommendations, incident reports, and the small daily journals I keep for court and other purposes. Writing up stellar agents for recognition has been one of my favorite things to do as a supervisor over the years, and therefore it may appear as if every agent featured here is some kind of superhero. What makes them super is that they are ordinary guys motivated to do extraordinary things.

There may be a lot more of these types of agents than the average person might think, but they are still the exception as opposed to the rule. Outstanding agents simply do not always get the recognition they deserve due to the constant press of operations and the workload of supervisors who can easily put off and then forget to write award recommendations in a timely manner.

One Border Patrol Agent, Jason, is an example of an ordinary agent who made an outstanding effort to rescue a person, whom he did not know, from the top of a ridge line in very inhospitable terrain at the end of his shift when it would have been easy to just not answer the radio.

A radio call came out that an alien, stranded in the mountains, could not go further and had dialed 911 on his cell phone. He was able to stay on the phone long enough for the 911 operator to obtain the GPS coordinates of his approximate location on the Tohono O'odham Nation. That location was on the side of a small mountain range north of State Route 86 between San Simon and Quijotoa, known as the Sierra Blancas.

The Border Patrol Search, Trauma, and Rescue Team (BORSTAR) was available, in the air and in vehicles, but had an "extended ETA." Jason was close enough to respond, so he answered up, parked at the end of a road, and headed a mile in to the foot of the mountains with some extra water. Then he started climbing.

Jason eventually made it up into a ravine that appeared to

be leading to where the caller was located. It was hard going; the loose rocks giving way underfoot take a toll on anyone trying to climb up a mountainside. He ended up climbing into and back out of the ravine several times due to rocky outcroppings and heavy brush. Eventually, he came out on a spur and spotted the caller, a young Guatemalan suffering from heat exhaustion. Though it was only May, the Sonoran Desert was heating up for the summer and the daytime temperatures were in the 90s.

As he tells it: "I tried to drive in as close as I could to the 911 caller but drove to a large wash that impeded my path. I had to go in from there on foot. I put on my camelback over my bulletproof vest and my long arm. Knowing that the subject was more than likely suffering from dehydration and heat stroke, I grabbed a gallon of water as well..." He then "hiked for over a mile just to get to the mountain where the individual was. I hiked to the top of the mountain calling for the individual but I had no response. After searching for quite some time, I located the patient. He was cold and was in and out of consciousness. He was only able to mumble but was able to understand what I was saying. Knowing that our BORSTAR team was coming, I just needed to keep the subject alive until our medically trained agents could arrive. I picked up the patient and moved him into the shade under a tree. I covered him as best I could and wetted down his clothes with the water from my Camelback."

Continuing his attempts to rehydrate the alien with what water he had been able to carry up with him, Jason reassured the semi-conscious patient that help was on the way.

BORSTAR units came in on quads. Jason: "The BORSTAR guys came in on ATVs. I had to guide them in. By the time that they arrived, all of the water that I had brought had run out." On the mountain, "one of the BORSTAR agents started the IV and was successful on the first try." This is very hard to do with patients that are dehydrated; the veins all but disappear as the body redirects blood away from the extremities and into the torso where all the major organs are. "[Later] when we got the Guatemalan male to the ambulance, one of the EMTs tried over 10 times to put in an IV before he asked the experienced EMT to try. It took the experienced EMT 6 tries to get it. Note that this was after four bags of fluid and he was more hydrated. Our [BORSTAR] guy was awesome."

They were able to rehydrate the Guatemalan with IV fluids; Jason was still in good shape. He continues: "The helicopter came after the BORSTAR Agents arrived and tried to find a place to land. Sadly, there wasn't anywhere safe to land for miles. In an attempt to help, the helicopter pilot tried to drop us some water. Each of these water bottles exploded on impact. Without much that they could do, they ended up leaving to work other traffic."

The agents started on their way down to the waiting vehicles, but the alien was unable to walk steadily due to his condition. They ended up carrying him all the way down, resting often, and changing positions. Their physical conditioning and will to succeed in treating the patient probably saved his life and saved him from permanent kidney damage due to Rhabdomyolysis, a severe form of dehydration common amongst illegal aliens and sometimes, Border Patrol Agents.

"We took turns carrying the subject down the mountain," said Jason, "we had to take him to a paved road where we met an ambulance."

Jason's name was submitted for Employee of the Month. Agents usually got a nice plaque or a small gift from the Patrol Agent in Charge, usually something like a flashlight, pocketknife, or a gear bag. This particular agent is well-known as one of our Chaplains, as well as a member of the Peer Support Unit. His recognition was well-deserved.

Rip Crew Pre-empted

Sometimes you get to them before they make a hit.

In January of 2019, I hung around the station too long doing admin stuff and got hit up to respond to an Other Agency (OA) call. The Pinal County Sheriff's Office (PCSO) was requesting Border Patrol over near State Route 87 in Eloy. I grabbed my stuff and headed out. The reporting indicated a vehicle with three occupants had been stopped by Deputies in a remote rural area of fields and dirt roads to the east of the highway, north of Interstate 10. One guy from the previous shift, BPA D., also answered up.

BPA D. got there first and saw the three subjects handcuffed, sitting on the side of a dirt road in front of the marked PCSO Tahoe. On the hood of the PCSO vehicle were three long arms: a Del-Ton 5.56mm AR-15, a Smith & Wesson AR-15 in .22 caliber, and a .22 caliber Marlin Model 60 semi-auto rifle, along with several magazines and loose ammunition. The subjects' white Chevy Cobalt was parked further up with all of the doors, the trunk, and the hood open.

One of the Deputies told BPA D. that they had been responding to a call of a suspicious vehicle in the area. Upon their arrival, they encountered this white Cobalt, registered to the driver, Francisco. The driver stated that they were looking around for deer to hunt. This being January, at night, in an area of farms and distant industrial buildings that is known for a high volume of drug and alien smuggling, the Deputy's suspicion was aroused. When he spotted a 5.56mm cartridge in the console cupholder, one of the Deputies asked if there were any weapons in the car. Francisco replied yes, in the trunk. At that point, all individuals in the vehicle were identified.

Two of them could not speak or understand English and were not entirely cooperative in Spanish. Their body language, lack of eye contact, and evasive, mumbled answering of the Deputies' questions indicated to them that they might be illegal aliens. Therefore, they called for Border Patrol Agents to determine citizenship.

By the time I got there, BPA D. had already questioned all three as to their immigration status. We determined that Francisco was a Guatemalan Citizen, but a Lawfully Admitted Permanent Resident of the United States. His two passengers were illegal aliens from Guatemala with no documentation to enter, remain in, or pass through the United States. We took custody of the three on suspicion of Alien Smuggling and Entry Without Inspection, towed the vehicle, and loaded the rest of the weapons and other items into our patrol vehicles. Records checks revealed that none of the weapons or the vehicle had been reported stolen, and Francisco was not wanted for any crimes currently.

The investigation would continue at the CAG Station.

We requested assistance from a Special Agent of Homeland Security Investigations, as is common when illegal aliens are encountered with weapons. In this case, we thought that the three were either a load and that Francisco was smuggling the other two further into the United States, or more likely, they were a rip crew intent on taking down an as-yet-undiscovered dope load. Either or both could be true.

The Deputies left to search for the outstanding dope load which probably had been spooked by all of the law enforcement activity. Pinal County in general, and Casa Grande-Eloy-Arizona City specifically, are at the intersection of two Interstate Highways, the 8 and the 10, as well as a well-used railroad. This area is frequently transited by narcotics and alien smugglers due to the proximity to the International Boundary and the fact that the Tohono O'odham Indian Reservation is a heavily used funnel for smuggling activities. Terrain and infrastructure doom Pinal County to the constant presence of and operations by various Transnational Criminal Organizations. Luckily for the local citizenry, their Sheriff, Mark Lamb, is a real-deal lawman.

We met with HSI agents at the station. Interviews were conducted, checks were run, and fingerprints and photos were taken. In the end, there was nothing to tie the illegal aliens to the weapons. We could only tie LAPR Francisco to them by his fingerprints, and he was the legal owner of the weapons. This is not a crime in Arizona, a strong Second Amendment State. The aliens had entered long ago and were considered "domiciled." That meant that smuggling charges were not sustainable.

It was with great remorse that we released Francisco with his car, guns, and ammunition. Everything about the encounter screamed to me that they were criminals and that they were targeting someone or something. Most likely, they were laying in for a specific load of dope mules on foot, or more likely a load vehicle with narcotics, which they could hijack. This type of crime happens regularly and repeatedly in border communities across the four border states, though it is rarely encountered by law enforcement, much less prosecuted!

Their ridiculous story about looking for deer was not even the least bit believable. It was nighttime. They had no tag. There are few or no deer in the area. The 5.56mm rifle was the only one capable of a humane kill on a deer, with the ammunition present. The 5.56mm was military full metal jacket, not hunting ammunition. The .22 rifles would not suffice for that.

The two Guatemalan illegal aliens were arrested and set up for deportation. That was the best that we could do. At least they didn't get their dope load, or murder anyone, as far as we could tell. Thanks to PCSO for that.

Border Violence

Border violence is nothing new. There are the vulnerable populations of illegal aliens who get murdered, raped, robbed, kidnapped, and/or extorted into smuggling dope for the cartels. Then there are the people who live on the border that get their houses broken into, fences destroyed, vehicles stolen, or are otherwise intimidated and victimized and even sometimes murdered on their own property. And then there are the different kinds of predators. There are the dope smugglers, alien smugglers, scouts, foot guides, rip crews, rapists, and bandits; there are Border Patrol Agents, local police, and citizen militias, either the good ones who observe and report or the bad ones who are LARPing at best or ripping off the aliens at worst.

Most of the drug smugglers, scouts, and even most rip crews are not there to do anything that might negatively affect their business. Their guns are for each other, bandits, and for opposing gangs' rip crew activity. When law enforcement arrives, they usually discard any weapons as soon as possible to avoid the extra charge. Usually.

The most notorious rip crew event in recent times was the murder of Bryan Terry. In the area south of Tucson, Arizona there had been years of rip crew activity before this event. Details vary but the official version of events is a team of BORTAC operators near Peck Well in the Nogales Border Patrol Station's AOR encountered a rip crew and engaged with a bean-bag shotgun. The bad guys answered with gunfire and killed BPA Terry. The bad guys were armed with semi-automatic versions of the AK-47 rifle, at least one of which was linked to the BATFE Operation Fast and Furious. The bandits were pursued and one was arrested on the scene. The rest TBS'd back to Mexico and were eventually caught and prosecuted; a total of six were convicted for this murder. Books have been written about Operation Fast and Furious, which allegedly aided and abetted the smuggling of thousands of weapons from gun shops in the United States to Mexican drug cartels. The truth of this horrific criminal enterprise, perpetrated by United States government agents, will probably never be known. Suffice it to say, the emotions surrounding this murder are still pretty raw for many of us, especially the family of Brian Terry. HSI Special Agent Jaime Zapata, operating in Mexico, was also murdered with a weapon allegedly trafficked through Operation Fast and Furious.

(CBP.gov; odmp.org)

There were other events. A vehicle ambush near Green Valley, AZ, where a rip crew opened fire on a load vehicle with the intent of robbing and/or kidnapping the aliens inside which resulted in deaths and injuries. In the same area south of the mines, a journeyman agent was introducing his trainee to the local back roads when bullets began landing in the dirt all around them. The agents thought a nearby armed group had been startled by their stealthy approach and fired shots in order to clear the area. The subsequent response, delayed due to bad radio reception, turned up nothing. Running car chases on Interstate 10 between Tucson and Phoenix, Arizona between rival gangs were not unknown, not to mention various high-speed pursuits initiated by law enforcement.

Most reports of border violence go relatively unaddressed. The victims, usually the illegal aliens and/or drug mules, are usually unsure of their location at the time of the incident they have survived, may or may not have known their attackers; it may have taken them days and many miles in order to find agents to give up to.

In one instance, illegal alien Jose crossed with his group at approximately 4:00 AM on a cool November morning near Las Lesnas Mountains. They made good time, reaching an area known as El Elefante by noon the next day. As they climbed up into El Elefante, a group of five men accosted them. Of these five, two carried backpacks and three carried "*cuernas de chevo*," AK-47 type rifles. Jose's foot guide, in the lead, was swiftly stabbed to death by one of the assailants. Jose, next in line, was struck on the head with the butt of an AK-47. Jose was then forced to carry a backpack of marijuana for the gunmen. Fortunately, he was able to escape the following day by running away. He ran several miles north to State Route 86 where he was able to flag down a passing Border

Patrol vehicle and report his story. The Border Patrol in turn informed the Tohono O'odham Police Department, whose officer assigned a case number, and nothing further was learned or done.

In the same area years later, a woman was apprehended with her group and at the station, she reported a sexual assault. The group she had been traveling with was stopped by rifle-armed males speaking Spanish, who marched the group to one of the many caves in the area of the Quijotoa Mountains. The young women were then separated from the men and taken to another cave where the assault took place. Other apprehended aliens on other occasions have reported this practice of separating the young females from the males for this purpose.

Again, in the same area, an illegal alien reported to agents that he and a companion were taken captive by armed Spanish-speaking males in the vicinity of the Quijotoa Mountains, about 20-plus miles north of the US-Mexico Border. They were taken to a cave complex, where the reporting alien stated there were up to 25 other men staging, all with AK-47s. The two kidnapped aliens were forced to call family members in their home countries in order to raise ransom money for their captors. At some point, the leader of the armed group received a phone call and told his men they had to move out. They all marched off leaving the two illegals free and unhurt.

On yet another occasion, again in the Quijotoa-South Mountain area, several dead bodies were found by an agent on foot face-down in a hole with plastic bags tied over their heads, hands secured behind their backs. TOPD was called, responded, and recovered the bodies. A report was taken and nothing further was heard of the incident.

A report was taken in 2013 regarding Hugo, an illegal alien from Mexico, which was more typical of what happens in and around the border area. Hugo was what we call a "quitter," an alien who has had enough and just wants to get caught, get some food and water, and get sent home. They are usually dehydrated, exhausted, and stressed out from being lost after becoming separated from their group.

After getting out of the hospital where he had been treated for dehydration, Hugo reported to agents that he had been taken against his will by unidentified armed assailants near a small village on an Indian Reservation. He had initially crossed illegally with a group of six east of the Baboquivari Mountains. They walked for about eight hours, according to Hugo's report, and it was around midnight when they were accosted by two masked individuals. The two bandits wore "military-type" clothing, black boots, and were armed with three pistols and a "short rifle." They also used small handheld radios. The pair demanded money from the group of six and told them to count to three and disappear, or they would all be killed.

Hugo told agents that the group complied, gave up their money, and scattered. Because he was unable to see well in the dark, Hugo fell and was recaptured by the bandits. They walked him into the mountains further north and into a cave where bundles of possible marijuana were stored. The bandits alternated between watching Hugo and scanning the surrounding terrain with binoculars from a hilltop. They tried to get Hugo to contact his family in Mexico and arrange to have them send $50,000 to secure his release. Hugo also heard the men arguing about the "packers" being late to pick up the marijuana.

The presence of the marijuana, binoculars, and the subject of the argument, indicates that these two assailants were cartel scouts. Scouts are sometimes assigned a specific terrain feature or a specific route. Backpack loads of marijuana are relayed through by various groups, dropped off by one group to be picked up later by another until it is loaded in a vehicle and taken to a stash house. Many scouts, as seen here, are not averse to kidnapping as a side hustle.

At one point, both of his captors fell asleep and Hugo used this opportunity to flee, running down the hill and away from them. He claimed to have been held for two days and to have evaded the scouts for another two days before giving himself up to Border Patrol Agents at an FOB. It was a very happy ending for Hugo; the desert is littered with the bones of those not so lucky.

Not far from where Hugo gave himself up to agents at the FOB, another "quitter" presented himself to agents near the International Boundary with a gaping wound in his neck. He had had his throat slit from ear to ear, somehow missing the major blood vessels, and the yawning wound leaked saliva, blood, and mucus uncontrollably as he sobbed seeking medical attention. The bodies of the other members of this poor alien's group were found later, bled out from similar injuries. Their mistake was crossing the fence line dividing one smuggling crew's territory, or "*plaza*," from another crew's area.

On the Mexican side, there was a ranch right next to the border, within sight if you were up on a hill, where cartel smugglers and the Mexican Military alternately occupied the property. On one occasion when the smugglers had it, they slaughtered several aliens by taking them from the ranch where they were waiting to cross, into a brushy wash where they were all shot. Later the "Mike-Mikes," or Mexican Military, came in and reoccupied the area, recovering the bodies. Border Patrol Agents from Sector Command and the International Liaison Unit were staged at the border north of the ranch in case some of the bad guys tried to evade the Mexican Military northward into the United States. This did not happen, but one of the Mexican Government helicopters was circling overhead in support of the operation. At one point, this aircraft crossed into or very close to US airspace and fired several shots at the agents on the ground, for an as-yet-unknown reason. It should be noted that the border is very clearly defined in this area, with a border road, fence line, and vehicle barricades that can be seen from space.

Border Patrol management claims that the Mexican Government apologized for the mistake. Some BP Agents on the ground at the time said later that there was no mistake and no apology. As with many stories, there are multiple versions of this one.

More Border Violence

In the case of Hugo, he had been twice accosted by scouts moonlighting as bandits before his escape and evasion all the way to a US Border Patrol Forward Operating Base. Hugo was very lucky.

In another case, there is another lucky survivor who happened to have a cellular phone and enough signal to call 911 after witnessing a mass murder just south of the International Boundary. Felipe was no angel. Under oath in his custodial interview, he freely admitted to being an illegal alien, as well as a drug mule. He was hired on by his cousin, who worked for a drug-smuggling organization based in Rocky Point that was involved in, among other things, moving marijuana across the border on foot.

Arrangements were made and Felipe traveled up from the interior of Mexico to Caborca, Sonora. Many of the criminals and smugglers we had apprehended over the years were based out of Caborca. Pretty much every Mexican town along the border, some more than others, has a deeply entrenched criminal smuggling gang working out of it. Mexico being such a rich country with such a poor population, there is no shortage of recruits for these organizations. Felipe was pretty typical. He agreed to carry a pack of dope into the US for $1700 US cash, and in lieu of smuggling fees, to a destination in the US State of Wisconsin.

From Caborca, Felipe was taken to a ranch in the desert where a group of about fifteen individuals was formed. This group was loaded into a truck and driven to the immediate border area. They waited in the desert at the drop-off point until another truck showed up; this one had three heavily armed men inside. The men dropped off a load of burlap packs containing the narcotics. These homemade backpacks were made of burlap sackcloth, tied around cellophane-wrapped marijuana bales (usually two; sometimes one or three bales) with burlap straps tied on using thin rope or twine. The good ones use automobile seatbelts for straps and, while not as padded as the burlap straps, these had the luxury of being adjustable.

Thirteen of the mules were designated to carry the packs; one was probably the guide and another may either have been a guide in training, or the food mule. As is common, no one was obviously armed. Most backpacker groups have support personnel staged along the way to scout for them, provide food and water at designated locations, and observe for rip crews and/or law enforcement. Their job is to contact the guides via handheld radio with updates (such as the two who abducted Hugo). If anyone is armed, it is usually, but not always, those support guys.

It was July, easily in the 100s, and you cannot carry enough water on your person to make it through a 20-plus mile hump through the Sonoran Desert with a 50-lb pack of dope on your back. You would have to rest often and drink plenty. A support system would be set up for you ahead of time, with waypoints where supplies of food and water are stashed. In the case of this group, they were told that they were supposed to cover the distance between the International Border and the village of Quijotoa in two days. There, the packers would load their dope into a vehicle driven by a female tribal member (Quijotoa is on the Tohono O'odham Nation) and await another load vehicle which would take them further on their way to various destinations in the United States.

Felipe stated that the group walked for a couple of hours through the desert to the low mountains known as Las Lesnas, south of the border. As they went into Las Lesnas, his group encountered another group of five men in masks and camouflage, armed with "*cuernos de chevo,*" or goat horns; this refers to the distinctively curved magazine of the AK-47 rifle. The packers were walking along in a single file when they encountered these armed men. One of the armed men asked who they worked for, and Felipe's guide told him.

"*Los contras* (enemies)!" yelled one of the gunmen. They opened fire, shooting everyone in the group as far as Felipe could tell. He was in the rear and had time to dump his pack and dive into a wash for cover. Then he ran north towards the United States. Felipe stated that two of the gunmen followed him. He reached the International Boundary Fence, which in this area consisted of a barbed-wire fence backed by welded steel I-beams as a vehicle barrier. There was a group of five other prospective immigrants sitting at the fence, resting. He called to them to run away from the shooters as he ran past, over the fence, and into the US. Not taking any chances, he kept going. Just north of the International Boundary, he ran into another immigrant, Mario, who was walking alone. The two of them ran up a hill to hide and watch out for the gunmen.

Mario happened to have been traveling with the five that rested by the International Boundary; he had walked away to relieve himself. Felipe and Mario witnessed two of the armed men approach Mario's companions. The five unsuspecting prospective immigrants had remained at the fence. The shooters ordered them into a wash, still on the Mexican side. There, the four males out of the five were shot. There was one female in the group of five that was not murdered at that time and Mario and Felipe did not see her again. Felipe and his new companion used a cell phone to call 911 and report the situation to the Pima County Operators. Then they observed the gunmen emerge from the wash and cross into the US over the fence, still apparently searching for them.

Mario and Felipe took off northbound, trying to move fast and evade the shooters, who gave up after a short time. The two walked for a couple more hours before encountering a Border Patrol Agent and giving up to him. This single agent was the only available unit dispatched to investigate the 911 call made earlier.

OA Smuggling Case with Money

I had just gotten south around 10:00 PM. It was chilly for Arizona, being January, but not unpleasant. It was a rare day for me to get into the field, and I had sadly wasted a lot of time at the station doing paperwork. My usual routine when I got south into the border area was to pull off on a dirt road we called "the Piss Road." The Piss Road is a dirt road that breaks east from Federal Route 15 about a mile north of the intersection FR15/State Route 86. It goes east for about a mile to a big dirt clearing. The first 100 yards or so is dotted with puddles at all hours of the day or night from agents and motorists who take the opportunity to relieve themselves in an area that has no other discrete opportunities. Hence the name. Except for a single port-a-john at the gas station in Quijotoa, it is the most discrete opportunity to empty one's bladder within a few miles. You could not pay me enough to use a random port-a-john in a small desert town.

There wasn't much going on. I used the facilities and checked my G-phone for agent locations and sensor activations I had heard on the radio. A couple of sensors had banged off and were being checked, but nothing was positive yet. If I was the only sup down south, I would stay up on 86 until something good came up; then it would be easy to go east or west, depending on the location. Once you got down in the desert, moving laterally along the Border was more problematic with the crappy roads and so forth.

At around 10:20 PM, dispatch came on and informed us that the Tohono O'odham Police Department was requesting back-up on a traffic stop on 86.

"Any Charlie Unit, 860" called Dispatch. "TOPD behind a white SUV, possible load vehicle. Request BP back up for a traffic stop on 86."

"860, C-37, where on 86 are they?" I replied.

I got off the Piss Road and moved south to the intersection of FR1 and SR86, where the streetlights were bright enough to backlight the occupants of oncoming vehicles. There is a hill right by where the two roads meet where you can look into the beds of pickup trucks as well. As I turned to face the road, a small white SUV and two TOPD-marked Ford Expeditions sped by westbound.

"10-3, I have them. C-37 to back TOPD, at 15 and 86."

"37 to back, 10-4," she answered.

By the time I got on the road, they had pulled over the suspect vehicle. I rolled up behind them to see a TOPD officer on each side of the white Land Rover Discovery, holding the doors closed as the people inside were trying to get out. The windows were all fogged up, an indicator of sweaty people in a warm car, but I could see commotion in the back as well. It was good for a load.

I called out, "Border Patrol, coming up behind you" until one of the cops nodded to me. It is never a good idea to rush up behind law enforcement when they are on a traffic stop.

"860, it's a load," I said into the radio, "Roll agents to help out please." I called out the vehicle plate, make and model, and went to the passenger's side. The front passenger window was down, revealing a very nonchalant young black guy, eyebrows raised as if to ask "moi?"

"Border Patrol. Put your hands on the dash. Lean forward. Do not move."

"OK, OK," he said. I peeked into the back over his shoulder, placing a hand on his back so that I would feel him move if he got stupid. The smell assaulted me: bad breath, body odor, desert brush, and wood smoke. They were definitely aliens, a squirmy mass. Each wore camouflage, head to toe, over their regular clothes.

I shouted in Spanish into the back of the vehicle, "Immigration, don't move!" But they kept jostling each other to get further forward so they could bail out in a rush. One alien wriggled his way up, practically in between the driver and the front passenger, trying to decide whether or not to dive through the window on the highway side. "Hey asshole, get down!" I yelled and grabbed him by the hood of his camouflage hoodie, pulling his

247

skinny body back into the car. I again reminded the front seat passenger to remain still.

"There are other agents coming," I said to the older Officer. "When someone else gets here, we'll take them out one at a time." All the while, the aliens were jostling around trying to get out the passenger doors. One of them kept trying to open the hatchback, but it must have been locked, or we would have had a problem. Soon, a couple of guys from the previous shift arrived, one of whom was the transport agent. The aliens accepted their fate and stopped trying to get out.

We extracted them one at a time, searched them, and placed them in our vehicles. Alan, the transport guy with a van, took all of the aliens. After making sure that they were indeed illegal, and from Guatemala, they were thoroughly searched and placed in the van. The driver and his passenger up front were both USCs from Ohio. We placed them in separate vehicles, away from the aliens, for transport back to Casa Grande. They had rented the really nice Land Rover in Cleveland and, as their bullshit story went, drove out to Tucson because they wanted to see the desert.

We arrested the driver and the front-seat passenger for Alien Smuggling and loaded them and all of their IAs into the vehicles to take back to the station a hundred miles away for processing. Seven of the eight IAs were retained as material witnesses, while the eighth, a juvenile, was Voluntarily Returned back to Guatemala.

The driver was Davonte Williams, a USC. He carried a phone and $1600 USD in fifties and hundreds. His passenger, Brandon Wilson, had a warrant out of Lake County, Ohio, for cocaine possession; he was to be considered armed and dangerous.

Upon being read their Miranda warnings, Williams immediately clammed up and requested an attorney; Wilson agreed to make a statement. We wrote up the case, seized the cash and the phones, and turned the rental vehicle over to Elite Towing for storage until Hertz Rental picked it up. I don't know about you, but if I ever spring for a nice luxury rental SUV, I do not want it to have been used for alien smuggling; that thing will never smell the same.

When all was said and done, the two USCs were offered a plea agreement and took a misdemeanor "aiding and abetting" conviction. The remaining aliens were deported, and we agents worked a 14-hour day to accomplish next to nothing.

How do I know this? Well, two years later, I got a summons from the US Attorney's Office in the Northern District of New York to Williams' trial on a different crime involving drugs and guns. I met all of the other officers and agents who had arrested him in the roughly year and a half since my encounter with him on the side of the road. He had continued to get arrested for felonies involving guns, drugs, and large amounts of money until finally, a DEA task force had him with so much dirt that it could not be ignored. He fired his court-appointed attorney, who was threatened physically by Williams' mother, and represented himself at trial. I took the stand, for only the second and final time in my career, while he played attorney and generally made a fool of himself before being convicted by the jury.

In another case, I responded to some agents who had called for a supervisor after pulling over a vehicle in Sasabe, Arizona. They had witnessed the vehicle come through the small two-lane Port of Entry and pull up to a trailer home in this small border town in Pima County. The trunk was opened, and a tire was removed. A few minutes later, another tire was brought out of the trailer and placed in the trunk, at which time the car departed. The agents followed it northbound on State Route 286 for a while, while they ran checks on it, and confirmed it was the same vehicle that had crossed through the POE. Then they pulled it over.

The driver gave consent when the agents requested permission to check the trunk. The spare tire was found to be the wrong size for the car. It was also very heavy for its size and would not bounce on the pavement. These are all things that indicate a "tire load" of narcotics. An agent then read the woman her rights and asked her if she was willing to tell him what was in the tire. She said she did not know, but that the "guys at the trailer" had worked on it for a while before she had departed. I arrived and read her her rights again, asking again if she would tell us what was in the tire. She admitted to knowledge of the tire being placed in the trunk with the intention to smuggle the narcotics. Then, our K9 team arrived. The dog alerted to the tire, and agents cut the tire open; they found dope. I cannot remember what kind of dope, but it was a relatively small amount for us at the time, maybe 30-40 lbs., wrapped in cellophane and placed in little divided compartments in the tire.

We arrested her and seized the dope and vehicle. They were taken in for processing, but we ended up letting her go the next day. We couldn't get approval to prosecute a female.

FTY - Shots Fired

The biggest draw for many in the Border Patrol is that anything can happen at any time. No one expects you to be at 100% 100% of the time, but they notice what you do and how you do it. "Zero to Hero," on any given day, or back the other way.

One day on a noon shift, I was getting ready to go south. After roll call, checking and responding to email, completing some of the daily rosters, and checking out a ride, I was in the processing area for some reason when we heard, on the radio, a fragment of a call.

"Shots fired, shots fired!"

Everybody froze for a moment.

A vehicle had failed to stop at our immigration checkpoint on Federal Route 15, and agents were in pursuit. Shots fired was the only update I heard. After listening for a supervisor on the net and not hearing one, I went to the armory and grabbed my M4. An agent updated me as I ran out to my vehicle and jumped in to try to intercept the FTY vehicle.

There was no chance to intercept; once on the Interstate, I was passed by several vehicles from PCSO and DPS. There were two Border Patrol units in pursuit, Border Patrol Agents Rotceh and Scott (first names). They knew what to do; Rotceh was a seasoned agent, had been in several pursuits, and had always acted appropriately. BPA Scott had been detailed to the DPS Gang Task Force and was very productive both at the checkpoint and in the field, having written up many successful smuggling and narcotics cases that were accepted for prosecution. He was solid. The two agents in pursuit were among the first I would choose to be there, had it been my choice!

From I-8, I could see the smuggling vehicle, followed by PCSO and Border Patrol units as they crossed over a bridge. I had to turn around in the median and exit to get on their route. For several minutes, I hadn't heard any other supervisor on the net, so I took control of the pursuit.

Since they were entering Casa Grande and PCSO had the

lead in the pursuit, I called on all BP Agents to fall back. By policy, we are not allowed to "caravan," meaning no more than two units behind any FTY. Everyone else has to stay back. I had seen the DPS and PCSO units moving up the on-ramp to assist, so the BP (with our more limited jurisdiction) had a role, but it wasn't to be right on the ass of the bad guy.

I followed them at a distance, warning agents to watch for civilian traffic and to let the DPS and PCSO units handle the pursuit. This was as much for anyone (management, dispatch, or the press) listening to the radio, as it was for our agents. As a supervisor, you want to put out there, "on tape," that no one is caravanning and no one is tearing through the city with their fangs out and hair on fire: everyone is cool. It eases the bosses' minds.

It was a nightmare moving through the streets of Casa Grande around 3:00 PM on a weekday. The loader went past schools letting out, there was heavy traffic, and he was really moving. The deputies and the troopers were right on him, with BP a ways back, as it should be. Had there not been shots fired from this vehicle, we would have terminated the pursuit as soon as the suspect approached the first populated area, much less the city of Casa Grande, but with his reckless and violent behavior, there was no way he was going to be let go.

The bad guy got back on I-10 towards Phoenix and really got up to speed before being "PITted" by a DPS Trooper. The PIT (Pursuit Intervention Technique) maneuver is when law enforcement places their front fender on a suspect vehicle's rear fender and pushes the rear end around, causing the suspect vehicle to spin out. There is more to it than that, but that is the gist of it. This time, the ballsy DPS guy did it at about 100 miles an hour with, unbeknownst to him, a couple of illegal aliens in the trunk. No one but the pursuing agents were aware of aliens in the trunk until it was all over, due to the lousy Border Patrol radio reception.

It was very fortuitous that there was not a catastrophic accident. I can only imagine those two aliens in the trunk were begging the driver to stop, knowing that shots had been fired and hoping nobody shot back through the trunk lid. In the event, the vehicle was successfully stopped, and DPS, with Border Patrol and PCSO in support, were able to place cuffs on the driver.

I arrived on the scene and called all tertiary BP units to leave the scene. I saw a few units turn around and go back south to CAG. The guys I saw were the agents you would want around if things got hairy: the agents that looked for work and knew how to do it. But they were not needed now, so I asked them to clear out from the mess on the freeway. That done, I looked for the senior DPS Trooper on the scene. I found that my own Patrol Agent in Charge and his deputy were pulling up, relieving me of responsibility for the Border Patrol element of the incident scene. Then I noticed: my holster was empty.

When the call came through I had been in processing and had locked up my pistol in a lockbox. I had remembered to get my rifle out of the armory but had forgotten to get my pistol out of the box. It was an embarrassing situation, downright shameful! I am sure my face was beet-red. If there had been some kind of gun battle, my M4 would have been the go-to weapon anyway, but for the rest of my time in the Patrol, I never forgot my pistol in the box again. I turned over the scene to my boss and cleared out.

For a taste of what led up to this, I have parts of the agents' accounts to rely on.

At about 2:35 PM, a silver Ford Taurus approached the primary inspection lane of the FR15 Checkpoint. Border Patrol Agent A. was the primary agent performing immigration inspections on vehicles at the time. The vehicle stopped in primary, with all of the windows rolled down. Border Patrol Agent Scott noticed that the driver had a large visible tattoo on his neck; while this was not necessarily indicative of criminal or gang activity, Scott was always more attentive when people presenting themselves for inspection had such tattoos on their necks or faces due to his experience as a member of the DPS Gang Task Force.

BPA A. requested permission to look in the trunk. The driver, identified as Stewart, replied "Sure," and popped the trunk open from inside the car. Scott and Rotceh were at the rear of the car waiting to look inside the trunk. As it opened, the agents saw that there were two individuals concealed within the trunk of the Taurus.

Stewart put the car into gear and took off; Rotceh attempted to throw a spike strip under the tires, but Stewart was able to swerve and avoid the spikes. Rotceh jumped in the Dodge Charger pursuit vehicle and Scott into a 4x4 Chevy Silverado patrol vehicle. They called out an FTY (Failure To Yield), a description of the suspect vehicle, and the registration information, but due to poor radio communications, not all of this was received at the station. Also, though a supervisor answered up to control the pursuit, we were not aware of this at the station either, again due to the poor radio signal.

The pursuit reached speeds of about 80 miles per hour with no traffic on the highway at that time. As they sped northbound, the fleeing suspect and the two pursuing agents approached an unmarked Border Patrol truck also going northbound. The agent in the unmarked truck activated his emergency lights in an attempt to slow down Stewart in his Taurus and end the pursuit. Stewart slowed and didn't try to pass but remained "boxed in" by the Border Patrol units fore and aft. After a couple of miles, he pulled out a black semi-automatic handgun and stuck it out of the sunroof of the Taurus, firing several shots into the air and then at the vehicles behind him.

The agents pulled back to gain distance, and it was then that Rotceh called out "shots fired" on the radio. The agent in front pulled over. Stewart passed him and accelerated the Taurus to high speed again. He drove northbound until leaving the Indian Reservation at the village of Chuichu and then continued over the bridge spanning Interstate 8 towards the city of Casa Grande. This is when the Pinal County Sheriff's Office took over the pursuit. As it approached the city, PCSO set up to spike the Taurus, but there was too much oncoming traffic, so they aborted.

Stewart continued through Casa Grande, getting pinched at a stoplight near a school and driving his car up onto the sidewalk to get around traffic. A third attempt was made to spike him, this time from DPS. They had set up near the Casa Grande Airport;

Stewart swerved into oncoming traffic to avoid the spikes and kept on going back onto Interstate 10. Finally, a DPS officer PITted the Taurus at mile marker 175, and they were able to quickly take Stewart into custody as well as the two subjects in the trunk, who admitted to being Mexican citizens present in the United States illegally.

The whole mess was transported to the Casa Grande Border Patrol Station where the various agencies coordinated with the FBI and the AUSA to pursue charges for Assault on a Federal Officer, High-Speed Flight from an Immigration Checkpoint, and Alien Smuggling, as well as other state charges to follow. With any luck, it will be a long time before Stewart gets out of prison.

Controlling Pursuits

Whenever there is a flight from the checkpoint, or any FTY from a Border Patrol Agent, the supervisor on scene is expected to control the pursuit. If there is no supervisor on scene, then the Duty Supervisor or Watch Commander are responsible for controlling from the station. If there is no response form a supervisor or above, the agent is expected to terminate the pursuit unless there are exigent circumstances, such as an assault or shots fired, etc.

It is not always the case that this happens. Agents, and cops in general, pursuing fleeing suspects often have "their fangs out, hair on fire," and get caught up in the excitement of the chase. It is up to the supervisors to exert control in these situations.

In the early nineties, a pursuit in Southern California got out of hand, which resulted in a stolen Chevy Suburban with 13 illegal aliens in it, driven by an illegal alien juvenile, losing control and crashing into another vehicle and pedestrians in front of a Temecula, California high school. Six people were killed: an adult, four students, and one of the IAs in the load vehicle. The Suburban was going so fast that when it hit the smaller Acura, that vehicle was torn in half and all three occupants were killed. According to the Border Patrol at the time, the pursuing agents reportedly had a malfunction with their lights and siren (a not unheard-of occurrence) and had backed off the pursuit before the load vehicle ran a red light and collided with the Acura and the pedestrians. The driver was convicted of six counts of second-degree murder.

Many blamed the Border Patrol for pursuing the vehicle. Many others blamed the actual driver of the stolen vehicle for running a red light in a school zone at 90 miles per hour as students were arriving for school. The driver went to prison, and the Border Patrol changed its pursuit policy. While not explicitly banning pursuits, the result that I experienced in San Diego Sector was that no supervisor would authorize one unless he was prepared to be heavily disciplined. The only pursuits I can remember before the rules were relaxed after 9/11 were one in which a vehicle tried to run over an agent near Tecate, California, and another one in which the irrepressible Agent Ski and his partner chased a kidnapping suspect on Interstate 8 eastbound from El Cajon with local law enforcement.

This incident was always in the back of my head whenever pursuing a suspect vehicle or monitoring one. I had made up my mind that whenever I was in charge, there would be no car chases through populated areas (a notable exception being when the driver shot at my agents).

Fast forward to 2021: As Duty Supervisor, I was just coming into the control room when I could hear the radio traffic involving a car chase. A vehicle had reportedly fled from the checkpoint and was driving north at speed. The pursuing agent said, "I can still see tail lights," which I interpreted to mean "the suspect vehicle is getting away." I waited a minute to see if there was another supervisor on the net in control and heard nothing.

The next step is to try to contact the agent. As usual, comms were terrible and I could not reach him. I telephoned dispatch and requested her to get the agent on the air. Agent J came on and said that he was not speeding and he could still see the suspect vehicle northbound ahead of him. He was in an unmarked vehicle and had not activated his emergency equipment. If this was the case, then it was not a pursuit, so I authorized him to follow at a distance.

Another agent north of them said that he would wait by the side of the road until he could see them and attempt a vehicle stop. As it happened, the suspect, in a black Nissan SUV, picked up speed passing through one of the Indian villages and blew past the waiting agent. The agent got onto the roadway and activated his red and blues and hit the siren.

Since the suspect was traveling at high speed towards a populated locality in a 4x4 SUV, and had failed to yield to the agent, I told all units to stop pursuing and come to the station to write it up. Due to Covid-19, almost all prosecutions were being declined at the time. Federal Courts were largely closed, so it wasn't worth the potential carnage just to get a smuggling case. We notified the Casa Grande Police Department of the situation as the vehicle entered their city, and then set about the reporting process.

It wasn't thirty minutes later when I heard on the radio that the Casa Grande PD had spiked the vehicle as well as one of their own vehicles and that an unmarked Border Patrol unit was taking over the pursuit down Florence Boulevard in Casa Grande. Needless to say, I was taken aback that the agent whom I had told to stop the pursuit had re-engaged. While my Watch Commander got on the radio to terminate, I telephoned dispatch and again asked her to relay to the agents to stop the pursuit and turn around.

As we were doing this, the Nissan came to a halt in the park and the occupants bailed out. Responding Border Patrol and CGPD units converged and arrested three IAs and the driver, a 27-year-old female USC. We tried to set her up for High-Speed Flight from an Immigration Checkpoint, as well as Alien Smuggling, both felonies. We then called in our Prosecutions Agent several hours early to write it up while our agents processed the rest of the case.

It turned out that the initial reports were incorrect. Rather than fleeing the checkpoint at high speed, the driver had been inspected by the primary agent and released. She further claimed that she never saw the red and blue lights behind her, nor did she hear the siren. I thought this was bullshit, but it wasn't about what I thought; it was all about what her smart-ass legal aid attorney could convince a jury. The lack of a High-Speed Flight case made the smuggling case a turd, since regular alien smuggling was no longer being prosecuted under Covid protocols.

I was not happy, the agents were not happy, and the prosecution guy was definitely not happy. I attempted to explain to Agent J. that he had already been instructed to stop the pursuit, but he did not see it that way. He preferred to define it as two separate pursuits, one which was called off and another that was completely different. He meant well, but that would not have been sufficient had there been chaos and destruction: he would have been in deep trouble.

Luckily, the Casa Grande Police had their chance, and they went hard on her for felony flight, reckless endangerment, and other charges.

Rescue at Dead Man's

I had no idea it would be one of my last days down south as a supervisor for the Casa Grande Border Patrol Station, and as a Border Patrol Agent.

As the "down south" Supervisor, I sat in my Tahoe at the Piss Road, right in the middle of the Tohono O'odham Nation (TON), an Indian Reservation in Southern Arizona. It is about the size of Connecticut and straddles the US-Mexico border. It was still early, only around 9:00 PM, and the boys were working a couple of groups, but it was handled. My practice was to wait a bit before committing myself to any particular calls, so as to maintain awareness of what everyone was doing, and direct air support or transport to them if they needed it. First rule of supervising: give them what they need to do the job. I checked the tracking app on my G-phone, confirming where I thought the agents were working; they were represented on the map by little green dots.

A radio call came in regarding two individuals approaching one of the rescue beacons near Big Fields, or Gu Oidak in the native tongue. Gu Oidak means "big field," but agents all called it Big Fields anyway. On all of the major east-west roads in our area, there were these towers with bright blue strobes on top, cameras pointed down to a button which basically says: if you want help, push this button. It is in English, Spanish, and O'odham, the language of the Native American population of the TON. You didn't have to press the button; just being close to it, would activate a sensor and take your picture. This didn't always work, but when it did, it saved a lot of time. A lot of the beacon activations were cows and other animals.

According to dispatch, two persons, one armed with an AR-15 type rifle, had approached the beacon and activated it. Per policy, every activation needed to be cleared, especially when there was a picture. The Tribal Police were also responding. The Tohono O'odham Police Department (TOPD) was pretty hard-up for personnel, and their response times off-road were usually extended.

"Anyone available to check out the beacon? C37." I asked

the radio. Hopefully, someone was close.

"I'll get it," replied Dave, "C119, 10-13 from Sells." He was one of the more senior guys. He was a good bit closer than I to Big Fields.

"10-4, I'm inbound from Quijotoa, just in case." I paused and then called the station. "863, C37. Did you copy last for the beacon?"

"37, we copy. Will advise TOPD."

While armed individuals were not necessarily anything alarming in rural Arizona, especially close to a village, it is always a good idea to send more than one guy to such a call. Also, I had a long arm with me, which most agents did not. You never know. Innocuous calls can sometimes go dynamic, and dynamic calls often turn out to be nothing.

It was about a 20-minute drive to get to Sells, taking State Route 86 east heading south in Sells, and then 15 minutes west again on Big Fields Road; it would be another 10-20 minutes to get to the beacon. I was tempted to haul ass, just to be close in case something terrible happened, but had to watch out for horses, cattle, deer, and dark-clothed people who could cross, lurch drunkenly into, or be sleeping or dead on the road.

I kept the windows down as I drove off Piss Road onto the highway; FR15 south for a mile, then east on SR 86. It was summer, but a pretty nice night. On 86, the windows had to go up though or I couldn't hear the service radio.

The Quijotoa Trading Post was deserted, it closed at 8 even pre-pandemic. There was very little traffic on 86, but I dared not go too fast for fear of catching a cow. The red-brown ones were especially very hard to see until you got right up on them. My process is to look left and right down the road at the reflectors or the fog line, and if they were broken I would slow down until I knew for sure there wasn't something in the road.

Sells was deserted as well. Usually, the Shell Station had a lot of activity but because of the pandemic, it too closed at 8. So, there was nothing there except a lone coyote looking for some bunnies or garbage to eat. A metaphor for something. I went south on Main Street, passed the Sells Indian Hospital, and turned back west on Big Fields Road. Leaving town, I had to go even slower as Big Fields Road was not really fenced. Frequent groups of cattle forced me to slow down or stop.

"37, 119... TOPD already cleared the call," it was Dave again. "I met up with them before hitting the dirt. It was 10-19."

"OK Dave, I'll meet up with you in a minute. I'm almost there." I still wanted to cut around the beacon. Why would someone with an AR weapon be wandering around in the dark? Drunks? Shootin' at some food? Ripping off the aliens?

I saw headlights coming and, thinking it was Dave, pulled over and rolled down the window. No dice, it was TOPD, and they were moving out smartly; they did not stop to talk. Those poor guys probably had calls stacked up; never a dull moment on the rez. I briefly flipped the red and blues on and off to acknowledge them (it's kind of like waving or nodding but is going out of style).

The next set of lights was Dave. The road was clear for miles in each direction, so we just sat there in the middle of it, each looking down his lane, chatting. He said he had almost made it to the end of the road where it turns to dirt and is called Federal Route 24. The TOPD guys came eastbound from there. They had told him they cut the beacon and had two sets of prints going into town. More importantly, they relayed that the call was an old one from earlier that afternoon. My concern evaporated: the call was old, TOPD cleared it, and the AR-15 guy was long gone.

The real police had requested BP support in case it was immigration-related, and because we had more of a presence on the TON than they did. Imagine an area the size of a small state with only four to six cops working it. Granted, there are only around 20,000 people living in this area, but those cops definitely earned their pay as far as I'm concerned.

Another agent, Frank, showed up. We got along well. Frank, and Dave, are among a core of agents who can always be counted on. It is my great fortune to have always been surrounded by such people in my career. Frank was our union guy, was always solid, and there were none of the adversarial union-vs.-management confrontations at the shift level. We could talk things out like reasonable people. Also, Frank would work down south or at the checkpoint just like everyone else. This was unlike some of the union guys I had worked with in San Diego who used their gig to skate their way through life and were rarely seen anywhere close to an illegal alien. Frank had a box truck and was assigned 4x4 transport.

We cleared the call and commenced shooting the shit for a while. Dave and I had a good rapport. He had previously worked at the Ajo Station, which is CAG's western neighbor. Ajo has more border area than all of the San Diego Sector, and was even more out of control than CAG, with dope and aliens all over the place. After a few years, Dave transferred up to the northern border for a while before coming back south to CAG about the same time as me. Dave is, ahem, outspoken, but I always appreciate that when it comes from real-deal agents.

Before long there was a call for a group further south near a place called Middle Gate Road. Then, a minute later, a 911 call was relayed by the station for two aliens on top of a mountain near Cowlic, AZ, also on the TON. Two agents responded to the 911 call, while only one responded to the group near Middle Gate. Things were getting busier.

"Could you guys help out with the group, and I'll head towards the 911 stuff?" I asked. If it was a good call, the 911 thing might need some level of coordination with air or medical assets. Some were just lost aliens who wanted a ride and a shoulder to cry on; others were in serious trouble, especially in the summer months, like now.

"Right on."

We all took off back east to Sells, turning south on Main Street and then Federal Route 19. Then westbound on FR20, south on FR31, to Cowlic, FR12, and dirt. It would take 30 minutes or more to get anywhere close to the calls, but we were the only ones on the east side, plus the two ATV agents responding to the 911 call who were already there. Some nights were like this the whole time, driving hither and yon, but never getting anywhere in time to make a difference.

Cory and Lance were two of the hardest working agents in the Border Patrol as far as I am concerned; these guys and a couple more accounted for most of the mountain apprehensions on shift. Giving them ATVs just got them to the mountains more quickly. The 911 call, after I inputted the coordinates into my GPS, showed it almost at the top of Devil's Peak in the Alvarez Mountains. I hit dirt and turned south on Mule Deer, one of the crappier of the washed-out dirt roads. I made contact with the agents as they were dismounting and getting ready to climb up. It is only another 900-1000 feet up from the road, but there are not exactly escalators to get you up there. The washes and crevices have all kinds of spiky, nasty cactus and brush; there is uncertain footing on the rocks and deadfall. And it's still hot in the ravines, especially when you're humping straight uphill with body armor, belt gear, and Camelback.

As I turned east into a wide cul-de-sac road where the mountains formed a "C," I could see the flashlights of the two guys heading up to Dead Man's off to the south. The space between them was opening up, even as I watched. The guy falling behind would be Cory, who was a little older and wore his vest; Lance was younger, lighter, and did not wear his vest; he was really moving up the hill. I found where their ATVs were parked and turned my Tahoe around before shutting it down, in case there were a bunch of rides parked here later. I didn't want to be blocking the road or have to back out when surrounded by other vehicles.

Lance made it up to the caller, and I could see her cell phone light moving back and forth as his light got closer to hers. She was pretty excited but okay, and able to take him to her traveling companion, a middle-aged overweight guy who was in and out of semi-consciousness. I could hear her chirping away in the background as he passed on the information via handheld. Lance called out the particulars and commenced hydrating the guy with the extra water he had brought.

I guzzled water while putting on gloves, Camelback, and a hat. Another vehicle arrived on the scene with a BORSTAR supervisor. They had heard the call and he was responding with a team of three guys in a side-by-side (basically a four-person ATV or dune buggy). That was great, now I could leave all of the coordinating to him and get up the hill with my guys. He said he would stay on the radio at the bottom, and his guys would be along shortly. Even better, with an agent presence here at the vehicles, I could leave my M-4 locked up in the rack so I could get uphill quicker. I told him my plan and shoved off.

About 20 minutes later, the BORSTAR guys, much younger and in much better shape than my 52-year-old ass, passed me in their side-by-side heading to the base of the mountains. When I got there, I saw their vehicle parked and headed up from there. As I huffed and puffed my way up, I had to turn back a couple of times and wrap around some of the worst rock faces and inclines. My arthritic knees, back, and shoulder reminded me why climbing mountains was no longer my primary job.

It took me a while to get up there, but upon meeting up with the others, I saw the BORSTAR agents had the middle-aged male stuck with an IV and fully conscious. One of them had a look at me and offered me a pouch of "Liquid IV," which was gratefully accepted. It had me feeling pretty good after about 5 minutes; that stuff is gold out in the desert.

Looking at the alien on the ground, he was pretty round to be humping up the mountains. How he thought he could do it in his condition was beyond me, but I guess plenty of them had made it over the years. Of course, plenty of them had left their bones in the dirt picked clean by buzzards, too. This guy had a large surgical scar over his abdomen, and several recent-looking healed bullet wounds as well. He was telling the BORSTAR guys that he got shot up as a taxi driver in Guatemala City.

For the next few hours, we were on the radio with the BORSTAR guy down the hill and Dispatch, who was trying to get us an air unit to lift the guy off the mountain. While the alien was able to talk, he was definitely not going to be walking off the hill. For that matter, neither was the female. Both were at the end of their respective ropes, although the male was in worse shape. The female also had an IV inserted, and kind of zoned out while they got some fluids into her.

There was one Blackhawk in the air as well as another Omaha (CBP Helicopter), but neither of them had long-line extraction capability. There was an ongoing conversation on the radio regarding the ETA of a DPS Ranger unit. Ranger-1 was a Search and Rescue (SAR) bird with a flight medic and long-line capability. They were far away and it was going to be a bit of a wait to wake up the crew members and activate them for an op. Lance, Cory, the BORSTAR guys, and I all hung around chatting while we waited, really hoping it would not be necessary to carry these people off the mountain. It is hard going uphill, but the potential for injury increases when you are moving downhill. Gravity and friction will ruin you. When assisting or carrying others, you can imagine the possibilities. While all of us were trained in this and had done so before, nobody relished another stretcher carry without a stretcher.

Dave called me on the radio; he was going to go north with the three they had apprehended near the District Fence Line/Middle Gate area. Frank called too; he volunteered to hang around for transport if we needed it.

"Never mind, you can head back in, sir," I told him. "We might be up here all night until they can get a bird in. " It was already late, and there was no reason for anyone else to wait around when the oncoming shift was southbound already. I then called the station to make sure oncoming had agents going to the hospital to sit on these aliens. "Two hospital watches, one male one female, and we'll try to make it to Sells."

The DPS guys ended up coming in around 3 AM in the morning. It was pretty cool watching another extraction like that. Some of the ones I had seen years before were not nearly so technical and methodical. The little boy in me never got tired of watching the hovering helicopter lowering the medic, who then hooked up the aliens, one after the other, and then went back up herself. The bird lifted out the female alien first and dropped her off with the BORSTAR supervisor at the bottom of the mountain, then they came back for the male. He was then flown all the way to Chandler Regional Hospital.

From Lance: "That is... how I remember it. From what I saw when I first got up there, the male was unresponsive and when I first got to him, I thought he had already passed away. I checked for a pulse and breathing... and then immediately started cooling him down with extra water, because I thought he was heat-stroking out. It took quite a while of me pouring water on him, and giving him the occasional shake, to get him to respond. I think a lot of it was him just being beyond exhausted. I still can't believe those two chunks thought the mountains were a good route in the summer."

Lance is a prolific agent, as are many of the guys in this book. He remembers another rescue, on another day: "If you need a few more good rescues... I can remember a few good ones. Jason and I stumbled into a scout on the top of the mesquite mountains in the summer, after we climbed the mountain on a whim. The guy we found ended up having a broken femur and it was almost a compound fracture. The terrain was so bad, we had to take turns fireman-style carrying him to a landing zone that the third helicopter coming in finally managed to find. I can still remember his screams every time we would lose footing and stumble with him on top of our shoulders."

Back to Dead Man's - once the aliens were gone, we slowly filed down the mountain. I walked last, several paces behind the others so that if I fell they wouldn't get hurt, too. A painful lesson learned long ago. Lance and the BORSTAR guys, one of which was at least as old as me, scampered down with aplomb. Cory and I got down right before sunup, had a snack, and then made the 100-mile journey back to the station.

Though I still had a couple of months before I actually retired, the crush of huge groups of "quitters," the lack of supervisors, and shuffling assignments meant there would only be a couple of "down south" nights left. What Dave, Frank, Cory, Lance, and the BORSTAR guys did that night embodied all that I love about the Border patrol. They are all first-class agents and I was happy to be out there with them.

There are seldom any dramatic shootouts with desperate bandits and not a ton of exciting car chases. Border Patrol work is a grind. Many of our arrests are rescues of one sort or another, but most are pretty routine and involve nothing more than running around in the desert or mountains before tracking out a group, gathering them up, and walking them out. Most of our felony arrests are not prosecuted or prosecuted to the least possible extent. It is dirty, sweaty, and not terribly rewarding work; the money is good but the job is pretty hopeless, so it is sometimes hard to appreciate how cool it is just to do the job. That being said, the agents reminded me every day.

For every alien we get, another one gets by. For every ten that get away, only a few get counted... from those ten, you probably have at least two or three career criminal aliens who have left a trail of victims, known and unknown. They will likely leave many more. Those are the ones you might read about later.

Rescue North of the Checkpoint

A phenomenal effort happened a couple of summers ago. A few agents were sweltering at the FR15 Checkpoint in the 110-plus degree heat when a motorist heading south stopped and addressed them. The driver reported that there were a couple of people trying to flag down traffic about a mile north of the point. The Supervisor had the point closed and sent his three agents to investigate.

Dan, Scott, and Jeff responded. Dan was a certified EMT. They made contact with the two subjects who reported that they had left others on the other side of the mountain to the east of them. Dan and Scott grabbed their Camelbacks and headed that way on foot, while Jeff stayed with the first two aliens. About a mile or so into it, they arrived at the location. Dan evaluated a female who was suffering from heat exhaustion. She had stopped perspiring and her skin was cool and clammy. This is an extremely dangerous situation for anyone. The agents knew from experience that a life flight helicopter would not land on an unpaved surface; they called for additional medical support to meet them on the road.

Dan and Scott took turns carrying this woman over broken ground in the extreme heat for over a mile back to the road, having to take frequent breaks to hydrate the alien as well as themselves. After a fashion, they made it back to where their partner Jeff, and an ambulance, were waiting.

Dan tells the story:

"It was late summer, but still ridiculously hot out. It was 115 that day. I spent the day down on the border road investigating tire and foot sign on the border road as I suspected someone was taking advantage of the construction traffic on the border road to smuggle narcotics.

"I was on my way north and just passed through the checkpoint when a DISRUPT agent [Jeff-author] got on the radio to say that he had encountered some illegal aliens about a mile north of the checkpoint. These aliens had relayed to him that they had left some people behind in the bushes and a woman from the group had passed out. I was already going to go over my 10-hour shift by the time I off-loaded my gear, fueled the truck and turned it in, but I knew that there wasn't an EMT closer than me. In fact, it was a good bet that there wouldn't another EMT within a 45-minute response time (a fact we deal with given our large area of operation and the small number of agents). So, I pulled over to help.

"The DISRUPT agent relayed to me that the aliens had said the woman in distress was "just over there" pointing to the southeast. Since my patient was supposedly very close, and the cause of her losing consciousness was most likely caused by heat stress and dehydration, I opted to bring my oxygen/IV therapy bag. This meant that I would leave behind my Camelbak which I normally use to stay hydrated myself when I'm out of the truck. I grabbed two 20oz water bottles and shoved one in each of my cargo pockets. I also grabbed two electrolyte powder packets and stuffed them in my pocket as well. I then set out southeast to look for persons who had been left behind. Agents Scott and JB were already searching when I got to the area." Dan then linked up with them, and as they continued the search, two other agents joined the effort, K and JT.

"The terrain was rocky, hard pack [crusty, dry dirt from being baked in the sun-Author] with your regular mix of creosote bushes, ocotillo, palo verde, and mesquites. The area was crisscrossed with numerous steep and deep wadis. We continued southeast as the DISRUPT agent kept trying to give us more information from the aliens he had in custody back at the road. We zig-zagged all over the area looking for any sign of the distressed aliens. I eventually decided that they were probably further east from our current position." Dan turned hard east, leaving JB, K, and JT to continue searching the washes.

"As I headed east, Scott notified us that he had found the group. I asked him where he was and he said he was in the bowl of the Slate Mountains due east of me (the direction I was traveling). I picked up the pace and asked him for his exact position. In response, he just shouted and I could hear he was off to my right front (east and a little south). There appeared to be a deep wadi between us, so I navigated my way down into it and up the other side. Once on the other side, I continued east. After a minute or two, I got a visual of Scott only to realize that the wadi had taken a hard turn and he was in fact on the same side that I had started on. So, I had to find a way back down into the wadi and across to the other side again. Scott was carrying the woman on his shoulders in a fireman's carry and two other individuals were following him on foot. He began to look for a way to get to me, but I instructed him to remain on that side and I would move to him." Dan put out a radio call that he had found Scott with the patient and gave the GPS location so that the other agents in the area could find them. "I then made my way down into the wadi and up the other side. I had to backtrack a bit to find a place that was safe to traverse.

"When I got to Scott, he put the woman down and I began my patient assessment. She was conscious and alert, but her responses to my questions were slow and her responses weren't appropriate. Her skin was warm and dry to the touch. This was a very bad sign given how hot it was. She also had a hard time sitting up straight. Her body would kind of flop around. The other two individuals who were traveling with her were able to give me some basic biographical information on her, an estimate about how long they had been in the desert, and the last time she had drunk water."

While interviewing the aliens, Dan pulled the two water bottles out of his pockets and mixed in the electrolyte powder. He gave one bottle to the woman and the other to her companions. Initially, the woman tried to drink the contents of the bottle without opening it first.

"I opened the bottle for her and she drank some. I continued my assessment. Her breathing was rapid and shallow, her heart rate was weak and fast. As part of my assessment, I would have gotten her blood oxygen level and heart rate, but I can't recall what they were. By this time JB, K, and JT had shown up. Now my patient began to vomit up the electrolyte drink she had just consumed. This was another really bad sign."

JT had taken over communications, letting dispatch know what was going on. The agents knew this lady needed help, and fast. She was tiny and severely dehydrated.

Dan continues: "I had my IV bag with me and could have given her fluids, but it was getting dark soon and I was never super confident in my IV abilities. I figured that her best chance was just to move her to the road as quickly as possible and pass her off to more experienced EMS personnel who would have better equipment and would be in a better environment than in the dirt on the side of a mountain."

While reassuring his patient, Dan asked JT to request an ambulance to meet them on the road, and a "life flight" helicopter (the EMS helicopter company operating in our area won't land off the pavement). "Looking at my GPS we appeared to be about 1.5 kilometers from the road. I asked Agent K to take care of my medical bag if possible, otherwise, I was going to leave it."

"At this time I had been an EMT for years and had taught TCCC (Tactical Combat Casualty Care) to most of the agents at the station. I was an expert compared to everyone else on the scene, but even as such, I was out of practice. The Border Patrol as a whole doesn't put a premium on training (either initial training or continuing training). I knew that the best way to carry this woman would be a technique called 'the backpack.' This technique requires putting the patient's arms over your shoulders like the straps of a backpack. To do the technique correctly you need to make sure the patient is high up on your back so that your shoulders are in their armpits. You're also supposed to crisscross their arms on your chest and grab onto their wrists."

"Well, I asked the agents there to help get her onto my back so I could start moving her to the road. Scott offered to carry her, but I declined. He had been huffing and puffing pretty hard when he carried her before. He was also smaller than me and I felt a strong sense of duty to do it myself since I was the EMT. So, I took a knee and they draped her on my back. I took her wrists (forgetting to cross her arms) and took off at a brisk pace northwest. I just walked a general line and the agents with me would occasionally point slightly left or right to adjust my course. Every so often I would have to pause and ask Scott to help push her back up high on my back (that wouldn't have happened if I had remembered to cross her arms)."

After a few minutes, another agent, Mark, showed up in a four-door pickup truck after plowing through the desert off-road and offered to drive the agents and aliens the rest of the way out. Dan: "I climbed in and pulled her in behind me. Scott then climbed in last. I had my back to the door, she was sitting sideways between us, and Scott had his back to the other door facing us. Mark started driving us out over the rough terrain. The woman kept slumping over and began to vomit again. At that time, I was trying to keep her upright, but leaned forward enough to let the vomit fall out and keep her airway open."

After driving for a few minutes, Mark came to the conclusion that it was no longer prudent to continue in the truck. In the waning light, he kept coming to wadi after wadi and wasn't able to find a path through. Scott and Dan got out of the truck, put the woman on Dan's back once more, and started walking.

"Thankfully, Mark had pointed out the direction to the road," Dan says. "Having been in the back of the truck was disorienting and I wasn't immediately sure of which way to go otherwise. So, we headed off. I had to cross several more deep and steep wadis on the way. I'm not a religious man, but before entering a couple of the wadis I made a split-second plea to any higher power that might be listening to give me a hand. I was terrified to fall as it would have been disastrous for both myself and my patient. The wadis were so steep that while going down, only the heels of my boots were in contact with the ground. And going up the other side, only the toes and part of the ball of my boots were touching the side of the wadi. Each time I rose out the other side, I was grateful to have made it. I was so glad that I was wearing my Salomon Forces Quest 4D boots that day. They were the best boots I had found for hiking in the mountains.

"As we finally approached the road, the sun had dipped behind the horizon and twilight was setting in. We were headed to a spot between the checkpoint and where the initial group was encountered. By this time, there were several vehicles at the initial encounter with their red and blue emergency lights on. We notified dispatch that we were coming out to the road and they told us the ambulance was on the scene."

The agents then watched as an ambulance drove by them and went to where the emergency lights were, up the road. "We called on the radio to have them come back. They turned around and drove past us the other way. We called again and this time they drove back to the other emergency vehicles."

Around this time, another agent showed up and walked with them the last hundred yards or so to the road. Since the ambulance had gone to the wrong location again, he offered to give the whole group a ride to the group of Border Patrol vehicles, where the ambulance had gone.

Dan: "I placed the woman in the back of his Suburban and climbed in with her. We started to drive north to where the other vehicles were, and the ambulance once again passed us southbound. Someone, somehow, was able to get them to stop. We got out and started to pull the woman out to carry her the last 30 yards or so to the ambulance. This entire time she had been in an altered state of consciousness. Not unconscious, but not really alert either. Suddenly she looked into my eyes and a look of terror came over her. She grabbed onto the rifle rack between the front seats of the vehicle and would not let go. I tried to calm her down and reassure her that I was going to help her, but she wouldn't let go. I had to pry her hands off the rifle rack and ended up carrying her to the ambulance... Thank God she was so tiny."

Once the patient was loaded in the ambulance, dispatch was called to get the status of the life flight helicopter. It turned out that there was a new dispatcher, and after hearing that the ambulance was on the scene, she took it upon herself to cancel the helicopter. Such things are not okay in emergency services. The agents were exhausted and exasperated at this point after the Benny Hill-like fiasco with the ambulance.

Dan continues: "I told her that the ambulance was going to try to stabilize the patient, but we needed the helicopter for

273

transport. It took a little convincing and I had to say some 'magic words' to get the helo airborne again."

A section of the two-lane road was blocked off for the helo to land on.

"I checked on the patient and the ambulance EMS personnel let me know that her body temperature was 107. They had placed a bag of ice on her groin and started an IV to try to rehydrate her and lower her temperature.

Finally, the life flight arrived and took her to the hospital.

Dan concludes: "That was the end of my interaction with the patient. I don't know what hospital she went to or what her treatment was. I heard from the Watch Commander that she survived. That's all I know."

All of the agents involved did a great job. For their actions that day, both Dan and Scott were written up for awards based on the recommendations of some of the other agents present. It should be noted that similar efforts are made by your Border Patrol Agents regularly and routinely all year around. These feats generally go unrecognized.

On a side note, this all happened about 6 months or so into the COVID scare. In fact, the EMS workers on the ambulance were wearing full respirators. Meanwhile, Dan and Scott had just carried this woman through the desert while she vomited on them. They both knew full well that they were putting themselves at risk, but guys like that have always answered the call, and always will.

Super Agents and Dirty Agents

It may seem to the reader that almost every agent in these stories is some kind of cool-guy cowboy or something. Nothing could be further from the truth. What makes Border Patrol Agents so special, to me, is that they are regular guys and gals that do incredible things. It happens all the time.

An agent from the CAG Station found himself chasing a group up the side of a steep hill, almost a mountain. He pushed himself to the limit, until he started getting chest pains. At that point, being so close to the International Boundary and possibly being in distress himself, he called it out on the radio. Amongst Border Patrol Agents, this is not done lightly.

There were a couple other agents out on foot nearby who were also trying to apprehend the group that heard his call and responded to his GPS coordinates. One of them was an EMT. As they evaluated the agent with the chest pains, the EMT called for life flight or further medical assistance from EMS. While he monitored the agent, his partner ran back down the hill to the vehicle to get the EMT agent's medical bag, then ran back up with it. About a mile each way.

It turned out not to be a heart attack, but such a performance should not go unnoticed. We have a whole BORSTAR unit of highly fit agents who are trained EMTs and spend all of their time training for such a thing. None of them were available at that time. The "regular" agents, who were on scene when needed, took care of business.

On one dark night, there were two agents, out with a Mil-cam (a thermal night-vision device), that had spotted a group of approximately 20 IAs as the aliens dropped into a wash near a place called Little Baghdad. The agents laid in at a likely spot behind some cover and waited for the group to emerge. After a time, a small group of individuals carrying large square backpacks emerged from the wash. They were heading in the direction of the agents. When the group was close, the agents broke cover and announced themselves, issuing commands to halt and give up.

In response, the suspects in front dropped to the ground, while the subjects in the rear raised rifles and opened fire on the agents, keeping it up for a long time. The pinned agents remained in position while calling for help from anyone else in the area via handheld radios. Members of the elite Border Patrol Tactical Team, BORTAC, were immediately requested but were hours away either at home or at Sector Headquarters. The two "regular" agents, on their own, held their ground until more line agents responded and the shooters retreated.

Every agent mentioned above is considered a "line" agent; none are on any Special Units like BORSTAR or BORTAC. They do not spend their days studying maps and intelligence reports or doing cross-fit or rucking. They go out every day and greet each situation as it unfolds, whatever that means at that time.

There is a flip side to this coin, another type of "dirt" to look at. These are dirty agents. Agents have been arrested selling sensor maps to the cartels, running loads of dope north in department patrol vehicles, and more.

One supervisor at the Tucson Station was caught selling reports of apprehension or seizure to the cartels, who presumably would use these reports to cross-check against their own smugglers' reports of loads that had been seized. It doesn't take much imagination to envision what happened to smugglers caught by their bosses in a lie.

Another agent, a BPA Ortiz, rode with me as my trainee for a short time at El Cajon. While some reports at the time spoke of him in favorable terms, it was my opinion at the time that he was on the verge of "settling in," or becoming a slug. He seemed disinterested in the job. Apparently, he had been very interested: He and his brother were partners in a scheme to smuggle OTMs into the United States. Ortiz's brother's phone had been tapped by law enforcement due to gang activity in North San Diego County, leading authorities to BPA Ortiz. Former BPA Ortiz turned out to be an illegal alien, and was convicted, and sent to prison for his crimes. How an illegal alien somehow becomes a Border Patrol Agent is beyond me, but clearly, the system failed in this case.

At the Sonoita Station, the lead Union Steward was caught on a DPS patrol vehicle's dash cam as he took seized narcotics from one Department vehicle and placed them into his own, apparently intent on selling them to his own contacts. He admitted to the crime, was prosecuted, and convicted.

At the El Cajon Station, it was well-known that an agent who had been caught loading duffel bags of narcotics into his marked Border Patrol transport van, on duty, and convicted for the crime, was back working for the cartels as a scout after his release from prison years later.

When caught, dirty agents are likely to face prison. Every agent knows that if he or she succumbs to the temptations of the criminal lifestyle, they can and will be prosecuted to the fullest extent of the law, far and away more vigorously than smugglers or other criminals. The badge is worn over the heart for a reason: it is a symbol of public trust, the betrayal of which should be harshly dealt with. Why such a huge risk, for what seems like pennies on the dollar compared to a successful career, is beyond comprehension for most normal people.

But that is a subject for a different sort of book. There will always be criminals, slugs, and scammers in every profession. The USBP is no less vulnerable to this. There are long periods of attrition followed by frantic spasms of poorly executed hiring, according to whatever the prevailing attitudes towards law enforcement happen to be at the time.

My purpose here has been to highlight a few instances of Border Patrol Agents at work.

Why would anyone sign up for this job, which is simultaneously dangerous, fun, heartbreaking, and hopeless? Why would anyone keep doing it for twenty or thirty years? I suspect the answers are as varied as in any other law enforcement organization. Patriotism is one, though this idealism must be tempered with cynicism, the knowledge that Uncle Sam will never love you back. As jobs go, the Border Patrol is a pretty good one. For the mercenaries, the pay and benefits are excellent, but with the right education and experience, you can do better in the private sector. There is camaraderie and purpose in trying to prevent illegal aliens from entering without permission, but frustration and anger in that half the ones you catch are then released into the interior.

The years 2020 to 2022 have been a disaster at the border. Agents who had planned on working until mandatory retirement (Federal Agents must retire at age 57 unless given special permission to continue) are retiring as soon as they become eligible. Some are just resigning, in frustration and disillusionment. The ones left behind are keeping their heads down and trying to make it through.

Marijuana may be largely decriminalized in many states, but opiates such as fentanyl are more easily smuggled and far more profitable than simple weed. Human trafficking, or (as it is also known) slavery, is on the rise. Unlike drugs, humans can be bought and sold repeatedly; using drugs, they can be made more compliant by traffickers. This is one of the most underreported tragedies of the open border crisis currently underway.

Then there is the terrorist threat. Many laugh it off, as has been the case since before 9/11. In the flood of illegal aliens coming across, most of whom are not being apprehended, there will inevitably be terrorists. It only takes a few. The mass migration from North Africa and the Middle East into Europe after the Arab Spring is instructive in this regard - see the book *America's Covert Border War* by Todd Bensman.

The immigration system is not broken; it is largely ignored by those tasked with administering it. All of the necessary laws are in place, but they need to be enforced. That goes for drug smuggling as well.

V. The Way Forward

The Way Forward-The Line Agents' Views

What follows are comments from current and former agents regarding where the Border Patrol is going wrong, where it is going right, and what can be done to make it better. It doesn't take a genius. Humans respond to incentive and disincentive: prosecute the smugglers and the criminals and immediately deport the illegal aliens. Follow the actual law, instead of constantly re-defining what the words mean to satisfy your favorite ethnocentric special interest groups. If you don't like it, change the law; if you can't, you can't. Sadly, none of these things are under the control of the US Border Patrol.

"From my perspective, the Border Patrol is failing their mission in many areas for several reasons. Many of those reasons could be addressed quickly and some are probably far more complex than I view them."

"I think the most obvious and difficult-to-swallow problem is the lack of prosecution of the criminals we catch and the unwillingness to enforce the laws on the books. It is demoralizing for agents to work hard to catch a case, do the effort to present their case, and then have it declined over and over for what seems to be ridiculous reasons. The lack of punishment for the crimes we enforce encourages other individuals to commit the same crime again [as well as] repeat offenders. It's sad hearing guys that you respect say that they avoid vehicle loads or dope cases because they know it will be declined. It's understandable at the same time after you experience it yourself." The last comments refer to agents who do not like pulling over obvious load vehicles, or if at the checkpoint, do not question the occupants of vehicles at all. Some agents will go so far as to intentionally not go to the right place to interdict foot traffic, or "take the long way around" to avoid becoming involved in what might become a criminal case. While such incidents are not featured in this book, they are common knowledge within the ranks of the Border Patrol. There are plenty of occasions where agents go to the wrong place or do the wrong thing honestly with the best of intentions. But this is not always the case and when it gets noticed, it is very hard to shake off being labeled a slug.

Unfortunately, one of the first things you hear in the Border Patrol Academy is the saying "You will never get in trouble for not doing your job." While not always true, it's true enough. The more demoralized a failing agency, the more common this phenomenon becomes. In the last year, there has been a concerted push to get agents out of the field, performing processing, transporting, detention, and housekeeping tasks at the expense of enforcement. It has been deliberate and ongoing. This does not bode well for the nation, border communities, or the Border Patrol. Again, this is beyond the control of those that run the agency but it sure would be nice if someone spoke up publicly more than every once in a while. Since the dismantling of immigration enforcement with the new administration, millions of aliens have poured in. The numbers are always changing, but remember the real numbers are going to be way in excess of anything officially stated.

"Tactically, I think the Border Patrol is not good at collecting information from their line agents. I think too often people making decisions on asset deployment and ops are decided by people who are out of touch and uninformed or misinformed. For instance, the IFT towers [static day/night cameras]... had so much potential, but several were poorly placed... " says one experienced agent. "Any

SST agent would have told them that. The same goes for [MSC] truck deployments. I think command spends too much time looking at maps and looking to cover areas with a supposed view shed generator [a computer program used to determine what locations a camera or scope can 'see' into] and not enough time asking agents what current trends are and how to work them. [Recently, we] told command about a dozen or more groups of 20-30 [that] we cut in a small area up north (Pinal/Pima County, Arizona) and nothing has been done for weeks. That sort of find should warrant a response with shifting assets around within a few days. The word is that [an MSC] truck will go up for an op many weeks if not a month later. That is way too late."

"I also think the Border Patrol as a whole is very bad at pushing good press and highlighting our need for help. The Border Patrol could probably push positive stories harder but what runs on TV is beyond their control. We are all bad at this. Last night alone I cut probably 40-50 bodies that were fresh and had not been worked, and none of us there called it in since we were already busy with a group of 14. If we all called it all in and pushed the numbers up I think someone would have to listen. Your excerpt from your book was spot on that few are detected and even fewer apprehended."

"I love the job and the agency but it is certainly frustrating seeing us miss the mark consistently."

"I feel we aren't failing but our elected officials are failing us. We abide by a constitution that has three branches of government. When a law is passed and the judicial upholds said law, then all branches abide by the law. Well, that's how it should be. How can Congress pass laws, i.e., IRCA [Immigration Reform and Control Act 1986], and then the executive just tells us that we can't enforce said law? Allow us to do our job and deport these people. As it stands today under the Biden administration, we are more Ubers than Federal Law Enforcement Officers. Plain and simple, allow us to do our job. When we are allowed to do our job, we do it well. Hell, we are so good [President] Kennedy sent Border Patrol Agents (Inspectors) to escort the black children who were going to white schools during desegregation. That's how good we are. No more allowing everyone to come in with no consequence."

"We just run around catching what we can with what we have. Everything and everyone else goes around us."

One suggestion floated is a mobilization of the National Guard, backed up with regular military forces, under a cadre of experienced Border Patrol Agents. A certain number of experienced agents accompany each unit on its patrols providing arrest authority with confirmed illegal crossings. The military provides the bulk of the field assets, along with transport, escort, and detention of the apprehended violators. A cadre of experienced Border Patrol and CBP leaders is embedded at each level of command along with prosecutors and HSI Agents for investigatory purposes. Many senior military officers would probably get the vapors at the thought of their soldiers patrolling the border of the United States under arms, but that is what the situation calls for in my opinion. There would be few if any, shootouts with cartel operators who would have to find another way. If I am wrong, well, I would bet on the United States military every time in a tactical environment. Look at what is happening in Texas without much help from the feds. Our National Guard troops are calm, competent, confident professionals that are more than up to the task of defending their country from criminals and drug smugglers. They can be just as compassionate and professional with the "regular" illegal aliens as any NGO worker.

Matt - The Way Forward

Matt is a former Special Forces soldier who joined the Border Patrol in 1998. He had a background in such things as establishing rapport, training, and leading members of indigenous foreign personnel in combat long before putting on a badge. With twenty-plus years of experience as a Border Patrol Agent/Supervisory Border Patrol Agent, he has a perspective on training that I think would be beneficial to the Border Patrol.

I spent several hours with Matt intending to get some of his stories of twenty years patrolling the border from the Casa Grande

Station. We ended up talking about training, specifically training for Border Patrol leaders. It is clearly something that fires Matt up, as we have had the same conversation many times before while we were still working together.

Matt came to the Casa Grande Station in January 1999. There was a short period of acclimatization to learn the area and the job before the traffic took off in the early 2000s. With the construction of the border fencing in both El Paso and San Diego, and the expansion of the agency in general to man the fencing, alien and narcotics traffic moved away from the large cities and into the mountain and desert wilderness.

"There were so many bodies," he says of the early 2000s, "FTYs, pursuits, rip crews..." It was overwhelming. "Agents were just getting burned out..." Between the FTYs, pursuits, multiple groups, and dope, "twelve-hour days were normal. At least once a week, on a 16–18-hour day... one guy, 'Repo Joe,' would get 4 or 5 vehicle loads a day and process them. The agents were amazing. I could go on for days [about] all the incredible work they did, all the extra effort despite insurmountable odds. For a very long time, Casa Grande averaged 4-5 apprehensions per agent per day. The station was much smaller and so was the number of agents on shift. The agents would go to extremes to help each other."

Matt continues, "I loved when there was a traffic jam on the freeway and all the vehicles backed up..." Agents would drive along the shoulder picking out the loads and arrest the bodies. They would leave the vehicles there; for a time, a ruling by the 9th Circuit Court (as interpreted by the Border Patrol) forbade the seizure of vehicles used for alien smuggling.

"I had this trainee once who had experience as a Sheriff's Deputy somewhere back east. I took him out to Queen's Well one night; we had seven bail-outs that night." That trainee ended up quitting. This job is not for everyone.

"You had these rip crews, led by smugglers, who knew where and when the dope was coming. They would take out a separate crew to steal the drugs from the people who had carried them across the border." They would then resell the "ripped" drugs to their own contacts in the U.S. Ideally, untraced by their cartel bosses back in Mexico.

"You have these backpackers (drug mules) out in the desert, and they're getting ripped off in the middle of the night on the U.S. side by somebody with guns," says Matt, "Rip crews who have the benefit of not having to do all the coordination of getting people up into different areas of the border, deciding who's going to smuggle who... they just grab them [or their dope] once they're here!"

There were other rip crews operating "especially on I-10; crews driving down the highway, see a load, and steal the bodies. Just pull up to the load vehicle driving down the highway and point a gun at them." The hapless aliens would be kidnapped at gunpoint, taken to a stash house somewhere, and forced to contact their families to arrange ransom. Some of the assailants "acted as law enforcement..." One off-duty agent "got pulled over by someone who was acting as a cop. He [the impostor] was looking for bodies."

Just such a thing was going on where I was at that time, working out of the Tucson Station. A Ford F150, made up to resemble an unmarked Border Patrol K9 vehicle, would pull people over in the Sahuarita area. It was reported, and passed on at musters, but I never heard any word of the perpetrator(s) being caught.

Matt continues: "[We] had management... I'm not speaking bad about these people; it [the chaos and disorganization] reflects badly on them because the Border Patrol does not train them. That causes a huge lack of synergy. We all make mistakes individually. I've made lots of them. By lack of sound managerial training, the Patrol ultimately brings big problems on themselves."

As the Casa Grande Station filled up with apprehended aliens, a solution was implemented known as the BSI (Border Safety Initiative). Part of this solution placed a square of cyclone fencing, such as those used at construction sites, in the desert near San Miguel, Arizona, on the Tohono O'odham Nation. A PA with a shotgun was assigned to guard it. Field agents would drop off their bodies with field processing forms and take off to go catch more. There were not enough vans to transport the aliens north to the station, so buses were contracted to pick up forty or fifty at a time and take them to sector headquarters all the way in Tucson.

"It just sits on the ground," says Matt. "You would have 100-200 bodies in there and buses would come," to pick some up. There was really no system; some bodies would be there for a few hours, some for days. "Totally unsafe."

The aliens in the cage could have picked it up and walked it back to Mexico if they wanted to. It just sat there, and so did they. There were escapes, known and unknown... The single agent posted there would not have been able to pursue them anyway. Nearby agents would have been busy with other traffic. It was a mess. When the roll was called, if no one answered up to a name, then the Field Processing Form was thrown away. Papers got lost; blown away in the wind. Aliens who gave fake names would forget what names they gave and not answer up to roll...

Word got out. "A reporter went down and got a picture of a little kid in the cage... they didn't stop it; they just put some tarps out." Spread over the corners of the cyclone fencing, the tarps at least provided some shade. Some heavy plastic platforms, somewhat resembling upside-down coffins, provided a way to lay down off of the ground. When there was room to lay down.

When money was allocated for a processing facility, agents thought they would be allowed to use the Customs facility in Sells, which made a lot of sense. The agents had already been using the facility for a couple of years to transfer aliens to the buses for further transport to Tucson for processing. It was already built; there was room to expand and facilitate buses coming in and out. It is right off of State Route 86, on the way between Tucson and Ajo. Perfect location for efficiently processing and prepping aliens for transport out. But it was not to be.

"Even worse, it had been explained to me how extremely difficult it was to work out a deal with the TON Government to get the land in San Miguel. By then, we were already restructured after

9/11 to be under the same command as Customs, aka U.S. Customs and Border Protection. The land and facilities in Sells being used by Customs were already available to us. Agents working the border south of Sells had to drive right past the Customs facility going to and from their assignment anyway, so strategically, it was a great location."

"They decided no, we'll build it (and a lot of agent camps all along the Mexican border) in San Miguel because it looks good on a map," Matt told me. "We spent crazy millions." It was built near the site of the old BSI in San Miguel. They renamed it LEC for Law Enforcement Center. It was basically a processing facility, with an office for the TOPD officers to use.

With this set-up, an agent who caught a group near Sells had to get them twenty-five miles south to the LEC and then go right back through Sells again at the end of their shift. The buses coming from Tucson to get the groups then had to do an extra 50-mile round trip from Sells to pick up and take them to Tucson. You add this up over the course of a year or even a month, and its insane amounts of money and man hours, and for what? As we say in Wisconsin: "Now help me understand this..."

I never had access to senior-level managers back then. I suspected that the LEC was placed down on the border because it looks good on a map. I can hear it now, "See, we have a presence in San Miguel now! Right on the border."

The logic of Border Patrol management at the time was to keep lots of agents right on the border to deter illegals from even trying to enter the area. A huge flaw in that logic was failing to realize how insanely difficult and self-defeating it is to attempt border management along 45 miles of border that is 100 miles from the Casa Grande station. There are no paved or even gravel roads in that area and it is many miles of very rough jeep trails to get to 40 of those 45 miles. When an agent starts the [10-hour] shift, it can take them up to 3 hours to get to these areas.

Meanwhile, the bodies kept coming.

Another feature of the early 2000s at the Casa Grande

Station was detailers. These are agents sent to the "hot spots" from sectors that are not so busy. While there are advantages to this, if the detailers are not properly used, it can also lead to a lot of problems. Detailed agents [being from other stations, sectors, and states] get lost easily in the field. They may have been mandated, at very short notice, to go out of state for a 30 or 45-day detail. These guys are not as motivated to help out as it may seem on paper. Typically, the best use of detailed agents is for processing, transport, and custodial actions. Even at their home stations, these are the least desirable assignments. When I was a young agent in 1999-2001, we were getting ordered on details from San Diego Sector to the Tucson, Yuma, and El Centro Sectors for 30-day stretches, sometimes with a few days' notice. While not that big of a deal for my wife and me, I can only imagine what it must have been like for PAs with working spouses, multiple children, and no support network.

Matt was a supervisor at a small station of 40 that quickly grew to over 200. On top of that, they were getting a large contingent of detailers; it was difficult, if not impossible, to supervise operations under these conditions, so they just had to make do. Even without detailers doubling the number of agents on a shift, the station was extremely short on supervisors. This was due to senior management missing their yearly window of time where they could report their supervisor-to-agent ratio and be allotted more supervisors for the rapidly growing number of agents.

"One day, I come in the station and find my FOS [Field Operations Supervisor, a position later changed to Watch Commander] is off, which means I'm the only supervisor on shift. I go look in the cells; there are 180 bodies in the cells." Way over capacity and unsafe for the agents and aliens. The maximum capacity is around 75-80 people for the cells at the Casa Grande Station.

"I got [aliens] beating on the windows, 'I been here five days, when am I getting out?' It was on the verge of a riot."

Matt called down to the new LEC to see how many they had in custody. "They didn't know exactly, but it was over 400." Again, way over capacity. They couldn't get an accurate count with the few available agents and the constant stream of incoming bodies. It is a lot to ask of a first-line supervisor to walk in and take ownership of a 100% overcrowded detention area at the station, as well as a 300-400% overcrowded satellite facility located 88 miles away. Add to that the daily routine of FTYs, pursuits, dope loads, etc....

According to Matt, the backlog was the result of the FOS cadre "not screwing over their guys with processing assignments." If six or eight agents were needed for processing, they would assign two so that more agents could go out to the field and catch more groups. At the time, "FOSs wanted to be loved by the troops," and leave all the dirty work to the supervisors.

The bodies kept on coming.

"Don't do this to me. I'm gonna do something about it. And I did." Matt had heard from a friend at another station that, under severe overcrowding, one of the workarounds was to only run two index fingerprints instead of all ten fingerprints to speed up processing. All he needed was to get the approval of an Assistant Chief Patrol Agent. He called the prior shift's FOS to suggest this; [the FOS] agreed and told him which A-Chief to call for approval.

"I told him what we had, and he was silent." For a moment. Then he started asking Matt to repeat himself. How many do you have? How many files? Does the PAIC know? Matt repeated what he had; it was up to the FOS to call the PAIC; [the FOS] never did.

The A-Chief did an incredible job. He approved the move to 2-print processing, vectored in all available buses; they had all of the bodies almost cleaned out by the end of the shift. "Nobody said anything to me."

Matt had called his only available superior. He reported what he had and asked permission to adjust processing and clean out the cells. It was agreed, and Matt was advised which A-Chief to call for approval; [the FOS] was duty-bound to report this to the Patrol Agent in Charge. That was where it ended, from Matt's perspective.

Not quite. As usual, the chain of command had missing links.

The FOS did not inform the PAIC and remained silent later when Matt's name came up as the Supervisor who called an A-Chief, supposedly jumping the chain. It all got cleared up eventually, after much wasted time and effort. In hindsight, it's very possible that the FOS knew exactly what they were doing, forcing their peers and superiors to face the implications of their poor decisions which were putting the agents in jeopardy.

"I don't mean to speak badly about these people; they're good people. I'm trying to give an example of extremely disappointing ways management acted. It's inexcusable except for the fact that the Patrol does not train its managers. That's why these things happened... and many, many more. Don't even get me started on all the things managers all the way up to the Chief of The Patrol have done. Oh Lordy. If they were properly selected, trained with proper guidance and proper oversight, it wouldn't even have gotten close."

"You must understand the culture and promotion process in the Border Patrol. If an agent wants to become a supervisor, you take what I call a 'multiple-guess' or multiple-choice test. If you score high enough on that, you are put on a list of selectees; higher-ranking managers (who were promoted by the same means), as far as I have ever been able to tell, pick who they want. If you are a ladder climber, you kiss someone's ass early on and take the ride up with them. As far as I know, that's pretty much how promotions work all the way up. Very little, if any, formal training is given in planning and conducting operations, personnel management, administrative management, and how to make all three of those aspects work together as efficiently as possible. Again, 'Now, help me understand this...'"

"I wish the patrol would go to a selection-type promotion system. If you want to promote, you go on a selection course. You are simultaneously trained on the position you are competing for and subjectively evaluated by tests, scenarios, etc., and scored. Only the best in the tough selection courses get promoted by merit. A separate course for each promotion all the way up to the Chief of the Border Patrol." This would create a common foundation for all managers, established priorities, shared formats, managing techniques, and thus synergy within Border Patrol management. The overall lack of synergy is one of the top reasons for the agents' lack of confidence in their command.

"To paint a better picture of the chaos, let's look at the typical daily personnel management of a shift at my old station. A shift supervisor comes in one hour early to assign agents available that day. A typical roster may show 25 agents for the shift. 18 to 20 of those agents get assigned to mandatory non-border duties such as station assignments, traffic checkpoints, and transport. Shift supervisors have several mandatory duties to fill, then the last priority is maybe you have an extra supervisor to go to the border. Everyone is working with different agents every day. Supervisors work with random different agents every day. No consistency.

"Several times I tried to implement a more structured and manageable environment at the Casa Grande station. The area of operations is huge, the size of Connecticut. I broke it down into 3 more manageable areas. The shifts were made into 3 teams so there were agents and supervisors who worked together on a consistent basis in one of the areas. This gives the teams a more predictable work environment. They have an area they are responsible for, as a team, on a consistent basis. With this, management can foster a better sense of purpose and accomplishment for the agents, thus better morale.

"I was able to implement this plan on some shifts and once, station-wide for a whole year. Each time it was eventually rescinded. No good reason was ever given but I suspect the core of management's reasons revolve around their lack of understanding, spite, and fear of being held accountable.

"It all goes back to the failure of the Border Patrol to train its managers. They need a common foundation of operational, personnel, and administrative management and to integrate these three areas to become more efficient and effective."

Attempts have been made to remedy this situation in the past, but they are localized and fleeting. The Tucson Sector had several Chief Patrol Agents in a very short period of time in recent years; the Border Patrol went through four in the last five years. If they all had the same priorities and objectives it would still be problematic but they didn't seem to, which made it worse. This of course is not necessarily something that can be helped by the Border Patrol, but it illustrates one of the obstacles to implementing what could be a positive change.

What Was the Point?

So, what was the point? To work with people like the ones portrayed here, doing something worth doing. Sure, there were some successes but did we succeed? No. But we did our jobs as best we could, to preserve, protect, and defend the Constitution, while obeying the lawful commands of those appointed above us. How could it go so wrong?

As commentator James T. Harris says, "If it doesn't make sense, there's probably a buck in it."

Look at the dirt!

VI. Afterword

The purpose of this book was to tell anyone who cares to read it the stories of the fantastic agents with whom I have worked. I grew up reading others' books about the military and law enforcement and was inspired by them. Hopefully this modest attempt will educate some who wish to learn a little about what their Border Patrol does every day, inspire others who wish to serve, and maybe convince others who are not suited to BP work to find something else.

I would not trade my time in the Border Patrol for anything, however, keeping in touch with my former colleagues leaves me conflicted. I greatly miss them and the job; on the other hand, the job is now completely different, and I am glad not to be there in the current environment. On one hand, I am very proud of my brothers and sisters in green for what they do every day and night. On the other hand, everything that the Border Patrol was instituted to defend against is worse than it ever has been since anyone has been keeping track. This, in spite of the fact that the Border Patrol has steadily grown in manpower, equipment, and budget since at least the 1990s. Of course, that is now changing with the negative view of law enforcement prevalent in popular culture currently.

The very day I write these words, an 18-year-old driving a compact sport-utility vehicle failed to yield to the Arizona DPS Troopers on Interstate 10 near Picacho, Arizona. The result was a heinous crash, killing from three to five people (reports are still coming in). The tiny SUV was designed to hold five persons; there were nine inside when it struck an eighteen-wheeler while trying to evade law enforcement. Again, from reports, the dead and injured are "possibly tied to smuggling." This alleged teenage load driver thought he could run from law enforcement and get away clean. Why? Because we taught him that.

I would bet money that, in the nearly 20-mile-long backup resulting from this accident, there are many more load vehicles packed with aliens and/or dope that will make it through unmolested by law enforcement.

Stupid kids, addicts, convicts, single mothers, and other persons who need fast cash are recruited in large numbers by smugglers via WhatsApp or Snapchat with promises of easy money by picking people up and transporting them from point A to Point B. Most of the time, they make it (although they are not always paid, go figure). We shall see what happens with this young person, but I would be surprised if he doesn't know others who have gotten away with it repeatedly and routinely, or if they were caught, swiftly released. The smugglers' risk profile drops dramatically; they anonymously recruit the drivers who use their own (or their parents') vehicles. The pickup and drop-off locations are sent to them through smartphone apps. Sometimes the recruiter, or an accomplice, follows the load drivers in a separate vehicle, "remote-controlling" them along the way. If things go bad, the professionals cut the cord and disappear; the load driver, and sometimes the aliens being transported, face the music. Not to mention innocent passers-by and motorists.

Probably any law enforcement professional would feel the same way after a career. Bad guys getting away, victims left forgotten in their wake, triumphs fleeting, few and far between. But a country has a right to its own borders, ours is no exception. We have a right to decide who gets to come in, how they do it, and when. The frustration is that while this has all been decided, high-handed government appointees take it upon themselves to effectively change the laws by re-interpreting them, or simply ignoring them, without the consent of the voters.

VII. Glossary, Phonetic Alphabet, Other Items of Interest

GLOSSARY

ACOG - Advanced Combat Optical Gunsight. A low-powered prismatic scope that gathers light in the daytime with a fiberoptic light pipe, and at night with an internal tritium phosphor. Issued to all branches of the US military, and limited issue for Border Patrol M4 carbines.

Agent - any Border Patrol Agent of any rank. Also known as BPA or Border Patrol Agent, PA or Patrol Agent, or Journeyman.

Alien - a legal term defined in Title 8 of the Immigration and Nationality Act meaning an individual who is not a citizen or national of the United States.

App - Apprehension, "Alpha," or "10-15."

ASID - Alien Smuggler Identification and Deterrence team. These guys interview all incoming aliens if possible, identify foot guides, scouts, and facilitators. They assist agents in the completion of smuggling and other criminal cases. They, along with the field agents, generate most of the intelligence of value that is then consumed by management.

AK - generic term for AK-47, AKM, AK-74, and similar pattern rifles in various calibers in common use by cartel soldiers, bandits, and rip crews, as well as legally armed USCs.

AR - generic term used for any rifle in various calibers based on the AR-15 platform. M4 carbines are also ARs, as are M-16s.

AOR - Area of Operational Responsibility. Each station and sector has its own AOR; there is some overlap for better coverage.

ASO - Alien Smuggling Organization

ATF - Bureau of Alcohol, Tobacco, and Firearms

ATV - All-Terrain Vehicle. A four-wheeled, off-road vehicle for one person, used by the BP for harsh terrain enforcement activities. Made by Kodiak, Polaris, Honda, and Yamaha, they are very effective at getting agents to the hard places quickly. Also, at injuring careless agents!

AUSA - Assistant US Attorney. Border Patrol Agents cannot prosecute people; they can only set up a case file and send it to the AUSA or one of his designees. Sometimes there are Border Patrol Agents who are detailed to work with the AUSA office, and they can determine yea or nay. This is most common on the Southern Border where the sheer volume of apprehensions makes it impossible for the AUSA to stay on top of all the criminals.

Backpacker - a drug smuggler carrying his contraband on

foot. Also known as a doper, packer, mule, or *burrero.*

Bandit – the lowest form of human life on the border. These guys hold up aliens for whatever meager possessions or cash they have on them for their trek to the United States. See also "Rip Crew."

Bang, Bang-off, Bang-in - to activate or perform, or to call in sick. "Just go down 188 and bang a left at the first big dirt road." Also, when a sensor activates, it "bangs off." To call in sick is known as "banging in," especially when nobody believes you are actually sick.

BCC - Border Crossing Card

BM - Border Monument. Large concrete obelisks posted at intervals along the International Boundary back after the west was won.

Booties - shoe coverings made for illegal aliens to evade detection by Border Patrol. They are made from various materials, but the best ones are cloth with carpet for soles and are fastened on top of the normal shoes by baling wire. These are easier to put on and take off quickly. Aliens frequently walk without the booties, and only "bootie up" when getting close to roads or washes.

Border - referred to in this book alternatively as the line, the border, International Boundary, the fence, the barriers.

BORSTAR - Border Patrol Search, Trauma, and Rescue team. Highly trained EMTs who also have training in swift-water and technical rescue, long line extractions, and advanced lifesaving techniques. Some have reached paramedic status, though this is somewhat rare. Most rescues are still performed by regular line

PAs; they are the ones who are already there, after all.

BORTAC - Border Patrol Tactical Unit; the USBP SWAT team. They are mainly used in high-traffic areas to catch dope, or they go on international missions to train other countries' police forces. Now that dope is legal in most places, they just work traffic where the chief tells them to or assist other agencies. BORTAC trains very hard and is rarely seen in the field.

BP - Border Patrol. In Spanish, *la Patrulla de la Frontera*. Also referred to as Bravo, the Patrol, Green, Border Control, *la migra*, *la Patrulla*, and various other names depending on who you're talking to.

BR - Border Road

Bravo - Phonetic alphabet for the letter "B." In some places, radio slang for Border Patrol Agent. Also, "Green."

"Is that green traffic on the sensor behind Amerimex?"

"10-4, Bravo."

Brush out - as a verb, to clean up the sign, with a jacket, blanket, twigs, or even a leaf blower. Often the brush-out is easier to spot than the actual foot sign. Also, as a noun - "I have a brush-out at POE east; getting out on it now." Can also be used as a term for covering up wrongdoing. "Danny was cheating on his wife on duty, but he brushed out really good and got away with it for a while."

Brush up - also "bush up." To rest and hide from detection. Sometimes aliens "brush up" by actually pulling the brush over their bodies while they rest to hide from agents or aircraft.

Bug - slang for a sensor. "Somebody go cut that bug; I think it's good."

Bust or **Busted** - the dispersal of a group. "Jerry busted a group; they ran everywhere." Also, to get in trouble.

CAG - Casa Grande Border Patrol Station. BP Agents also refer to the town of Casa Grande as CAG.

CAG PD, CGPD - Casa Grande Police Department

Camelbak - the brand name of a backpack-style hydration bladder you wear over your shoulders. It has a hose with a bite valve on the end so you can take a drink without stopping. They come in various sizes; the 100-oz. version being most popular with BP Agents. There are various makers, but the Camelbaks hold up best in my experience.

CARP – (used to be) Criminal Alien Repatriation Program. Later it evolved to mean any Criminal Alien. "That guy there with the tattoos on his face, print him first, he's probably a CARP."

CBP - Customs and Border Protection. **CBP** is divided between the Office of Border Patrol (**OBP**) for Border Patrol Agents, the Office of Field Operations (**OFO**) for the guys who work the air, land, and sea Ports of Entry (**POE**s), and the Office of Air and Marine (**OAM**) who crew and support the air and watercraft in use by CBP. There are other components, but these are the main enforcement arms.

CHP - California Highway Patrol, the state law enforcement agency of California. Also known as "chippies."

CIS - Citizenship and Immigration Services. Evolved from the old, non-law enforcement INS.

Connex box - those big metal shipping containers you see on flatbed rail cars or semi-trailers.

El Corralon - the corral. A jail-type place in El Centro, CA, where the aliens awaited deportation.

Cuernos de Chevo - Goat horns. An AK rifle. This term refers to the curved 30-round magazine of AK-47 pattern rifles.

CTDD - Controlled Tire Deflation Device, otherwise known as spikes, or Vehicle Immobilization Device (VID). These are thrown under the tires of fleeing suspect vehicles or can be pre-staged and pulled across the road in front of a fleeing vehicle.

Days on the Beach - Involuntary unpaid suspension.

DISRUPT - This team is a plainclothes interdiction unit that is assigned known smugglers and follows up on intelligence-generated information, both at station and sector level. They are tasked to disrupt (hence the name) and deter local smuggling organizations.

DPS - Department of Public Safety, the state law enforcement agency, and Highway Patrol of Arizona.

Drag - as a noun, a bunch of old tires or other objects (branches, blankets, lumber) attached to each other in such a way as to be pulled over the ground to flatten and smooth it. As a verb, to pull such a thing over the dirt and make it smooth for the follow-on agent to cut for sign. Also used at prisons and sensitive facilities to detect intrusions or escapes.

Drop Scoots, or **Drop** - to remove UTVs, ATVs (scoots), or dirt bikes from a trailer.

DTO - Drug Trafficking Organization

DVU - Domestic Violence Unit. A San Diego Sector detail of agents who pored over court records looking for criminal alien domestic abusers, many of whom were CARPS. Agents would "lay in" at the local judicial proceedings, identify these aliens, and prioritize them for deportation. It was so successful that the San Diego Union-Tribune ran an article on how the Border Patrol was tearing families apart by deporting the abusers, resulting in political pressure that caused the BP to eliminate the program.

EWI - Entry Without Inspection or Entered Without Inspection; this term is used both as a noun and a verb in the Border Patrol. It does not necessarily mean an illegal alien, since all persons entering the United States must present themselves for inspection. A person can EWI, that is, enter without inspection, or be an EWI – someone who has entered without inspection.

Field Processing Form - otherwise known as "826," a form filled out by field agents giving the basic biographical information and circumstances of an apprehended illegal alien.

FLIR - Forward Looking Infra-Red. The company that manufactures Night Vision Devices that sense differences in heat signatures, such as the difference between the ground and a human on the ground. Mounted in and on trucks, aircraft, and other vehicles if possible.

FN-FAL - a 7.62mm rifle used by the Mexican Federales as well as legally armed USCs.

FOB - Forward Operating Base, known amongst agents as "camp." These FOBs are located right on the border, or very close to it, to save the Border Patrol commuting time and gain "time on task" in the most remote areas of the border. They are supposed to be fenced-in, secure semi-permanent structures with living quarters, kitchens refrigerators, helipads, and processing areas. Agents are usually assigned to camp a few times a year for a week or so.

Foxtrot - Border Patrol Helicopter call sign from the days when the Border Patrol had its own air units.

FTY, or **Failure To Yield** - When a suspect vehicle does not pull over for a law enforcement vehicle's red-and-blue emergency lights and siren.

Good Traffic - meaning that whatever you are following is likely illegal and amenable to arrest and/or seizure.
"That bug banged off and Homer checked it out; it's gonna be good traffic."   "Did you see that vehicle? I think it's good for a load."

G-phone – government-issued cell phone all agents must carry. Has numerous apps that track agents' location, speed, and direction of travel, as well as many other things.

Green - slang for BP. "That's green traffic at the cattle guard, 10-3."

G-3 - standard issue 7.62mm rifle for the Mexican Military.

House Mouse - an agent who seeks out administrative tasks in lieu of Patrolling the Border. Not every administrative agent is a house mouse.

IBF - International Boundary Fence

ICE - Immigration and Customs Enforcement, responsible for enforcing customs and immigration laws in the interior of the United States. THIS is your Deportation Force, Mr. President.

FI - Firearms Instructor

FOS - Field Operations Supervisor (second-line supervisor before 2012). One who supervises the supervisors and runs a shift. Considered a member of management.

Gotaway - Also "Getaway," "GTA," "GOA." Suspects who successfully evade apprehension. Usually, any group that has had no updates in 48 hours is considered GOA, but there are exceptions.

Hard pack, hard pan - the kind of dirt that is so baked by the sun that you don't leave much foot sign on it.

HMMWV - High-Mobility Multipurpose Wheeled Vehicle, a military truck with excellent off-road capability. Too wide for normal USBP use, but there were a few at some stations. Widely used on the Mexican side by their military.

Huera/huero - white girl/guy.

IBF - Internation Boundary Fence

IFAK - Individual First Aid Kit. Personal first aid kit purchased by or issued to Border Patrol Agents, similar to the ones in use by the US military.

Knock and Talk - the process of knocking on a door and talking to the occupants of a home. Border Patrol Management is very uncomfortable with this and has policies and procedures to cover it to make sure only qualified personnel perform these tasks. Basically, getting the local police to knock is best.

LAPR - Lawfully Admitted Permanent Resident, or "green card" holder. Legal alien. Pronounced "lapper."

LARP or **LARPing** - Live Action Role Play. This is what I suspect a lot of the so-called border militia groups were mostly engaged in. The Minutemen got a lot of bad press, but most of the ones that I met were good-natured, normal people who wanted to help out in a tough situation by spotting groups and calling them in. Folks in lawn chairs with binoculars and cell phones were often a great help to the Border Patrol, and I appreciated them. However, the cammied-up "Tactical Ted" types who enjoyed sneaking around the desert at night were the guys I worried about. Some of those guys were okay, and some were complete psychos, allegedly setting up booby traps on trails. I firmly believe some were involved in ripping off dope loads, but I was never able to catch them.

Lay in - to hide in ambush for suspected groups of illegal aliens or smugglers.

Lay up - to stop for a rest. Aliens usually lay up, and BP Agents usually lay in for them.

LEO - Law Enforcement Officer

Load - illegal cargo. A load can be twenty bodies in a truck, bundles of dope in backpacks, or even counterfeit toy action figures.

Loader - vehicle used to transport illegal cargo, bodies, or dope, etc.

LP/OP - Listening Post/Observation Post

Maglite - The best flashlight ever made for Border Patrol work. A large and somewhat heavy flashlight taking anywhere from two to six C or D cell batteries. Very rugged and long-lasting.

Mica - generic slang term for a green card or Border Crossing Card. Pronounced "mee-kah."

Mil-Cam - a handheld thermal night-vision scope.

Mochila - an alien's bag or backpack containing his or her belongings. Usually identity documents, spare clothing and shoes, food, and water.

MSC - Mobile Surveillance Capability. The latest (for the BP) in a series truck-mounted array of forward-looking infrared optics (FLIR), powerful day-scope, and ground sensing radar.

MSS - Mobile Surveillance System. An older version of the MSC.

M4 - Standard issue 5.56mm carbine in use by the US Military, US Border Patrol, bandits and rip crews, as well as legally armed USCs.

Naturalization - the legal process of becoming a United States Citizen, or USC. When the applicant is sworn in as a citizen, he or she is "Naturalized."

NGO - Non-Governmental Organization. Groups like *No More Deaths*, *Angeles de la Desierto*, or the *ACLU* are all examples of NGOs.

November Bravo - Phonetic alphabet for Northbound. I wonder sometimes why we say these things, when the actual verbiage is quicker and easily understood.

NVD – Night Vision Device

NVG - Night Vision Goggles

OAM - Office of Air and Marine. This component operates the air and watercraft for CBP.

Omaha - call sign for OAM helicopters after the Border Patrol gave up its air units to Customs and Border Protection, Office of Air and Marine.

OTM - Other Than Mexican; not necessarily an illegal alien.

OBP - Office of Border Patrol. They enforce Customs and Immigration law in between and around the land POEs, as well as in some interior stations and seaports.

OFO - Office of Field Operations. They man all POEs, enforce Customs and Immigration law, and levy duties and fines.

Patrol Group - a shift, or a "watch." Led by a Watch Commander and several Supervisors, ideally, although smaller stations might only have a Supervisor and a few Agents. Not all stations are 24/7, so there might just be one shift at some of the smallest stations. Larger stations have three or four.

PCSD - Pima County Sheriff's Department; works the county around Tucson, AZ

PCSO - Pinal County Sheriff's Office; works the county around Casa Grande and Florence, AZ

Pit - the Processing Area. The lead agent is the Pit Boss. In some stations, the Processing Agents are known as the Pit Crew.

POE - Port of Entry. These can be the sprawling multi-lane inspection stations you see in San Isidro, CA, or Nogales, Arizona, to the two-lane checkpoint-looking things you see in Lukeville, AZ and Tecate, CA. Border Patrol Agents patrol in between the land POEs, while Customs and Border Protection Officers (CBPOs) are responsible for the POEs themselves, as well as the airports and seaports.

Processing - This is where the aliens are brought to be entered into a biometric identification system, photographed, fingerprinted, and ultimately identified. Their disposition is determined based on what comes back from various criminal databases. Some will be formally deported, others are considered Expedited Removals, and some are charged criminally with other outstanding crimes if the AUSA decides it should be so.

Pushing a group - following sign for a group; signcutting.

RDU - Rough Duty Uniform, the standard field uniform of the Border Patrol Agent. The equivalent of the US military BDU, or Battle Dress Utilities. For a while in the San Diego Sector, agents were authorized to wear a certain brand of green BDU trousers because the polyester RDU trousers were so terrible.

Real Police - my half-joking reference to those agencies and officers who are POST-certified peace officers in their respective states. Half-joking because their powers of arrest far exceed your average Border Patrol Agent in most law enforcement scenarios. For instance, when protestors got inside Tucson Sector Headquarters and handcuffed themselves to the building, the Sector Chief at the time called 911 for Tucson PD to respond and make arrests.

Our agents thought it was a weak move. The protestors were amenable to arrest and prosecution for impeding/obstructing, but management uses the "real police" to do the jobs that they and the Assistant US Attorney will not do. It's sad.

Rip Crew - these are sometimes cartel-sponsored hitters who specialize in ripping off other cartels' dope and sometimes aliens. They are usually armed and are absolutely willing to kidnap for ransom and/or to murder their victims. They generally do not mess with law enforcement or "civilians," such as campers or naturalists in the desert. There are also rip crews consisting of foolish USCs who also attempt to prey on any illegals or dope mules they find. This is rare, but not unheard of.

SDSO - San Diego County Sheriff's Office

Sector - a Border Patrol organizational unit consisting of several stations. Several Sectors make up a Joint Task Force, or JTF.

Sicario - comes from the Latin *sicari*, or dagger. Mexican slang for hitman or killer.

Side-by-side - a four-wheeler ATV designed to hold two to four people.

Sign - traces or tracks on the ground, or any visible indicator of persons or vehicles passing through an area. There is foot sign (prints), vehicle sign (tracks), high sign (fibers), etc.

Signcut - to track, or cut for sign is to signcut; looking for sign. Usually shortened to "cut" or "cutting."

"BPA Smith is cutting the drag on the Border Road; hang out north to respond."

Slug - A lazy Border Patrol Agent; the opposite of a hard-charger.

Soldado - Spanish for soldier

Staging - a group or vehicle(s) preparing to cross illegally into the United States.

Station - generally the lowest level of Border Patrol commands; there can be and are substations, which are smaller, and resident agents, who work alone out of Sheriff's Offices, but not many.

Supervisor - Supervisory Border Patrol Agent, a first-line supervisor who would supervise five or ten journeyman agents administratively, as well as in the field. Also known as "sup," "SBPA," or "first-liner." NOT considered management.

Terry Frisk - A limited search around the subject's outer clothing or areas in reach for weapons or things that can hurt you; to make the officer safe while conducting an investigation. See

Terry vs. Ohio.

TBS - Turned Back South; successfully deterred. "That sensor was good for 4 apps, 5 TBS, and a getaway."

TFO - Task Force Officer

TO - a member of the Tohono O'odham Nation

TON - Tohono O'odham Nation, an Indian Reservation in southern Arizona comprised almost half of the Casa Grande Border Patrol Station AOR.

TOPD - Tohono O'odham Police Department; police agency operation on the TON.

Tonk or **TONC** - an illegal alien of any ethnicity, nationality, or religion. Traveler Out of Native Country.

TCO - Transnational Criminal Organization

Trique Bag - Slang, pronounced, "Tricky bag." A gear bag containing an agent's personal gear for his shift; usually a posse box (clipboard) with field processing forms, maps, sensor list, flashlights(s), spare ammo, gloves, flex-cuffs, etc.

(Los) Triques - slang for "things;" personal items.

TTP - Tactics, Techniques, and Procedures

UOF - Use of Force, generally referring to a less than lethal use of physical force to effect an arrest or prevent escape. Can also refer to the use of spikes, see CTDD. Defensive Tactics Instructors are renamed UOF Instructors nowadays.

US or **USA** - United States of America. Everyone wants to come here for a reason!

USC - United States Citizen, born or naturalized.

USG - United States Government

VIN - Vehicle Identification Number. Unique ID of each vehicle, usually found on the driver's side dashboard through the windshield, on the engine, or a sticker inside the door.

Voluntary Return - otherwise known as a V/R. Non-criminal aliens used to be given this option as opposed to formal deportation; now it is usually only offered to unaccompanied Mexican children and sick or injured aliens.

Watch commander - lowest level of management; after 2012, runs a shift and supervises supervisors. Participates in Command-staff meetings, finds fault in accident investigations.

Phonetic Alphabet

A-Alpha N-November
B-Bravo O-Oscar
C-Charlie P-Papa
D-Delta Q-Quebec
E-Echo R-Romeo
F-Foxtrot S-Sierra
G-Golf T-Tango

H-Hotel	U-Uniform
I-India	V-Victor
J-Juliet	W-Whiskey
K-Kilo	X-X-ray
L-Lima	Y-Yankee
M-Mike	Z-Zulu

I hope you have enjoyed *Look at the Dirt!*

Here are some other books in the realm of law and border enforcement that may be of interest:

Unrepentant Sinner by Charles Askins

America's Covert Border War by Todd Bensman

Uniform Decisions by John Caprarelli

Guns, Bullets, and Gunfights by Jim Cirillo

Fireforce by Chris Cocks

Arresting Communication by Jim Glennon

El Narco by Ioan Grillo

Gangster Warlords by Ioan Grillo

War on the Border by Jeff Guinn

Jim Cirillo's Tales of the Stakeout Squad by Paul Kirchner

FBI Miami Firefight by Ed Mireles

Bandit Mentality by Lindsay O'Brien

Newhall Shooting: A Tactical Analysis by Mike Wood

Out on Foot: Nightly Patrols and Ghostly Tales of a US Border Patrol Agent by Rocky Elmore

First Line of Defense: Inside the US Border Patrol by James R. McFadden

This is a small sample; there are many, many others. A few of these titles are from Rhodesian military and law enforcement folks who fought a long bandit war in the 1960s to 1980 and are included due to some similarity in their work to today's BP agents, mainly signcutting groups. Their mission, terminology, and objectives are somewhat, ahem, different, but the signcutting is the same.

About The Author

Paul Eberle is a retired Border Patrol Agent. He was assigned or detailed out to several stations in the San Diego, El Centro, and Tucson Sectors, over a 24-year career. His experience included many ups and downs working as a field agent, firearms instructor, all-terrain vehicle agent and supervisor, and as a first-line field supervisor. *Look at the Dirt* is his first book.

www.ingramcontent.com/pod-product-compliance
Lightning Source LLC
Chambersburg PA
CBHW052121270326
41930CB00012B/2705